HISTORIC COSTUME

A resumé of style and fashion from remote times to the nineteen-sixties.

KATHERINE MORRIS LESTER

Co-author of ACCESSORIES OF DRESS

AND ROSE NETZORG KERR

Artist and Designer, Albuquerque, N. M.

Additional illustrations by Ila McAfee and Helen Westermann

SIXTH EDITION

Chas. A. Bennett Co., Inc. PEORIA, ILLINOIS

Library of Congress Catalog Number: 61–16745
PRINTED IN THE UNITED STATES OF AMERICA

Preface to the FIFTH and SIXTH Editions
of HISTORIC COSTUME

THE years between 1940 and 1967 quickened and intensified the already changing living habits of the American people. Occupations, transportation and travel, entertainment and scientific achievements sped ahead at breathless pace. These years were fraught with wars, political problems here and abroad, and with expanding economic and social complexities. The dress of both men and women was a direct outgrowth of these developments. Greater numbers of younger people, today, have formed new ways of weighing old ideas of education, life, occupations and professions, daily schedules, health, entertainment, and sports. Clothing is of the first importance in recording these changes.

Long before 1940, changes in clothing design, novelty appeal, and chemical fibers had inspired a following. Like pageantry, the changing clothing designs passed before the viewers and the wearers, giving them pleasure or shock but not indifference. Today, students at schools, colleges, and universities have unwittingly become critics of clothing designs by their acceptance or rejections of styles manufactured *for* them.

Early in the 1960's, women's clothing began to be designed for the 18-year-old girl. Then it was adapted for the older women as well as for younger persons. Men's clothing, widely manufactured from wrinkle proofed or treated fibers and fabrics, began to hug the figure more closely. It was designed for younger men with such styling as the shorter coat, more fitted hips and waist, and narrower trouser legs. The wider range of styling included clothing for business wear, for specific occupations, for all seasons and activities as well as that designed especially for sports, leisure, and athletic wear.

Because the sixth edition of HISTORIC COSTUME contains sixteen new full-color plates of costumes from ancient

3

Biblical times to the present, with seven or eight figures each, the colors will help the reader visualize more vividly the actual historic appearance of costumes. The last chapter has been extended considerably to bring the costume history to the present time.

Katherine Morris Lester wrote about costume and fashions, but real people moved in and out of her pageant of time. It is a distinct privilege and a pleasure to extend her work with color drawings, descriptions, and text.

Rose Netzorg Kerr

☆   ☆   ☆

(From) Original Preface and Notes on Earlier Editions

COSTUME has always been influenced by contemporary conditions—social, religious, and political. For this reason the author believes a résumé of such study limited to a single volume will be helpful to the student of the subject. Though nothing worthy of the name costume can be considered as existing before the discovery of the arts of weaving, dyeing, tanning, and working in metal, the faint beginnings of dress may be detected in the prehistoric decoration and ornamentation of the body.

From the marble figures in relief found in the ruins of the ancient city of Persepolis comes much of our knowledge of the dress of the Persians. On the Trajan column in Rome, the arch of Septimius Severus, and that of Constantine, are pictured the Parthians and Dacians in the characteristic costumes of their land. Moreover, sculptures and vases in the museums of Greece and throughout Europe yield authentic records of the dress of these Asiatic peoples.

Greece represents the zenith of achievements in ancient arts and letters. Sculptures, mosaics, vases, and sepuchral monuments furnish an accurate and detailed record of the classic world. Likewise, the Roman world is preserved to us in sculptured monuments, portraits, busts, and ancient paintings.

In the Middle Ages we find the sculptured tombs, stained glass windows, and wonderful old tapestries picturing the men and women of the period with truth and accuracy. From the beginning of the sixteenth century France has been the acknowledged leader in matters of fashion. For this reason the writer has considered French Fashion through the period of the Renaissance (1500-1700) and in succeeding time periods. By studying the French a knowledge of fashions may be applied to Europe and the colonies of America.

American sources may be traced, also, to Spanish and Italian influences, which made their contributions to modern styles. In the works of eminent French painters and sculptors, on down to the array of modern fashion books, are presented a galaxy of costume bewildering in its diversity, yet bold and direct in the *leading* types which stand forth in each period.

This work is the result of extensive travel, study of ancient monuments of Greece and Egypt, combined with much research relative to modern dress.

CONTENTS

LIST OF PHOTOGRAPHS

LIST OF BLACK AND WHITE PLATES

LIST OF DRAWINGS

LIST OF FULL-COLOR PLATES

CHAPTER ONE

The BEGINNINGS of Costume

FROM the beginning the subject of costume has received a full share of the world's interest and attention. Dress in this twentieth century is so much a matter of course that we scarcely ever think of its beginnings in the remote past. And yet the impulse toward adornment was just as marked and vital in our primitive ancestor in his paint, tattoo, and human bones, as it is today expressed in milady's rouge, feathers, and fur. Looking back through eons of time we find that man, in that dim, distant age, lived in caves and under rocky cliffs. He was concerned mainly with the securing of food and the preservation of his life. Dress did not exist. However, the impulse toward dress grew out of this early life which was dedicated to the hunt and the chase. Evidence is unmistakable that costume as we know it today emerged after a long and tedious process of evolution. The beginnings of dress, that from which dress came to be, was in the form of body decoration. The painting, cutting, and tattooing of the skin are forms of body decoration, which were the first steps toward modern dress.

The ambition to be distinguished from his fellows no doubt stimulated the desire toward dress. This desire grew out of certain discoveries which had been made. When this primitive hunter, stained with his own blood or that of the vanquished, returned to his tribe, he found these evidences of his might greeted with respect and admiration. Physical power in this remote day was the only standard of worth. These blood-stains were mute witnesses to a courage and might which compelled the veneration of his fellows. So gratifying was this distinction to this primordial leader that he sought for more permanent badges of bravery. Now, the blood-marks of courage were left upon the body as long as possible. When finally they wore off, the scars remained. Out of this admiration of scars and blood-marks upon the human skin there arose a dim sense of beauty. Naturally the desire for continued notice and favor gradually led these early leaders to devise new schemes of decoration. The colored clays that were so plentiful about them were the next source of inspiration. They began to daub their faces, heads, and bodies with this colored pigment. Soon these daubs were expressed at regular, measured intervals. Thus a sense of rhythm and the idea of pattern began.

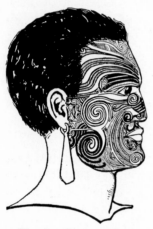

Fig. 1.   Tattooed head of the Maori, New Zealand. The form of design is traditional; every part has a meaning

The days of crude face painting, however, do not belong alone to the primitive past.[1] The present-day savage of Australia carries with him a supply of white earth and red and yellow ochres. Daily he touches up his face with spots of color, and on festive occasions he carefully paints his entire body in pattern. The Adamese, who live in the Adaman Islands of the Indian Ocean, and are the lowest order of savages, paint the entire body with a pale green when in mourning, with white for decorative purposes, and with yellow ochre, mixed with fat, for facial decoration. Even as late as the last century, the American Indian when about to go on the warpath covered his face with rhythmic patches of yellow, red and blue. The modern rouge and the patch, which had such a wide-spread vogue in the eighteenth century, are only later refinements of this same age-old body painting.

Soon another form of body decoration found expression. The cutting edge had been discovered. Knife blades

[1] *Color News,* June, 1924. Munsell.

were made of bone, horn, flint, and other stones and finished
with a fine point and edges. With these new tools the
primitive fashion leader amused himself by cutting and
slashing his skin in forms of pattern. This was followed
by tattooing, a method of marking the skin with slight
incisions and adding coloring material. This form of decoration expressed itself in elaborate pattern. (Fig. 1.)
Even today this custom is wide-spread, being found among
the South Sea Islanders, the Burmese, the Chinese, and
Japanese. Among the recovered relics of the ancient cave
men, remnants of ground ochre and other colors used in
painting and tattooing have been found.

The second impulse toward dress took the form of
body ornamentation. Now the coveted marks of distinction were ornaments added to the body. Various peoples
in many parts of the world have worn a bit of bone, wood,
or stone run through a hole in the lip, nose, or ears.

> Both he and his people were black as sloes,
>   For the region they lived in was torrid;
> And their principal clothes were a ring through the nose
> And a patch of red paint on the forehead.
>   —THOMAS HOOD, THE YOUNGER.

Bye and bye these bits of facial ornamentation were
supplemented by the trophies of war and the chase. The
leader now wore his necklace of teeth, bone, or polished
stones, and his waist-belt of skin. It is this same necklace
of teeth, bone and, in time, beads, hanging about the neck,
that later, after the discovery of the art of weaving, developed into the tunic, waist, and jacket. In like manner
it is the waist-belt of feathers, bones and other trophies
that gradually became the apron, and later was transformed into the modern skirt.

The protective dress, namely, the wearing of skins, furs,
and bark for protection, came after ages of decoration and
ornamentation.

The first problems in costume proper were worked out
by those early peoples living along the shores of the Mediterranean.

It was here after the art of weaving was discovered that the necklace of beads, teeth, and fringe developed into the tunic and mantle, and the primitive waist-belt lengthened into the skirt.

The ancient records picture the king and man of wealth wearing the long skirt dependent from the waist and the mantle hanging from the shoulders. Woman, whose life was largely restricted to home and home duties, soon adopted the long robes of her lord. The long skirt finally became an established form of conventionality in woman's dress, upon which the world of fashion has continued to play but never has completely changed. The long skirt and mantle are distinctly the dress of antiquity.

Modern dress, that is, the fitted garment as we know it today, emerged during the Middle Ages when Frank, Gaul, and Latin mingled. Climatic conditions in western Europe necessitated a more clinging garment which would sustain the warmth of the body. So the men of these parts wrapped their legs in cloth and skins. They were ridiculed by the Romans as "trousered barbarians." As the Romans, however, pushed their conquests farther north they were compelled to adopt the same costume. Though trousers are undoubtedly of oriental origin, it was at this period of the Middle Ages, during the fusion of the races, that trousers became the established type of men's dress, while the skirt remained the conventional dress of women.

REVIEW

1. Discuss the most primitive impulses toward dress—body-painting, tattooing, ornamenting.
2. How did the sense of pattern develop?
3. What was the probable forerunner of the tunic and mantle? Of the skirt?
4. What important discovery in the useful arts led to the development of dress?
5. Where were the first problems in dress worked out?
6. Discuss the outstanding difference between ancient and modern dress.

CHAPTER TWO

EGYPTIAN Costume Ancient Times

A MONG the great civilizations of the past, that of Egypt opens the first record of costume. This record is clearly and unmistakably written in temple, tomb, and mummy-case, in statue, design, and colored hieroglyphics. The Egyptians were the first to leave their records of costume in a form so durable that they could not be easily destroyed. The development of dress in that distant corner of Africa takes on a peculiar interest as we see not a few of our more modern types dating back two or three thousand years before Christ. Our sources of information concerning this remote period are quite as realistic as a modern fashion plate, for they are none other than the pictures of Egyptian life painted upon the walls of tomb and temple. Today these drawings are quite as distinct, and in many instances the coloring quite as fresh and bright as when left by the hand of the primitive artist. Here we may see the laborer, the merchant, the king, the rich, the poor, each clad in the garments of his class.

These ancient records show that the lower classes of this country, especially in the earliest periods (2900 B. C.-2350 B. C.), wore no clothing whatever, and the upper classes very little. Gradually clothing became more general, and in the Fifth Dynasty (2700 B. C.-2500 B. C.), the loin cloth had long become the dress of the peasants and a short skirt or apron was adopted by the higher classes. The materials were very thick and coarse, and in all probability made of flax, which was abundantly cultivated in Egypt. A kind of matting is also known to have been worn by the lower classes.

Though on the whole there is greater variety in the early costume of men, yet the tendencies in the general development of the costume of the two sexes are quite similar. During the early dynasties (2550 B. C.-1530 B. C.) there is a sameness in the costumes of the women of all classes. This characteristic dress consisted of a long, straight tunic, reaching from the bust to the ankles. The shoulders and breast were uncovered, and the tunic kept in place by straps over the shoulders. (Fig. 2.) These tunics were extremely scant, and drawn so closely about the figure that not even the suggestion of a fold appears. A small number of sculptured figures of this type have

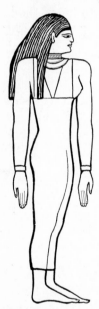

been found, and the only possible means of telling that the figures were intended to be covered is the almost imperceptible edge about the neck and ankles. Recently, while in Egypt, a number of American women secured photographs of this most ancient type, and delighted in sending them home to their American tailors, declaring, "Now we have found the original of the hobble-skirt." Other records show the woman of Egypt clad in a short, scant tunic of one piece of material, with a jeweled belt connected by straps with a jeweled collar. Sometimes a piece of material was thrown about the shoulders and fastened to the collar at either side of the front. Innumerable rows of rich beads were worn about the neck, forming a mass of color reaching to the waist.

Fig. 2. The Princess Sedet

From the earliest times the men of the higher classes wore a short simple skirt which became the foundation for all later developments. The skirt was usually a straight piece of some white material, and was wrapped about the body from right to left so that the edge came in the middle of the front. (Fig. 3, a.) This skirt later became longer and wider, reaching sometimes to the

ankles. Among the higher classes the form gradually
changed, and it was arranged with a triangular fold at the
front, which was so elaborated at times that it extended at
the lower edge from one side of the figure to the other. (Fig.
3, b.) As the coarser materials were given up, finer and

a   b   c   d   e   f   g   h

Fig. 3. Skirts of Egypt. a, ancient skirt; b, later skirt; c, the two
skirts; d, e, f, draped skirts; g, skirt with the golden border; h, oldest
form of royal skirt

more transparent materials were used. It was then necessary to wear a second skirt under the first. (Fig. 3, c.) Originally these two skirts were very similar, but as time went
on the outer skirt was gradually shortened in front and
lengthened at the back. At the close of the Eighteenth
Dynasty (1350 B. C.) the underskirt became longer and
wider and the outer one looped in puffs over it, giving the
first suggestion of drapery. (Fig. 3, d.) Gradually these
two skirts underwent another change; the under one became full and plaited, and the upper one evolved into a
strip or sash of linen folded about the hips and tied in
front. The manner of adjusting the sash varied; sometimes it reached down over the back of the legs, and was
gathered up short in front, and sometimes it was wrapped
twice around the body. (Figs. 3, e and f.)

For festive occasions the great lords of Egypt wore a
short skirt similar to the oldest types, made more elegant
with trimmings of gold and a golden clasp at the girdle.

The front of these skirts was rounded off, and from the center back to the front ornamented with a plaited piece of gold material, which gave an added touch of elegance to the costume. (Fig. 3, g.) The king's skirt was similar in form—that is, with the rounded edges—but with an added strip of material which, hanging from the girdle under the skirt, could be seen below. The addition of a lion's tail at the back completed this most ancient form of royal skirt. (Fig. 3, h.) In later times it became the proud privilege of others beside the king to wear the shend'ot, the royal skirt. Many of the ancient monuments show the same skirt minus the lion's tail worn by kings, priests, and other dignitaries.

The one badge of royalty in the king's dress which was reserved for him alone was the king's apron, which no doubt succeeded the earlier type. This apron hung from the girdle in front, and was richly ornamented with colored feathers, colored leathers, and opaque polychrome glass. Usually a row of asps, always the royal insignia, bordered the apron. (*C,* Plate I.) One of the rare treasures found upon the mummy of King Tutankhamen when his tomb was opened in 1923 was the handsome ceremonial apron. It was made up of several gold plates in graduated size and each was inlaid with small shapes of opaque polychrome glass. The apron was probably suspended from a finely chased golden girdle which encircled the waist, and under this was tucked a dagger. Two other girdles were found. They were composed of gold beads and faience. This again is mute testimony to the lavish use of beads employed by the ancient Egyptian in both ornament and dress decoration.

With the Eighteenth Dynasty (1545 B. C.-1350 B. C.) there were many changes in dress, due in great measure to the new relations with Western Asia and the far-reaching commercial interests of the country. It was during this period that the coarser materials gave way to the finer, and cotton and linen began to be extensively used. At this time the value of dyes seems to have been well

A   B   C   D   E   F

PLATE I—EGYPTIAN COSTUME—ANCIENT TIMES

A—The dress of an Egyptian princess. The bell-shaped tunic fitting at
the shoulders and flaring toward the lower edge is a type of dress
worn only in the royal household. The head-dress is an ornamented
wig of the period.

B—A simple white tunic worn with the mantle which in later days developed into the modern shawl.

C—A king of Egypt. The badge of royalty is seen in the king's apron,
which hangs from the girdle, and in the head-dress, or pshent, ornamented with the royal asp.

D—A queen of Egypt with the sacred bird, the vulture, as a head-dress.

E—A lady of rank wearing the straight tunic, armlets and ankle rings.

F—An Egyptian prince. The distinguishing mark of a prince was the
badge at the side of the head, descending to the shoulders.

17

known. This period witnessed the entrance of a new
fashion—that of covering the upper part of the body and
adopting a short shirt as an article of dress. These shirts
were usually open on the right side, while the arm passed
through a short sleeve on the left. This garment gradually
evolved into a robe with short sleeves which covered the
entire figure. (*D, G,* Plate II.)

The women's dress of this period resembled that of the
men in possessing a sleeve for the left arm, leaving the
right arm free. It is also in this later period, no doubt,
that the bell-shaped tunic belongs—fitting close at the
shoulders and flaring toward the lower edge. (*A,* Plate I.)

A painted wooden figure discovered at Thebes and dating about 2000 B. C. shows an interesting development in
the sheath-like tunic. (Photo A.) Here the upper part of
the tunic, for about three fourths of its length, is painted
in a dark and light pattern, forming lines which run around
the figure, while the lower part is in vertical stripes. The
tunic is supported by shoulder straps which are also in
dark and light pattern. The painted anklets, bracelets, and
neckpiece may represent either woven material or beadwork. The deep collar of strung beads was a conspicuous
favorite of Egyptian women and is frequently seen painted
upon mummy cases and also in much of the recovered
sculpture. Later all of these ornaments were made in gold
set with stones or enriched with enamel. The massive wig
falling in heavy lappets is typical of the early period.

During the Nineteenth and Twentieth Dynasties (1350
B. C.-1090 B. C.) the wearing of a long mantle became
fashionable. (*B,* Plate I.) This was draped sometimes under one arm and over the other; sometimes over both
shoulders and fastened in front over the breast. Later the
mantle became a short mantilla, which was often edged
with fringe (*D,* Plate I.) This type of wrap was, no doubt,
the forerunner of our modern shawl. The fringes were
made by the projecting threads of the warp, twisted
together and tied at the end in one or more knots to prevent their unraveling. Herodotus says that they had the

A   B   C   D   E   F   G

PLATE II—EGYPTIAN COSTUME—ANCIENT TIMES

A, B, E, F—A group showing the simple forms of skirt worn in the
  earliest periods of Egyptian history. The caps and head-dresses were
  a protection from the rays of the sun.
C—A peasant woman wearing the long straight scant tunic.
D—A priestess wearing the simple tunic, the embroidered collar, the head-
  dress, and carrying the key of life.
G—A priestess in robe of striped material and wearing the usual head
  covering.

19

custom of leaving a fringe to their pieces of linen, which, when the dresses were made, formed a border round the legs. This kind of dress was called a calasaris, but was not universally worn. The dresses in the peasant classes followed in the main the general tendencies of the upper classes—the women wearing the long straight tunics with or without sleeves (*C*, Plate II.), and the men clinging to the simple skirt and shirt.

In the oldest period, that of the Old Empire, the dresses of women were more often colored than white. Later, during the Middle Empire, various colors were worn, especially green. The use of color in dress, however, largely gave way among the upper classes to the finest and whitest of linen, the merit of the clothing consisting in its absolute purity and its fineness of texture.

The fashionable coiffure of five thousand years ago reveals a marvel of the wig-maker's art. (Fig. 4.) It may appear singular that so warm a covering for the head should have been adopted by both the men and women of Egypt. These coverings, however, were devised especially to keep the head cool, serving the same purpose as the modern turban. The women of Egypt often kept the hair short, and the men always shaved the head. The wig, built upon a netlike surface, allowed the heat of the head to escape, and at the same time served to protect the head itself. The fashion in women's coiffure varied according to the period. Under the Old Empire the fashion tended toward huge constructions reaching to the shoulders. (Fig. 2.) This style continued general, the only change being fringe-like arrangement of the ends. The Eighteenth Dynasty, which wrought so many changes in fashionable attire, also introduced a greater variety in the styles of hair dressing. The women of this period seemed to get away from the stiff conventional form of the past, and adopted a more graceful natural arrangement—the hair falling in soft curls without concealing the contour of the head. Later the styles reverted to the past, and the woman of the Twentieth Dy-

PHOTO A—A PAINTED WOOD FIGURE FROM
THEBES. (About 2000 B.C.)

The repetition at regular intervals of dark and
light pattern shows, even at this early period, a
fine sense of pattern. Note the heavy wig, also
the collar, anklets, and bracelets, which suggest
woven material or beadwork.

nasty allowed her wig to fall in a heavy mass over each shoulder to the waist.

Styles in men's wigs followed the dictates of fashion as did those of the women. Originally short hair arranged in little curls seems to have been the fashion. This wig

Fig. 4. Head-dress of a lady, from a mummy-case
(After Wilkinson)

was set low on the forehead and covered the ears. The second type was the long-haired wig, the hair falling thick from the crown of the head to the shoulders. Variations of these two forms of coiffure succeeded each other, until in the Twentieth Dynasty we find long freely waving hair.

We in our day have grown rather accustomed to the popular use of artificial hair, and in view of the modern weakness in that direction cannot judge severely our sister of antiquity. Another custom, however, closely allied to this, which the men of Egypt adopted, we cannot view with quite the same leniency—that of wearing an artificial beard. The Egyptian regard for absolute cleanliness led them to discard the natural beard. From the most primitive times

the beard had been regarded as a badge of manly dignity.
Consequently, in order to command respect from the popu-
lace, the dignitaries of the country, on certain occasions,
appeared with artificial beards fastened beneath the chin.
The style of the beard was determined by the importance

Fig. 5. Beards and crowns. a, beard of Osiris; b, crown of Lower
Egypt; c, artificial beard and crown of Upper Egypt; d, king's beard
and the pshent

of the person wearing it. Private citizens usually wore a
small beard, probably two inches in length. (Fig. 5, c.)
That of the king was of considerable length (Fig. 5, d), and
that of the gods turned up at the end. (Fig. 5, a.)

Aside from the wigs proper, members of the royal
family wore a covering for the head which was especially
symbolic of office and rank. The state head-dress of the
Egyptian king, the pshent (Fig. 5, d—b and c combined),
symbolized the union of Upper and Lower Egypt. A helmet-
like cap, probably derived from the Persians, was also
worn, made of thick stuff with a nap and ornamented with
the royal asp. The distinguishing mark of a prince was
the badge at the side of the head, descending to the shoulders and edged with gold fringe. (*I*, Plate I.) The vulture, the sacred bird, protector of the king in battle, appears upon the head-dress of the queen. (*D*, Plate I.)
This was a very elaborate arrangement, the plumage entirely covering the head. Besides these royal head-dresses,
wreaths, colored ribbon, and the lotus flower were often
twined round the hair.

In many works of art of the early Egyptian period the men in everyday life are pictured wearing close-fitting caps and hoods. In many cases the hood hangs down over the shoulders in two broad bands or sometimes plaited lappets. (*B* and *E*, Plate II.) This type of head-dress is also part of the kingly attire in the most ancient period.

The heads of female figures are frequently covered with a hood, which is often close-fitting and again often laid in a number of folds. The usual form of head-dress was made of one piece of linen or striped material, cut in semi-circular fashion with a band for the head left in the center of the straight edge.

With peculiar interest we have seen many of the Egyptian costumes revived down through the centuries, and we note that even the very modern fashion of carrying a walking-stick dates back to remote antiquity. (*D*, Plate I.) The Egyptian canes were usually four to six feet in length and surmounted by a flower or some similar ornament. Many were decorated with gilding and color, and were frequently inscribed with the owner's name.

Though we find that the earliest form of protection for the feet partook of the nature of sandals, it is perhaps true that shoes or low boots, many of which have been found in Thebes, were not in general use in Egypt until after the conquest of Greece. The warmth and mildness of the East rendered a close warm shoe unnecessary; and indeed at the present day they have much of the character of slippers. The foot thus unconfined by tight shoes retained its natural shape and freedom of motion.

Again we may go to the records written upon the walls of a temple at Thebes, and gaze upon the ancient shoemaker at his work in the early days of Thothmes III, who ascended the throne about 1495 B. C. and is now regarded as the Pharaoh of the Oppression. The shoemakers are both seated upon low stools (real specimens of such tools may be seen in the British Museum), and are both busily engaged in shaping the sandals then worn in Egypt. The first workman is piercing with his awl the leather thong at the side of the sole through which the straps were passed which secured the sandal to the foot. His fellow-workman is equally busy sewing a shoe and tightening the thong with his teeth.

The higher classes paid a great deal of attention to the beauty of their sandals. Those worn by men and women of the upper classes were usually pointed and turned up at the end. Some had a sharp flat point; others were nearly round. (Fig. 6, a, c, d.) Many were made of a woven or

a   b   c   d

Fig. 6. Egyptian sandals.

interlaced work of palm leaves and papyrus, frequently lined with cloth. Sandals have been recovered which show the painted figure of a captive upon the inside lining of the sole. (Fig. 6, b.) This humiliating position was considered as one befitting the enemies of the country.

Among the Egyptians, ornament and design as well as color were of serious moment. Color and pattern had real significance to these people of long ago. Down through the centuries these same designs have continued, and though their early significance is often unappreciated today, the inspiration which made them possible at this remote period found its source in the deep and sincere religious life of the people.

The winged globe (Fig. 5) is one of the best known of the Egyptian ornaments; it was the emblem of the great sun-god, Ra, who took precedence over all other gods. The sun symbolized life, power and eternity. The winged globe represented the sun being carried on wings through the heavens. The wings suggested the protection the sun-god assured to his people in life and in death. For this reason it was placed over the entrance to temples and tombs, and used as a decoration upon garments, head-dress and jewelry. It also ornamented the ruler's throne and his chariot. Further, a body was never placed in a mummy-case that did not have a winged globe as part of its decoration. The conventional form of the cobra, representing the generative power of the sun, is often seen on either side of the center.

"As Ra and his descendants are rulers of earth and heaven, all must be submissive to the great rising sun, or there will be no peace on earth or in the hereafter." This hymn, written to the rulers, was preserved on an old piece of parchment.

The scarabæus, or sacred beetle of the Egyptian, was the emblem of immortality and, according to Pliny, was worshipped as one of the gods of the country. (Fig. 7, a.) The designs inspired by this sacred beetle were used generally in decoration. When cut in stone they were used for rings, necklaces and other trinkets.

The lotus and papyrus furnished the inspiration for the more delicate patterns. (Fig. 7, b and c.) These were conventionalized in various ways. Many of the newly opened tombs disclose a wealth of design. Beautiful decorations in color not only embellish the interesting contents of the tombs but likewise enrich the walls of corridors and tomb chambers.

By its annual innundations the Nile fertilized the valley, giving life to the various crops. Hence the great water-god received the reverence of the people whom he protected. A simple wave-like design, symbolic of the life-renewing stream, is seen over and over again. The soft green color in which this has been worked out is known as "Nile green." (Fig. 7, d.)

The colors most generally used in fabrics and design appear to be green, yellow, red, light blue, tan and black. These colors are believed to have been produced by wonderful dyes. Many of the tombs have yielded cakes of color which indicate that mineral dyes and later vegetable dyes were used.

The Egyptian woman, as the women of other and later civilizations, had her jewels and ornaments, especially earrings, armlets, and ankle-rings. At all periods both men and women wore colored embroidery necklets, bracelets for the upper and lower arm, and anklets of the same material. Of course these were not confined to embroidered materials, but were of gold and silver as well. Many of the necklaces were made with pendants in the form of figures of the gods or of animals sacred to them, or of amulets to which magical powers were attributed. The rings were made of gold, silver, bronze, and faience. Sometimes the bezels were solid and immovable; sometimes they were inlaid with scarabs inscribed with various devices or the name of the wearer, and, as they revolved, were used as a personal seal. The red carnelian, carved in the design of a scarabæus, was the stone most used in the Pharaoh's ring, as his official seal. The seal was of great importance, for it took the place of a key in protecting treasure, at a time when keys were seldom if ever used. The door of the treasure house or treasure chest was secured by wooden bolts, set in mud and stamped with a seal. To break

Fig. 7. Egyptian ornament. a, scarabæus; b, lotus pattern; c, papyrus pattern; d, Nile pattern; e, f, Egyptian fans

a seal, particularly a royal seal, was considered a crime, and
the offender was severely punished. The seal ring carried with it all the power and prestige of the owner. The
bracelets were often inlaid with precious stones or colored
paste. After the Twenty-
sixth Dynasty, the ends,
owing to Phœnician influ-
ence, often terminated in
lions' heads.

Beads were used in
great profusion by both
men and women, and were
evidently considered quite
choice as an ornament.
They have been found cut
into various shapes, round,
rectangular, oval, and ob-

Fig. 8.   Lady rouging herself
(From the Papyrus of Turin)

long; and made of emerald, agate, carnelian, lapis lazuli,
amethyst, rock crystal, onyx, jasper, garnet, gold, silver,
glass, faience, clay, and straw. Several painted figures
show rows of beads about the neck, with pendants of beads
hanging over the breast like a mantilla.

In accessories of the toilette the Egyptian lady was by
no means behind her modern sister. Fig. 8, from the
Papyrus of Turin, shows a lady rouging herself. Oils,
ungents, and perfumes were in common use. Many of the
tombs have yielded beautiful vases and jars of the finest
alabaster and porphyry; filled with various oils and scents,
they were placed in the tombs at the time of burial. Chief
among all the devices which made for feminine beauty was
that of the application of stibium to the eyes. The ladies
were wont to stain the eyes and eyebrows with this mixture,
making the eye appear larger and adding to its beauty.
This custom still exists in Egypt. The same properties
are also ascribed to kohl, which is a mixture of various
ingredients. The kohl was kept in curious little "kohl-
pots," many of which have been recovered. These are of
various forms and made of alabaster, steatite (soap-stone),

glass, ivory, or wood. Usually they are from three to six inches high. (Fig. 9.) The stick with which the kohl was applied to the eyes was made of wood, bronze, or glass, and was thicker at one end than at the other. The thick

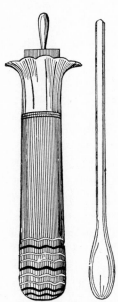

end was moistened, dipped into the powder, and then drawn along the eyebrow. The custom of painting the eyelids or the parts immediately under them is contemporary with the earliest dynasties, and seems to have been common all over the East. In II Kings 9:30 we read that Jezebel "put her eyes in stibium"; and in Jeremiah 4:30 the daughter of Zion is told that her lovers would seek her life even though "she rent her eyes with stibium"—referring to the wide-open appearance the use of stibium gives to the eyes of the women of the East.

Combs and hairpins alike were made of wood or ivory. The date of the appearance of combs in the East is un-

Fig. 9. Egyptian kohl-pot

known, but it is believed they were not introduced until a comparatively late period. Some combs had but a single row of teeth; others had two rows, one thicker and longer than the other.

The use of mirrors seems to be of great antiquity. They were frequently made of bronze, and were usually round, oval, or pear-shaped. The handles were of ivory, wood, bronze, or faience, and of beautiful design, usually suggesting the lotus plant and flower in form and color. They were also given the form of figures—one of the favorite types, judging from the number found, being that of a woman with arms raised supporting the mirror.

Of all toilette requisites, the fan is one of the most ancient, and its popularity has waxed and waned for something like three thousand years. The Egyptian fan is the original of all the later styles. (Figs. 7, e and f.) In that day the fan was not the "toy of the fashionable lady," as it was in the eighteenth century. The ancient fan was large, with flexible handles five to seven feet in length. The fan proper was usually made of leaves, and of feathers cleverly dyed and arranged in effective pattern. The support was ornamented with jewels or painted in color. A special attendant, usually a slave, carried the fan, holding it to shield the owner from the rays of the sun, or moving it back and forth to cool milady and keep the insects and flies away.

Gradually the articles of toilette as well as the garments of Egypt influenced those with whom she shared her commericial life. That which was distinctly Egyptian was borrowed by other nations, and variously modified to meet local need and environment. The influence of ancient Egypt is recognized again and again in the costumes of modern designers. Her contribution in design and ornament has lived through the centuries, and continues to be the inspiration of ever new arrangements and combinations that still hold the interest of humanity.

REVIEW

1. What great civilization of the past furnishes our earliest records of costume? What are the chief sources of information?
2. Describe the earliest form of dress worn by Egyptian women. What materials were generally worn? Why?
3. Discuss the use of color in the dress of ancient Egypt. Name colors generally used in later dynasties. How were these secured?
4. Give a short account of the Egyptian practice of wig-wearing.
5. How was the beard regarded? Describe various types.
6. Describe the official head-dress of upper Egypt. Of lower Egypt. Show how these were combined to represent the union of upper and lower Egypt.
7. Describe the general types of footwear.
8. Name and describe at length the various artifices of the toilette.
9. Discuss the favored ornaments commonly worn by women.
10. Has the civilization of ancient Egypt made any contribution to modern dress? Discuss.

CHAPTER THREE

ASIATIC Costume Ancient Times

A SIA MINOR plays a significant part in history as it became the channel through which the civilization and culture of Asia were transmitted to Greece and Europe. In matters of dress these less distant Asiatics, under the names of Phrygians, Persians, Medes, Syrians, Parthians, and Amazons, have passed on to the western world many types of costume which, though modified, have been preserved to the present day. Judging from the recovered coins, monuments, and engraved gems of this remote period, there seems to have been much similarity of costume among these near-Asiatic peoples. Though the monuments picture the costume of men far more frequently than that of women, we may be able to glean the general types of women's costume from the few instances left to us upon bronze, marble, and fictile vase.

The characteristic type of dress throughout the region is distinctly that of the Orient, whose one contribution to the world of dress has been that of pantaloons and sleeves. Invariably these figures of Asia Minor wear the vest with long sleeves reaching to the wrist, and the pantaloons descending to the ankle. (*A* and *B,* Plate III.) The pantaloons were frequently close-fitting, and perhaps just as often very ample, falling in great folds and caught in the shoes or sandals. (*A* and *B,* Plate IV.) The vest was always of the same material as the pantaloons, and was closed either in the front or back by means of clasps or studs. Over the vest was worn a sleeveless tunic of another material. (*A,* Plate IV.) This was girded at the waist, and if too long, was girded a second time lower down.

A B C

PLATE III—ASIATIC COSTUME—ANCIENT TIMES

A—An Amazon. The vest with long sleeves and the pantaloons reaching
to the ankles are the characteristic dress of the East. Over this the
short tunic is worn. The tunics were frequently richly embroidered
or painted in design. Studs or coins sometimes ornamented the belt.
The voluminous mantle and the little Phrygian cap are often pictured
as part of the Amazon costume.

B—Amazon dress—pantaloons, sleeves and tunic made from leopard's
skin. The Phrygian helmet and the half-boots with flying flaps also
suggest the skins of animals.

C—An Amazon from a vase painting (Hope). This figure is sometimes
classified as Greek. The tunic is short, girded at the waist. The
designs are probably painted.

32

ANCIENT BIBLICAL AND EGYPTIAN COSTUMES

A—Joseph, eleventh son of Jacob, wearing his long-sleeved coat of many colors.

B—David, as a shepherd boy in animal skin costume. Later, he became the color-ful King of Israel and Judah, about 1000 B.C.

C—Young Samuel being taken to the Temple by his mother, (*D*) for dedication. Note her softly draped blue costume.

E and F—Maid attendants to the (*G*) queen of Tutankh-amen, and to the (*H*) reigning young Pharaoh of Egypt 1358 B.C. In weaving linen, Egyptians have never been surpassed. The gold and enamel collars of both the Pharaoh and his queen are considered among the finest in jewelry. Colors were soft and restricted.

32A

ANCIENT GREEK COSTUMES

A—Dyed garments for Greek woman, 487 B.C., were favored over white or ivory.

B—Back view of Greek girl, Homeric period between 1200 and 850 B.C. Note hair arrangement, often repeated since.

C—Greek girl's bronze mirror and olive green costume with woven borders, 5th century B.C.

D—Greek woman wearing colored Doric Chiton and head scarf, about 480 B.C.

E—Brightly garbed boy adjusting his leather sandal, 5th century, B.C.

F—Greek citizen with ivory-toned draped mantle, 5th century, B.C.

G—Greek soldier (from a vase painting) with color-inlaid cuirass, helmet, greaves, and bronze shield.

32B

To this dress the dignitaries of the East added a voluminous mantle, which was distinct from that of other nations
in that it was edged with fringe. (*B,* Plate IV.) This
fringe was not a part of the woven material, but was added
as an enrichment. Though this mantle was worn by Grecian
ladies of later days, it was never adorned with fringe.
This style of decoration is frequently referred to by Greek
writers as being particularly characteristic of barbaric
and Asiatic races.

In contrast with that of Egypt, the records of these
near-Asiatic peoples show leather foot coverings enveloping the foot and extending to the ankles. (*A, B,* Plate IV.)
Here they were secured by thongs which passed several
times around the ankle and were then tied. Another type
of shoe worn by these people was the laced half-boot. This
was made of leather and often showed long flaps hanging
from the top suggesting the legs of the animal. (*F,* Plate
IV.) The idea of lacing the boot is a distinct departure
from the earlier tying. It is said that this custom was not
unknown among the peoples living along the Mediterranean.
Further, it is from this region that primitive foot coverings
have been found which exhibit a heel—probably the earliest
instance of that slight elevation at the back of the shoe.

The arts of dyeing, weaving, and embroidering were well
known to these people of Asia Minor. Tyre and Sidon,
the great commercial cities of antiquity, in course of time
became celebrated for their splendid dyes of scarlet and
purple, for their manufacture of fine linens and perfumes,
and for their skill in metallic work. Weaving with gold
thread is said to have been the invention of Attalus, King
of Asia. Pliny states, "to weave with gold thread was the
invention of the Asiatic king, Attalus." He then speaks of
the beautiful needlework practiced by the Phrygians, who,
he says, "were the first to divine the method of giving the
same effect with the needle,"—that is, to embroider.

Phrygia, a rather ill-defined portion of Asia Minor,
probably occupying the central plateau of Anatolia and
extending as far east as the river Halys, was wonderfully

A B C D E F

PLATE IV—ASIATIC COSTUME—ANCIENT TIMES

A—A Phrygian nobleman. The long sleeves reaching to the wrist and the pantaloons terminating at the ankles were characteristic of the costume of eastern peoples.

B—Costume of a Dacian king. The mantle edged with fringe distinguished persons of eminence.

C—A Dacian woman wearing the flowing skirt and long overtunic with a suggestion of sleeve.

D—A Phrygian lady of rank. The long flowing tunic and mantle of rich material, the head-dress, and casket of jewels suggest the wealth of the East.

E—A Phrygian lady of rank.

F—Figure attired for religious rites. (From a Greek vase, sometimes classified as Greek.)

34

rich in gold. The great quantities of this precious metal found in that region no doubt helped to frame the myth of King Midas, who was one of the Phrygian rulers. With this knowledge it is not surprising to read of the "purple and fine linen" of these ancient peoples, to note the beautiful designs which edge the costumes and mantles, and the silver and gold of their ornaments and arms.

Among the Phrygians the dress consisted of two tunics. (Fig. 10.) The under one was longer and terminated at or above the knees, the sleeves were wrist-length. Over this was worn a second tunic reaching to the hip. This was without sleeves and usually worn without a girdle. Sometimes this second tunic was quite full, girded at the hips, and fell to the knee. Often with this the sleeves of the under tunic were also full, turned and fastened very high with a hook.

The ancient records show the women of Phrygia wearing the long straight tunic, close fitting, with sleeves reaching to the wrist or elbow. This was of fine texture, many times embroidered in threads of harmonizing color. Over this characteristic dress was worn the mantle of rich material, with woven borders and all-over patterns. *D* and *F*, Plate IV.) The short skirted tunic is also pictured as a favorite costume of Phrygian women. (*E*, Plate IV.)

Fig. 10. A Phrygian (After Montfaucon)

The little cap worn by the Phrygians, and termed the "Phrygian bonnet," traveled as far westward as Venice, and the Doge continued to wear it to the last day of Venetian independence. The characteristic features of the Phrygian cap are its point or top bent forward, and its long flaps descending to the shoulders. Sometimes the cap was of soft pliant material and, unable to support itself, hung in folds. Again, when made in a more durable material such as leather or metal, it took on the appearance of a helmet, so well did it keep its erect shape.   Often these were richly ornamented. Usually two or four flaps descended to the shoulder, and these were probably the legs of the animals whose skins furnished the body of the casque or cap.

Among the statues and paintings of the Amazons, women celebrated for their courage and daring, variations of the Phrygian cap may be seen. Many

Fig. 11.   Head of an Amazon
(After Hope)

of their helmets terminate in the bill of a griffin, and the back of the casque takes on the jagged crest of that ancient animal of mythology.   (Fig. 11.) Minerva sometimes appears in a Phrygian helmet.   On many Roman coins Roma is pictured wearing the same type of helmet.   Fig. 12, from a cameo, shows Paris wearing the Phrygian cap and the long sleeves and pantaloons of Asia.   Many of the officers of the Byzantine emperors wore the same head-dress.   Later it was borrowed by the Turks and Greeks, and even in our day the children still cling to their "stocking-cap."

Fig. 12. Costume from a cameo (After Hope)

The costume of the Amazon women was quite similar to the usual Asiatic dress.   When at home and following peaceful pursuits they are pictured as wearing short skirts of fine material, richly embroidered or painted in spots, zigzags, checks, or stripes. The skirts were worn over the long pantaloons, which were very loose, hanging in numerous folds and caught in with the tops of the shoes. When engaged in war, they are often represented as wearing the long pantaloons of skins. A little vest closed in front was usually the upper part of the pantaloon costume, and was always of the same material. (Plate III.) Over this a wide sleeveless tunic of another material was sometimes worn. This was clasped at the shoulders, girded at the waist, and, if very long, girded a second time by means of a second belt about the hip, thus making the tunic reach about the middle of the thigh. Many of the ancient vases show a voluminous mantle added to this usual costume of the warring Amazons.

Among the Persians it was never the custom to go without clothing as it was among the Greeks; consequently the arrangement of dress among these people became of much importance. The vest and pantaloons, as with other Asiatic nations, were usually of linen, and the tunic also of linen. Later Cyrus (about 559 B. C.) brought the long robe or sleeved tunic of the Medes, and persuaded the people to adopt it. They found it of great advantage, not only in covering the defects of the body but in adding to the majesty of the figure. (Fig. 13.) These sleeved tunics were worn both long and short, depending upon the rank and power of the wearer. The dignitaries of Persia wore the purple robe lined with white. It was usually long, and shortened by means of horizontal folds arranged like steps.

On many ancient coins the kings of Persia may be seen wearing long beards and enormous wigs of curled hair. Sometimes the hair is arranged in long braids which fall over the shoulder. Bonnets, crowns, and diadems were worn, and it was also a common custom to bind a fine cloth about the head—a custom which has been perpetuated in the turban of the East.

Among the Persians the same garments were worn by both men and women. The latter, however, girded themselves with sashes made with fringes. Necklaces, ear-rings, bracelets, and rings on the fingers and joints, contributed not a little to the Persian costume.

Display and luxury characterized the Medes. Painted eyes, eyelids, and eyebrows gave an expression of power to the countenance. False hair in enormous quantities was worn by both men and women, and the latter added t h e further ornamentation, t h e aigrette. Long tunics descending to the feet were the fashion. These were of many brilliant colors and often embroidered. The successors of Cyrus wore a robe usually purple in color, without sleeves and richly embroidered. Subjects were compelled to wear the long sleeves, for they were not permitted to show the arm.

The Syrians wore narrow, close-fitting, plain clothes, in which dark blue threads alternated with red, frequently adorned with rich embroidery.

The Parthians, who inhabited a part of the Persian kingdom, were noted for their beauty. Their dress in the main followed the tendencies of that of Persia. A few of the rare

Fig. 13. A Persian
(After Hope)

coins collected from this country show the heads of the Parthians with their long hair and elaborately curled beards. Often they wear a cylindrical cap rather wider at the top than at the bottom, and called by the Greeks "mitre." (Fig. 13.) Sometimes this cap was enriched by a diadem, and often loaded with different emblematic ornaments. Its shape is to this day preserved in the head-dress of the Armenian priests.

The Dacians, though living on the European side of the Euxine, were of Asiatic origin, and seem to have adopted the same costume with but few changes. Their shoes or soles were fastened with long strings wound several times around the ankle, and their pantaloons were extremely wide. (*B*, Plate IV.) The dress of the Dacian women was equally voluminous and very long. The second tunic, which frequently descended to the foot, is often represented drawn up in numerous folds under the girdle. (*C*, Plate IV.)

Gradually through the extensive commercial relations existing between these countries bordering on the Red Sea and Mediterranean Sea, much of the dress which was purely local in character became more widely diffused. Types of costume which were characteristic of one country and appealed to the people of another were adopted by them, adjusted to the new conditions, and became a part of the national costume.

REVIEW

1. What outstanding contribution to costume has been made by the Orient?
2. Describe, in brief, the "pantalooned" figure of the East.
3. Name the various textile arts in which the people of Asia Minor excelled.
4. Name two cities which were commercially famous. In what particular fields did they excel?
5. Among what peoples was embroidery used as an enrichment on dress? Discuss colors used and general pattern.
6. Explain the use of fringe which usually finishes the mantles of the East. How does it differ from that worn on the mantles of the Greeks?
7. Describe fully the characteristic footwear of Eastern peoples.
8. Describe the dress of Phrygian women. Describe the Phrygian bonnet.
9. Name at least one distinguishing feature in the dress of the Medes, the Persians, the Parthians, the Dacians.
10. How did purely local characteristics in costume percolate through to other countries?

CHAPTER FOUR

GRECIAN Costume
(700 B. C. - 53 B. C.)

THE civilization of ancient Greece has left a rich heritage to posterity in her chaste and refined simplicity of dress. The saneness maintained in the matter of costume throughout the development of Greek national life is unequaled. Those excesses and barbaric splendors which so often appear in dress during a nation's most luxurious days were never seen in Greece. On the contrary, throughout her progress from primitive conditions to the highest point of refinement, dress remained exceedingly simple. It is to the costume of Greece of twenty-five hundred years ago that we turn for grace, beauty of line, refinement of detail, and unity of composition.

In approaching the study of Grecian costume one naturally recalls the many lines of Homer which sing of the beauty of Greek women—of the beautiful hair ornaments, veils, and diadems. The familiar sculptures of Greece and the realistic representations of costume seen in Greek vase paintings come to mind. However, it is not in any one of these sources alone that the wealth and variety characteristic of the dress of the classic world is found. It is only in study that combines all three sources—literature, painting, and sculpture—that one may develop an appreciation of the entire field of Greek costume.

It is in Greek literature particularly that we find reference again and again to the charming diversity in materials, ornament, and detail. It is in Greek literature combined with the expression of Greek life in sculpture and painting that we have an authentic and complete background for our study of classic costume.

The two garments always associated with Greek life and worn alike by men and women were the chiton and the himation. Today they are frequently called "tunic" and "mantle." The chiton was a form of tunic which was doubtless of Asiatic origin. Many of the oldest bas-reliefs show the

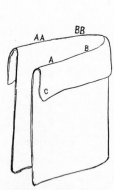

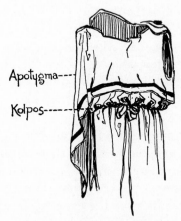

Apotygma---

Kolpos----

Fig. 14. The peplos

Fig. 15. Doric chiton, showing "apotygma" and "kolpos"

Assyrians wearing both long and short chitons. The earliest form of Greek chiton was called the peplos. This was in use during the period 1200 B. C.-600 B. C., and the later forms of chiton, notably the Doric and Ionic, superceded it.

The peplos was a rectangular piece of woolen material sufficiently large to wrap about the body. In adjusting it the upper long edge of the material was first folded over (Fig. 14), and the whole adjusted about the body, beginning at the left. Then the front and back of the folded edge were pulled up and fastened on the shoulder with clasps or brooches, points *A* and *AA* meeting over the right shoulder, *B* and *BB* over the left. It was then girded at the waist. The right side of the peplos remained open, and the over-fold covered the chest and the back. Since the material was heavy and closely wrapped the figure, the beautiful folds which distinguished the fifth-century chiton were absent.

The Doric chiton resembled the peplos. It was, however, more ample, of softer and finer material, and fell in numerous folds. It was girded at the waist and the superfluous length, pulled up through the girdle, fell in a baggy effect called the "kolpos." (Fig. 15.) The folded upper portion was known as the "apotygma." Great variety was introduced into the Doric chiton by making the apotygma long or short. When short, the garment was longer and consequently the kolpos was larger. With the longer apotygma, the length of the chiton was necessarily shortened, and the girdle was worn over two thicknesses of material. (*D, Plate V.*)

Among the women of Greece, the Dorians, particularly those dwelling about Sparta, were the conspicuous athletes. Superfluous length of dress hindered the graceful freedom of the body, consequently the Spartan women often wore the double girded chiton. This second girdle was adjusted about the hips and the material pulled up through this and the girdle encircling the waist. (Fig. 16.)

The names Doric and Ionic, given to the two types of chiton, correspond to those of the well-known columns of Greek architecture. The Dorians were soldiers and prac-

Fig. 16. The double girded chiton (After Hope)

tical men of affairs. These qualities were expressed in both the simplicity and strength of the architectural column, and the practicality of the Doric chiton. The Ionians were the artists, poets, and philosophers of Greece. Their every effort was marked by a fine feeling for grace and beauty Thus every nation expresses its characteristics in each field of activity which it enters, whether it be dress, architecture or political or commercial life.

4

Among the Ionians, linen is said to have been the choice material for the chiton. This was probably of sufficiently fine quality to lend itself well to easy and graceful folds

Fig. 17. Ionic chiton

when girded. In later times embroidery was added as en- richment. Greek vase paintings, in particular, show a great variety in these beautiful, patterned borders running along the lower edge of the chiton. Some of these were woven in the material while others as bands or borders were set on.

The Ionic chiton in its simplest form was an oblong piece of linen, twice the span of the arms in width. The length, from shoulder to feet, was always greater than the wearer was tall. In adjusting the chiton the front and back edges were caught over the shoulders and arms and held by means of clasps or brooches. The hands passed through the open spaces at the corners. (Fig. 17.) The front edge, spaced with two or three more inches than the back, gave the easy fall to the front which is characteristic of Greek dress. The girdle was added and the material

A   B   C   D   E   F

PLATE V—GRECIAN COSTUME—700 B. C.-53 B. C.

A—The Greek tunic with the added upper garment resembling the "bib" of the Ionic chiton and called the diploïdion.

B—The long straight tunic girded about the waist and hips, with the folds pulled up through the two girdles, making the tunic a convenient length.

C—The twice-girded Doric chiton. The little Phrygian cap became a favored head-dress of Greek women.

D—The Doric chiton girded over two thicknesses of material.

E—A flute player, wearing the chiton and himation.

F, G—Examples of Doric chiton showing borders and patterns found in vase paintings.

44

adjusted, forming the kolpos. The curved kolpos, or line
about the hip, was secured by drawing the material deeper
at the sides, making the skirt of equal length. There were
two other styles of girding the chiton. A band or ribbon
to be used as a girdle was first let down over the shoulders
to the waistline at the back, the ends of the ribbon passing

Fig. 18.   Ionic chiton, showing adjustment of girdle

under the arms were put through this loop, brought to the
front of the waist and tied. This gave the effect of straps
over the shoulders. (Fig. 18.) The second style shows
the ribbon let down over the back, but the ends were first
crossed over the chest before passing under the arms. They
are then caught through the ribbon at the back, brought to
the front and tied. (Fig. 19.) When it was desired to
shorten the chiton still more to give freer action in
walking, the hip-girdle was added. This was made by
carrying the ends of the ribbon down and around the
hips.

At a later date the chiton was fashioned of two strips
of material, frequently sewn together at the sides to within
a few inches of the top. The loose upper edges were then
caught over the shoulders. It was without sleeves and resembled a simple tunic. (*B* and *E*, Plate V.)

In many statues of Greek maidens, which have been
recovered, a kind of knitted chiton is seen. The knitted

effect has been given by means of minute lines seaming the figure. This suggests worsted work. As Greek women were accomplished in the arts of spinning and weaving, it is not unlikely that the art of knitting was known to them.

In earliest times wool was used for the Greek dress; then flax, then flax and silk, and lastly, pure silk. Silk in both the woven and raw state was introduced into Greece from Asia Minor. That which came in the raw state was woven into a fine transparent silk gauze which was frequently used in later times for the chiton and other parts of the Greek dress.

The outer garment worn by the Greeks was the himation. This was worn by both men and women, and seems to have been indispensable with the Ionic chiton. It was an oblong piece of linen or woolen material measuring about fifteen feet long by six feet wide. This particular garment was never fastened by clasps or brooches, but was wrapped or draped about the figure in ways so intricate that it was impossible for it to slip out of place. There seems to have been an endless variety in the arrangement of the himation, each indicative of the fancy of the wearer. As today one's dress is the expression of his taste,

Fig. 19.   Ionic chiton showing adjustment of girdle

so in ancient Greece the arrangement of the himation was an index to the character and culture of the wearer. When this garment was long and roomy it was wound twice around the body; first under the arms, and next over the shoulders. (*E*, Plate VI.) Another style which left the right arm free is seen in the painting and sculpture of the period. (*A*, Plate VI.) One end was drawn over the left shoulder from the back, and hung almost to the lower edge of the chiton. Then the material was passed across the back, under the right arm, and the remaining end thrown over the left shoulder. In still another style, one end was drawn from the back over the left shoulder, the material passed across the back and under the right arm as before; but, instead of throwing the end over the left shoulder, it was carried on the left forearm. With the Greeks the himation never had, as among the barbarians, the outer edge adorned with a separate fringe. In contrast with the Eastern custom of setting fringe on the garment as a decoration, the Greeks were sparing in their use of fringe. They never added this to the material; consequently, when it is seen, it may always be regarded as an integral part of the woven fabric. In order to preserve the folds and assist in keeping the robe in place, small weights were often sewed into the corners. In rainy or cold weather the mantle was drawn over the head, serving as a headcovering and cloak combined. In mourning, also, the mantle was drawn over the head. In this instance, however, the color—purple, dark green, or black—had much to do with the significance of mourning.

A second garment which afforded an additional covering for the upper part of the body, and resembled the folded hanging part of the chiton, was often worn. This seems to have been a square or oblong piece of material of various sizes, resembling the modern shawl, and called *diploïdion*. This, also, was frequently embroidered, the pattern being either woven in the material or, in the form of bands and borders, was set upon the cloth. It was folded double, the folded edge being upward and the bordered edge extending down to or beyond the girdle. This was placed around the figure so that the center of the material came under the left arm. It was then secured by clasps which held the front and back edges together on the shoulders. The clasps were frequently of beautiful workmanship, and the stone cameo was a favorite setting. If the material of the diploidion happened to be square, the ends would probably reach the waist, (*C*, Plate V.); if long, they fell to the ankles. (*A*, Plate V.) The shape of the garment was considerably mod-

A   B   C   D   E   F   G

PLATE VI—GRECIAN COSTUME—700 B. C.-53 B. C.

A—The himation, or shawl-shaped drapery, worn over the chiton. This
was the garment that expressed through its style of arrangement the
refinement and rank of the wearer.

B, C—Two mourning figures in robes of purple, dark green and black.
The hair was frequently cut as a sign of sorrow.

D—A short, ungirded upper garment.

E—A peasant girl.

F—A Grecian woman wearing the himation draped over the left shoulder.

G—A Grecian costume with sleeves. The free edges of the folds of the
chiton hanging from the shoulder are here held together by clasps or
studs, thus forming a sleeve.

48

ified by fashion, in later times it became a narrow slip hanging from the shoulders and resembled a semi-fitting jacket (*D*, Plate VI.)

The chlamys was a cloak worn by men. It resembled the himation in shape but was much smaller, measuring about seven feet by three and a half. When folded in two it formed a square. It was worn covering the left arm and side. The top edges were caught over the right shoulder and fastened with a brooch. The right side was open and the right arm free. This was the garment worn by men when riding. It was also used as a military cloak.

Veils were a charming note in the costume of Grecian women of rank; they were chiefly worn as a sign of modesty. Penelope when urged to say whether she preferred to stay with her father or to follow her husband, is represented as expressing her preference for the latter by drawing her veil over her blushing features.

> A veil of richest texture wrought she wears;
> —*Odyssey, xviii.*

And again:

> A veil translucent, o'er her brow displayed.
> —*Odyssey, xviii.*

At the adornment of Pandora we read that the goddess, Athene,

> held with her hands a curiously embroidered veil, a marvel to look upon.   —HESIOD, *The Theogony.*

Many references to veils appear all through the *Iliad* and the *Odyssey*. Of Helen we read:

> O'er her fair face a snowy veil she threw,
> And softly sighing from the loom withdrew.
> —*Iliad, iii.*

Embroidery distinguishes the veil of Athene:

> Pallas disrobes; her radiant veil untied,
> With flowers adorned, with art diversified.
> —*Iliad, v.*

The beauty and arrangement of the hair was given the greatest possible attention by these ladies of classic Greece. Since the general coloring of the southern races is dark, the lighter colorings, which were unusual, were considered more beautiful. The goddesses are often described as golden, red, or auburn haired. Paris has yellow hair; Achilles has ruddy hair; and Adonis wears a ruddy beard. In ancient painting and sculpture, red is often used for the color of the hair and beard.

Quite contrary to the custom among the Egyptians, the hair of both men and women was permitted to grow. The gods themselves rejoiced in the possession of long and abundant hair; Zeus, the king of gods, and men, is always pictured with "ambrosial locks" falling to the shoulders.

The young women often wore the hair falling loose in natural curls, or straight to the shoulders. (*A, C, F, G,* Plate V.) Others twisted or plaited their hair in various ways, sometimes confining it in a net spoken of as the caul. (*G,* Plate VI.) As a final touch the crown, wreath, or ornamental head-dress was frequently added. The head-band was probably a cord carried around the head and tied at the back with ribbons. In the following lines referring to Andromache's despair at the death of Hector, the head-dress is suggested; also the words band, net, and veil are used.

> . . . The ornaments
> Dropped from her brow,—the wreath, the woven band,
> The net, the veil, which Venus gave . . .

The ladies of fashion also adopted the mitre, the bushel-shaped crown worn by the goddess Ceres, and the tiara, the crescent-shaped diadem of Juno and Venus. Besides these, rows of beads, wreaths of flowers, nettings, fillets, and ornaments innumerable were worn by all the fashionable ladies of the period.

The wearing of hats seems to have been reserved for the women of later days. The men of Greece, however,

protected their heads while traveling by wearing a broad-
brimmed hat of felt, tied under the chin and known as the
petasus. When not upon the head it was pushed back on the
shoulders and supported by a string about the neck.

Though the Greek dress, when compared with that of
contemporary peoples, is always simple, there is a distinct
difference in costume between the Homeric period and the
later centuries. The distinguishing marks of the earlier
period were the quality and rarity of the cloth, the expense
of the dye, and the richness of the embroidery which often
covered the entire surface of the chiton. It is also a matter
of record that golden discs were glued over the surface of
the fabric, thus adding to the glitter and splendor of the
early dress. When a greater refinement of feeling developed, wealth, rank and social prominence were no longer
indicated by lavish display but it was the cut of the garment, the manner of wearing the chiton and himation, and
the more subtle distinctions at which the Greek leaders
aimed. In later times the early display was stigmatized
by Euripides as "barbaric finery."

The women of Greece were famed for both their work
with the needle and their skill at the loom. No doubt many
of the early stitches and designs were borrowed from oriental sources, for both Tyre and Sidon were now at the
peak of their glory. During the earlier years embroidery
had been wrought in cotton, woolen, and flaxen threads.
Silk was the last thread introduced into Europe, and that
not until the first century.

Over and over again the Iliad portrays the famed women
of Greece either at the loom weaving their precious patterns
or plying the needle in embroidery. Of Helen we read:

> Here in her palace at her loom she found;
> The golden web her own sad story crown'd,
> The Trojan wars she weaved (herself the prize)
> And the dire triumph of her fatal eyes.
>
> —*Iliad, iii.*

Lines of the *Odyssey* also sing with an equal pride of
this same skill attained by these women of ancient Greece.

PLATE VII—GRECIAN COSTUME—700 B. C.-53 B. C.

A, B—The traveling cloaks and petasos, or broad brimmed hat, worn by
the men of Greece.
C, D—Soldiers of Greece.
E—A Greek philosopher.
F—A peasant.

Of the wife of Alcinous we read:

> Her royal hand a wondrous work designs;
> Around a circle of bright damsels shine,
> Part twist the threads, and part the wool dispose,
> Whilst with the purple orb the spindle grows.
>
> —*Odyssey, vi.*

And Penelope says:

> The vest much envied on your native coast,
> And regal robe with figured gild embossed
> In happier hours my artful hand employ'd,
> When my loved lord this blissful bower enjoy'd.
>
> —*Odyssey, xix.*

Fig. 20.   Greek ornament.   a, b, frets; c, guilloche; d, e, anthemion

In many recovered statues of draped figures, painted borders and beautiful designs in color still remain, suggesting the borders woven into the garments by these women of Greece. Among these are the characteristic Greek patterns, the frets, or meanders, which were doubtless of textile origin. (Fig. 20, a and b. See also designs upon garments shown in plates.) The guilloche is another form of meander with the corners rounded, and suggests the Nile pattern. (Fig. 20, c.) The name "meander" is derived from the river Maiandros in Asia Minor, which flows in sinuous curves. All Greek ornament shows a great refinement of feeling for the abstract principles of design, rhythm, balance, subtle proportion, and spacing. The most notable feature of Greek ornament is the anthemion, or "honeysuckle ornament.'' (Fig. 20, d and e.) The beautiful large leaves, sharply toothed, of the acanthus tree and the laurel, the leaf of the bay tree, appear many times in jewelry, dress fabrics, and other decorative art. These plant decorations imitated nature in neither color nor form, but furnished the inspiration to creative design.

In early times white and gold seem to have been a favorite combination for feminine dress; this is referred to in the description of Nausica:

> The nymph's fair head a veil transparent graced;
> Her swelling loins a radiant zone embraced
> With flowers of gold; an under robe, unbound,
> In snowy waves flowed glittering to the ground.
>
> —*Odyssey, v.*

And again the white dresses belonging to the household of King Alcinous are mentioned:

> Then emulous the royal robes they lave,
> And plunge the vestures in the cleansing wave.
> The vestures cleaned o'erspread the shelly sand;
> Their snowy lustre whitens all the strand.
>
> —*Odyssey, vi.*

Penelope clothed herself in white when praying for the return of her husband:

> She bathed and robed in white with all her train.
>
> —*Odyssey, vi.*

This choice of white garment, however, does not preclude the use of colors. Among the colors in general use, occasionally one, no doubt, became the fad. At least we may presume as much from the many references to the ''saffron colored robe.'' These saffron colored robes are referred to constantly in the comedies of Aristophanes. In the *Ecclesiazusæ* of Aristophanes an old woman says: ''For I am standing idle, painted over with white lead and clad in a saffron colored robe and humming a tune to myself.'' In another part of the same play a young man describes

an old woman as "clothed in a bloody blister," alluding
to the flame or saffron color.   The *Agamemnon* of
Æschylus says in the chorus referring to Iphigenia: "And
pouring to the ground her garments of saffron dye."
Purple, usually suggestive of kingly or military rank, is
referred to frequently in Greek literature.   Though it is
usually worn by men, it is occasionally mentioned as worn
by women.

> Her purple garments veiled the falling tear.
> —*Odyssey, iv.*

Purple as well as black and other dark colors were worn
as a mark of grief or mourning.   In fact, black was never
worn by the Grecian women on any other occasion
than that of misfortune or sorrow.   When so robed, the
head was often covered with the himation.   (*B* and *C*,
Plate VI.)

> The face wrapped in a veil, declared her woes.

The closely cut hair completed the outward signs of
mourning:

> Will any means of grace appear or must I cut my locks,
> And clothe me even now in black array of garments?

The ancient form of stay, to which the modern corset
may be traced, was a very necessary part of the costume
of both Grecian and Roman women.   These stays consisted
of supporting bands of linen, wool, or soft skin worn round
the body in a manner similar to the way in which putties
are worn round the legs of the present-day soldiery.   There
were usually three supporting bands; the zone or loin band,
the thoracic band or strophion, intended to support the
breasts and conserve the figure, and lastly, the waist band,
which filled the space between the other two.   It was, no
doubt, from the combination of these three bands that the
modern corset evolved.

The Grecian women gave a great deal of attention to
the beauty of their sandals.   These were often one of the

most costly articles of feminine dress. The earliest form
of sandal for both sexes was only a wooden or leather sole
with thongs attached to tie over the foot. Later a
piece of leather covering the toes was added and the thongs
or straps were given a variety of beautiful arrangement
over the instep and about the ankle. Many times rich embroidery was added as a decorative feature to the strap
and the leather which covered the toes. Shoes or half-
boots were also worn by the women of Greece; these were
laced in front and lined with the fur of the cat tribe. The
muzzle or claws often hang from the top of the boot as
an ornament similar to those worn by Asiatic women.
(*E*, Plate IV.)

The men of rank and fashion seemed to be quite as
fastidious about the beauty of their sandals as were the
women. Often those worn displayed the finest workmanship. (*A, C,* and *D,* Plate VII.) The philosophers did
not appropriate this fashionable foot-gear, but preferred
to go about in very simple shoes or sandals. (*E*, Plate
VII.)

It is in the comedies of Aristophanes that we find the
vanities of the Grecian women exploited. Referring to
the painting of the face with white lead by elderly women
who wished to appear youthful, we read the words of a
young man to an old woman:

> Are you an ape covered with white lead or are you an old
> woman sent up from the dead?
>
> —ARISTOPHANES, *Ecclesiazusæ.*

Again, a young man holds a torch high and looks into
the face of an old woman, saying:

> O see, Poseidon and ye elderly gods, how many wrinkles she
> has in her face. Upon my word you'd be the better for it if one
> were to wash you clean. —*Plutus.*

Referring to the use of artificial hair we read:

> If thee doesn't make haste to get away from this with prodigi-
> ous speed, I'll forthwith be separating, even from thy brains, those
> falsified dandily arranged corkscrew curls of thine, with all their
> grease as well. —*Truculentus.*

The following lines are an interesting example of similar character:

> You have bought hair, paint, honey, wax, teeth, at the same cost
> you could have bought a face. —PALLADAS.

> You dye your hair; but you will not dye your old age, nor will
> you stretch out the wrinkles of your cheeks. Do not then plaster
> the whole of your face with paint, so that you have a mask, not
> a face, for it is of no use. Why, are you mad? A paint and
> wash will never make a Hecuba a Helen. —LUCIAN.

The desire to be admired evidently led the woman of Greece to adopt all the artifice that could be devised at that period. In this respect she is decidedly human and no doubt would be quite at ease before a modern toilette table.

Fig. 21. Pyxis and fans

Along with all the toilette accessories were the ornaments—the ear-rings, necklaces, bracelets, rings and beautiful pins for the hair. The recent discoveries of Dr. Heinrich Schliemann at Mycenæ prove that the wealth and beauty of jewels and decorative work, to which frequent reference is made in the Homeric poems, is not an exaggeration, but a description of the ornament of the period.

> What a quantity of gold she wears, like a virgin!
> —ARISTOPHANES, *The Birds.*

> Chains, bracelets, pendants, all their toys I wrought,
> —*Iliad, xxii.*

> Her soft white neck, rich carcanets embraced,
> Bright, and with gold in all variety graced,
> —HOMER, *Hymn to Aphrodite.*

All of these ornaments were kept in a small box or casket called pyxis (Fig. 21), which was the name of the wood from which the jewel boxes were made. Often on the vases and occasionally on the tomb monuments the Grecian lady is pictured holding this dainty casket from which she is selecting her ornaments.

The fan and sunshade were well known in Athens. Both had been used by Assyrians, Egyptians, and Persians. Grecian women adopted the fan soon after the fifth century B. C. The fans of this early day were made of leaves and feathers attached to a rigid handle. In the later centuries they were made by stretching linen or silk over a frame shaped like a leaf. In Greece, as in Egypt, the large fans with long handles were commonly used by slaves in the service of their masters. The sunshades resembled the Japanese parasol, being somewhat flat. They were made on a framework similar to the umbrella of today, and covered with linen or silk. Out-of-doors, the women were protected from the sun by the long handled sunshade carried by a slave.

The following lines from the *Iliad* picture in a poetic phrasing the fastidious toilette of the early ages of Greece:

> Swift to her bright apartments she repairs,
> Sacred to dress and beauty's pleasing cares;
> With skill divine has Vulcan form'd the bower
> Safe from access of each intruding power.
> Touch'd with her secret key, the doors unfold,
> Self closed, behind her shut the valves of gold,
> Here first she bathes; and round her body pours
> Soft oils of fragrance, and ambrosial showers:
> The winds, perfumed, the balmy gale convey
> Through heaven, through earth, and all th' aerial way
> Spirit divine, whose exhalation greets
> The sense of gods with more than mortal sweets.
> Thus while she breath'd of heaven, with decent pride
> Her artful hands the radiant tresses tied;
> Part o'er her head in shining ringlets roll'd
> Part o'er her shoulders rolled like melted gold;
> Around her next a heavenly mantle flow'd,
> That rich with Pallas' labour'd colors glow'd;
> Large clasps of gold the foldings gather'd round,

A golden zone her swelling bosom bound.
Far beaming pendants tremble in her ears
Each gem illumined with a triple star.
Then o'er her head she cast a veil more white
Than new fallen snow, and dazzling as the light.
Last, her fair feet celestial sandals grace.
Forth from the dome the imperial goddess moves,
And calls the mother of the smiles and loves.

—Iliad, xiv.

REVIEW

1. What elements of beauty distinguish the ancient Greek dress?
2. What are the authentic sources of information?
3. Name the textile arts which flourished in ancient Greece.
4. Name the materials in general use. Name the colors particularly favored.
5. Define: *chiton, chalmys, petasos, pyxis.*
6. Describe the characteristic Doric dress. The Ionic. Which do you consider more beautiful? Why?
7. How does the dress of Homeric times compare with that of later days?
8. Name the popular ornaments favored by Grecian women. Describe the fans and sunshades.
9. Describe the various artifices of the toilette.
10. What elements of ancient Greek dress could, with advantage, be introduced into modern costume?

CHAPTER FIVE

ROMAN Costume
(53 B. C.-500 A. D.)

THE life of the Roman Empire is commonly reckoned from 53 B. C. to 500 A. D. During this long period Rome exerted a dominant influence on the manners and customs of practically the entire known world. The Romans borrowed much from the Greeks in matters of dress, but the distinguishing feature of the Roman costume was different from that of all other nations. The toga may properly be called the Roman's national dress. (*B* and *C*, Plate VIII.)

In early days it seems to have been worn by both men and women over the long tunic or stola, which was similar to the Greek chiton. The exact form of the ancient Roman toga has long been a subject of controversy. Some contend it was a piece of square or oblong material, and resembled the Greek himation; others that it was circular in form. Be that as it may, the toga of Rome's imperial day was semi-circular in form, and measured from tip to tip about three times the height of the wearer. Though in this form it somewhat resembles the Greek himation it is without the four corners or points. It was sufficiently ample to envelope the whole figure, and could be so arranged as to allow a portion of it to be pulled over the head for protection. The arrangement of the toga was a matter of personal pride to the Roman.

It was usually draped on the figure by starting at the left foot. The straight edge was taken over the shoulder and arm, passed across the back, and under the right arm. It was then carried across the chest, over the left shoulder, and the remaining portion was left hanging down the back. The width of material under the right arm was often turned

over, giving the effect of a second drapery. The material
of the straight edge of the first section, which passed over
the left shoulder, was given a draped effect by being pulled
out and adjusted loosely over the top part. The loose portion at the back of the right shoulder was sometimes
fasten'ed at the belt, forming a sleeve.

If the ends were too long they could be shortened by
tying knots in the cloth near the ends. There were times,
however, when the ends were allowed to sweep the ground.
This was looked upon as a sign of the great dignity and
high rank of the wearer.

Soft wool, silk, and fine linen were used for the toga.
Undyed wool of a yellowish hue was favored by the higher
classes. In lieu of the toga, the lower classes wore a hooded
cloak of coarse gray or tan material.

The materials commonly used in Rome were woolen,
linen, and silk. Woolen was most generally used in the
earlier days. Augustus is said to have worn in winter no
less than four tunics beside the under one, and all of them
woolen. It is believed that linen was in common use for
women's garments long before it was adopted for those of
men. Some authorities state that it was not in use for
men's garments until a late period of the Roman Empire.
Silk seems to have been unknown to the Romans during the
Republic. In the time of the Emperor Aurelians (161 A. D.)
a robe of pure silk was so expensive that he refused to permit his empress to wear it. Heliogabalus (213-222) is said
to have been the first emperor who wore a robe of pure silk.
The Romans considered the silk imported from India too
thick and closely woven; consequently it was unraveled and
rewoven with linen or wool, and made so thin as to be transparent. Later, however, the silkworm was introduced from
the East, and the Roman manufactures soon equaled those
of India.

The story of the introduction of the silkworm into
Rome has to do with the ingenuity of two monks traveling
in the Orient. There they became greatly interested in the
silkworms of China. Knowing that the necessary expense

PLATE VIII—ROMAN COSTUME—53 B. C.-500 A. D.

A—Roman emperor in military tunic and paludamentum. This mantle, being less trailing and cumbersome than the toga, was frequently worn. It was fastened on the right shoulder by a clasp or button.

B, C—Roman citizens wearing the toga.

D—Military tunic of Roman emperor.

E, F, G—A group showing various types of dress worn by the Roman soldiery.

62

of silk was due to the fact that it had to be imported from the East, they hit upon the idea of carrying a gift of these curiosities back to their emperor. Fortunately, the monks in their travels carried the popular telescope canes which were a great convenience for transporting numerous objects, and forbidden objects in particular. In this instance they packed their canes full of the coveted eggs of the silkworm and carried them back to Rome. Thus it is that the great European silk industry owes its beginnings to the ingenuity of two monks and the telescope cane.

With materials of the finest texture, color began to play an important role in the Roman world. Both color in materials and color in embroidery rose to first importance. Since the use of gold thread appealed to the Romans, they made extensive use of it. Pliny mentions cloth made of gold thread without the usual background of linen or woolen material, making a veritable cloth of gold. Gradually colors began to be used as badges to distinguish classes. Purple and gold were reserved for those of royal birth; a purple striped toga was worn by men of rank; a purple silk toga embroidered in gold was the badge of a victorious general. Among the professions, blue was the color for philosophy; black, for theology; and green, for medicine. The costume of the soothsayer was white, with no ornament; that of the lower classes of a somber hue. The peasantry were permitted one color only; officers, garments of two colors; commanders of clans, three colors; and on up to the royal household where seven colors were permissible.

Though the toga was worn by both men and women in the earlier times, it was first laid aside by women, who adopted the palla, which corresponded to the himation of the Greeks. (*B, C, D, E, F,* Plate IX; Photo B.) This garment was oblong in shape; the four points or corners quite distinguished it from the toga. The palla was distinctly a woman's garment, never adopted by the men of Rome. It was worn over the long tunic or stola which resembled the Greek chiton, and fell in numerous folds about the feet.

A   B   C   D   E

PLATE IX—ROMAN COSTUME—53 B. C.-500 A. D.

A—The Roman military tunic, from a statue of Minerva.

B—A figure wearing the simple tunic with long sleeves and the palliolum with the flowing ends wrapped about the figure.

C—A Roman lady enveloped in the palla, the mantle worn by all Roman women. The style of hairdress is seen in many of the portrait busts of the Vatican Gallery.

D—A seated figure in tunic and palla. The sleeves are linked. The hairdress, the ear-rings and sandals are typically Roman.

E—The palliolum, or veil, is draped about the head and shoulders. In warm weather a transparent mantle replaced the veil.

F—A lady of rank wearing the ample palla wrapped about the figure in intricate fashion. The head-dress is distinctly Roman.

64

ETRUSCAN AND ROMAN COSTUMES

A—The Etruscan woman's semicircular outer wrap was worn over a form-fitted short sleeved gown. The two-tone garment and colored edging probably reflect the high culture of 283 B.C.

B and *C*—A Roman empress and her daughter, first century B.C. Similar in construction to Greek costumes, with plain colors, but lacking the simplicity of line.

D—A Roman general wearing a multi-color draped toga that conceals his cuirass and armor. 2nd century A.D.

E—A Roman lady wears a costume showing mono-hued draping in regular sequence of folds.

F and *G*—A Roman consul guiding his son in the use of a waxed stone tablet and stylus; first century, B.C.

MEDIEVAL COSTUMES

A—Theodora, Empress of Byzantium, 508(?)–548 A.D., after a mosaic portrait.

B—Charlemagne, King of the Franks, 768–814, A.D. His garments were woven from rich materials. From an old miniature painting. Actual colors were not known until 15th century.

C and *D*—English jester and Italian youth, 15th century, A.D., when the first printed account of the dyeing process was a 1429 Venetian work.

E—British knight, 1401, A.D., showing change from chain-mail armor to plate; with cuirass, coat of mail, and surcoat.

F—Young English girl with circular rose-colored cape, fifteenth century.

G—Titled lady with veiled steeple headdress, and high-waisted, fur trimmed, blue-green gown.

H—German woman, 13th century. Colors matched those of husband's coat-of-arms. The cape was held in place by a strap across the shoulders.

Originally it had sleeves reaching to the elbow, and later extending to the wrist; often the lower edge of the palla was trimmed with a border or fringe. (*E, F,* Plate IX.) Though the stola over which the palla was worn resembled the chiton of the Greeks, Greek simplicity was not in evidence in the Roman dress. The luxurious taste of the Roman women required several tunics worn one over the other, and each of a different color. The tunics usually varied in length; the topmost was looped up at the waist, displaying the several colors beneath; the sleeves, also, were made of varying length, thus giving the same color effects over the arm. With materials of finest texture and an almost unlimited range of colors, the Roman matron was free to indulge her every whim for display and luxury in dress.

The veil of exquisite quality, called palliolum by the Romans, was a favorite head-dress. It was arranged over the hair, held in place by bands or wreaths, and fell to the shoulders. There are numerous references in Roman literature to the theristrion which was a transparent mantle sometimes taking the place of the veil.

The belt or girdle was an indispensable article of dress. It was made of various materials, suited to the rank or wealth of the wearer. Often the girdle was hidden by the upper part of the stola falling over it.

> Most of the early Romans were peasants. The farmer, clad simply in his tunic, a loose woolen garment which reached the knee, and resembled the chiton, followed his bronze-shod plow drawn by a yoke of cattle. His narrow mind held only sober, practical ideas; for he saw nothing of the world beyond the mountains bordering the plain of the Tiber—mountains which inspired him with no love of the beautiful and the grand, but rather with a feeling of hatred for the enemies who were wont to sweep down from them upon his little field.[1]

He cherished no dreams of military glory or world conquest; only when an enemy attacked did he seize his weapons and join his neighbors to defend his home and

---

[1]George Willis Botsford, *History of the Ancient World* (New York: The Macmillan Company, 1911), p. 328.

PHOTO B—LIVIA, "PUDICITIA"—*Vatican*

Livia, wife of the emperor, Augustus Caesar, wears the typical Roman dress. Note the almost transparent quality of the shawllike mantle, the palla, often so ample that it was draped over the head as a veil.

66

fields. Cincinnatus, called from the plow to the dictator-
ship of the republic, is a typical Roman character. It was
in the early days of hardy, rugged life that the ideals—
social, economic, governmental—which dominated Rome
through her long history, were formed. In her later centuries, every reform in morals or politics was a harking
back to these ancient standards. As the great families
became powerful and wealthy, they acquired vast estates,
cultivated by armies of slaves; but the ancestral virtues
of simplicity, industry, and homely integrity were studi-
ously maintained. The increasing wealth and luxury incident to world dominion severely tested and finally destroyed the old system based on the homely ideals of the
farmer-soldiers of ancient Latium; but the best representatives of the old Roman families, true to family tradition,
fought to the end the vices and corruptions of the East.

One of the noblest and most interesting representatives
of the traditional Roman ideals is the wife of the Emperor
Augustus, Livia, descended from two of the most illustri-
ous Roman families. As Ferrero says:

> In Livia was concentrated the quintessence of the Roman aris-
> tocracy. In the palace of Augustus she preserved the beautiful
> traditions of simplicity and industry. Augustus never wore any
> other togas than those woven by Livia; woven not indeed and alto-
> gether by Livia's hands—though she did not disdain, now and then,
> to work the loom—but by her slaves and freedwomen. Faithful
> to the traditions of the aristocracy, Livia counted it among her
> duties personally to direct the weaving rooms which were in the
> house. As she carefully parceled out the wool to the slaves, watch-
> ing over them lest they waste or steal it, and frequently taking
> her place among them while they were at work, she felt that she
> too contributed to the prosperity and glory of the empire.[2]

Skill in the arts of spinning, weaving, and embroidery
was especially desired by the young Roman matron. It
was with great pride that she wrought out a length of
embroidery or a bit of design upon tunic, veil, or palla.

Many of the designs seen in Roman costume are easily
recognized as Greek in feeling. Rome derived her art

---

[2] *The Women of the Cæsars* (New York: The Century Co., 1912),
pp. 52, 58, 61.

directly from Greece, and shows individuality only in an elaboration of the original. The honeysuckle, acanthus, and laurel of Greek days are constantly used in the Roman scroll patterns. Beautiful rosette designs, inspired by the rose, are combined with the scroll patterns seen in the borders of costumes, Roman jewelry, and other decorated

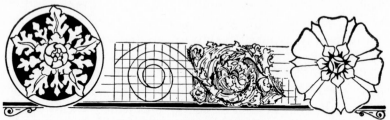

Fig. 22.   Roman ornament

forms. (Fig. 22.) This artistic influence touched Roman life after Greece had come under Roman rule. It was at this time that Greek artists were employed in the Roman households as teachers and designers. Wishing to please their luxury-loving masters, they elaborated the simple forms of Greek design until they took on the extravagant qualities always associated with Roman taste.

The Romans, like the Greeks, gave much attention to the hair. The ladies of the Empire frizzled and curled their hair in most elaborate fashion, adorning it with garlands of flowers, fillets, and ribbons of various colors, besides ornaments of gold, pearl, and precious stones. (Plate IX.)

> In perfect view their hair with fillets tied.
>
> —*Æneid.*

Arranging the hair was a matter of grave importance; it was usually frizzled and adjusted by the slaves of the household.

> His frizzled hair to coil,
> Hot with the vexing iron and smeared
> With fragrant oil.   —*Æneid.*

Sometimes women learned in the art of the coiffure attended to the proper arrangement of the locks, while the fair lady watched the growing edifice of curls in a mirror made of polished steel or brass, tin or silver. Ancient writers say that the lofty pile of false hair worn upon the head resembled a building. Even so, it was one of only moderate height as compared with the head-gear of later days. The back hair was often enclosed in a caul, or net, after the Greek fashion.

> Her head with ringlets of her hair is crowned,
> And in a golden caul the curls are bound.

Indeed, so important was her coiffure to the Roman matron that her care extended even to the sculptured portrait. These, it is said, were ordered with adjustable wigs, in order that with the varying style in coiffure the head-dresses might be changed and thus the portrait always kept in fashion.

The men of Rome usually wore the hair long, and gave it great care. The philosophers permitted the hair and and beard to grow, to give them an air of gravity. Lack of hair among the Romans was considered a deformity. It is said that Julius Cæsar wore a laurel wreath to conceal his baldness. Later, those who were bald wore a kind of peruke made of false hair, called capillamentum.

It was customary for both the Greeks and the Romans to go about bareheaded, but there were two kinds of head coverings which were quite common; the petasus, similar to the Greek hat of the same name, and the pileus, a closely woven cap worn generally at public games and festivals.

Of sandals and shoes the Romans had a great variety, adopted from Greece and from the far east. The Roman shoes had various names, and were distinct badges of the position held in society by the wearer. The baxea, solea, crepida, soccus, and corthurnus were the names of the leading types. The baxea were vegetable sandals, similar in construction, no doubt, to the palm leaf sandals of the Egyptians. They were worn largely by the peasant classes, and by the philosophers and priests as indicative of humility. The solea and crepida were worn indoors, being a species of sandal fastened about the foot or ankle by a fillet or thongs. The soccus was an intermediate covering for the foot; it resembled the modern slipper and could be cast off at pleasure, as it did not fit closely and was not secured by thong or tie. (Fig. 23, b, d.)

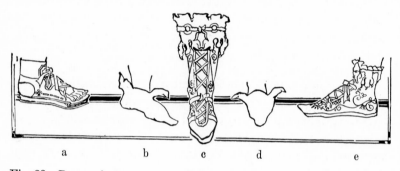

Fig. 23. Roman footwear. a, sandal; b, d, soccus; c, corthurnus (buskin)

The corthurnus (buskin) was anciently worn by the Phrygians, and was later introduced to the stage by Sophocles in his tragedies. (Fig. 23, c.) Hence the term applied to the theatrical performers, "brethren of the sock and buskin." This particular kind of covering was a very high boot, reaching above the calf of the leg and sometimes to the knee. It was laced very closely down the front. Sometimes they were dyed purple and other gay colors; very frequently the head and paws of wild animals orna- mented the top of the boot. If height of figure were de- sired, the ordinary thickness of the sole was increased by the insertion of pieces of cork. The shoes of the wealthy were made of fine leather, and were handsomely decorated. (Fig. 23, a, e.) They were often painted with various colors, and ornamented with gold, silver, and precious stones. It was the Emperor Aurelian who forbade men to wear red, yellow, white, or green shoes. These colors were reserved for women only. The Emperor Heliogabalus had his shoes set with diamonds and other stones, but prohib- ited the use of such ornaments to the women of the empire. Sometimes the shoes had turned up toes, a fashion undoubtedly of eastern origin, and which was carried to such extravagant lengths during the Middle Ages. The Roman senators wore black shoes or buskins reaching to the calf of the leg, usually ornamented on the top of the foot with a gold or silver crescent.

Cosmetics, washes, paint, and perfume were lavishly used by Roman women. White lead to soften the skin and vermilion to tint it were constantly employed by both sexes. The extravagant taste for ornament, for ear-rings, bracelets, and finger-rings brought scathing reprimands from contemporary writers. Pliny says: "They seek for pearls at the bottom of the Red Sea, and search the bowels of the earth for emeralds to decorate their ears." Seneca says that "a single pair was worth the revenue of a large estate."

In both classical and oriental dress, the easy flowing line is the distinguishing characteristic. Climatic conditions and the leisurely life of the people undoubtedly prolonged the fashion of the flowing dress. The citizens were practically nobles, and were not urged by the necessities of life to great activity. All menial work was done by slaves. After Charlemagne (800), the distinctly Roman costume disappeared, although this type of dress continued to be seen in countries under Roman influence.

REVIEW

1. What is the distinguishing garment of Roman national life? Describe fully.
2. What materials were most favored in early days? When was silk introduced? Discuss.
3. What textile arts were highly cultivated by Roman women? Give lines from literary sources verifying your statement.
4. Describe the *stola, palla,* and *palliolum* worn by Roman women.
5. Discuss briefly the use of ornament, cosmetics, and perfumes.
6. Give a brief account of the styles in coiffure.
7. Describe the principal types of Roman footwear.
8. What is the distinguishing characteristic of ancient dress?
9. What were contributing factors to this type of costume?
10. What is your reaction to its use in the modern world?

CHAPTER SIX

The Costume of the Middle Ages
—FRANCE
(476 A. D.-1500 A. D.)

THE period connecting ancient and modern history is vaguely designated as the Middle Ages. It is commonly supposed to begin with the fall of the western Roman Empire, 476 A. D., and to extend to the revival of letters in Europe, about the year 1500. These intervening centuries, often called the Dark Ages, represent a combination of pagan civilization, Germanic barbarism, and Christianity. It was during this period, when Frank, Gaul, and Roman mingled, that costume as we know it today evolved.

When the barbaric hordes of the North began to invade the South, and the Romans began to carry their conquests northward, a revolution in dress, as well as in the political and social condition of the people, followed.

The Northern peoples had learned to protect themselves against the severity of their climate by adopting a close-fitting garment which preserved the heat of the body, and by wrapping their legs in skins. The Romans ridiculed the men of the North as "trousered barbarians," but as the Romans pushed their conquests farther north we find a blending of the Roman and the barbaric custom.

After the conquest of Gaul by Julius Cæsar, Roman civilization was introduced into France. The natural consequence of gradual annexation to the Roman Empire of the various nations subjugated by Roman arms was an assimilation of Roman costume. It is especially interesting, however, to study its development in France, as this country was destined to become the fashion leader for the western world.

There were many conflicting influences in the dress of the people inhabiting this corner of Europe at this early period. The Roman occupation was followed by the invasion of the Franks (428 A. D.-752 A.D.), which caused another change in the style of dress. Under Charlemagne (752-987), still other changes took place, though not so marked. Later, with the accession of the Capet family (987-1328), until the time of the Renaissance a greater variety in dress developed, especially in the details of the costume.

It is quite natural that the Gallic women, becoming Gallo-Roman, desired to follow the fashion set by the ladies of the more influential Roman families. They adopted the palla and the stola, and gathered it in at the waist by a girdle. Thus the girdle became a part of the costume, and by its adjustment a long or short waist could be attained, according to the requirements of fashion. The garments fell in numerous folds about the feet, allowing only the tips of the shoes to be seen. (*B,* Plate X.) Often several tunics were worn one over the other, and frequently the sleeves of the under tunic, which were of a different color, extended to the wrist, while those of the upper one came only to the elbow. Beneath the tunic a close-fitting boneless waist was worn, which was no doubt the progenitrix of that more modern instrument of torture—the corset. The mantle which took the place of the Roman palla was draped about the figure. Gold tissue was a favorite material for this mantle; when occasion demanded, however, heavier stuffs were doubtless used. The mantle frequently took the form of a full cloak, opened in front and secured by a large clasp or brooch. Sometimes it was thrown across the left shoulder, leaving the right arm free. Squares of white linen or colored stuffs were draped over the head, falling to the shoulder. These were bound about the head by circlets of various design, ornamented with jewels. (*C,* Plate X; *C,* Plate XI.) The Phrygian and other little caps frequently covered the head, and, being small, permitted the beautiful hair to be seen. (*F,* Plate X.) Auburn and yellow were particularly admired by these women of Gaul, and if they were unfortunate enough to have dark locks, these were frequently dyed or concealed under artificial hair of a more fashionable hue. Hair dyes as well as cosmetics in general had, along with Roman customs in dress, made their way to Gaul. Drugs of all sorts were lavishly used and even the eyelids were stained to give brilliancy to the eyes.

The wardrobe of the Gallo-Roman woman was rich and varied. There were tunics of linen, cotton, and silk; violet-colored mantles often richly embroidered; veils, scarves, ribbons, and various kinds of shoes and sandals. The house shoes worn by these women of long ago were of soft and pliable material. They were very long, toes pointed, and without heels. The soles were of cork and the toes turned up. When going out of doors this light covering was exchanged for the sandal or a walking boot, which probably resembled the corthurnus of the Romans. In these early days hats had not yet arrived and women generally were wearing head draperies. Sometimes these were draped loosely over the head and shoulders; at other times a coronet was fixed about the brow to keep the veil in place. It remained, however, for the Gallo-Roman woman to adopt a large turbanlike cap which had come from Rome by way of Byzantium. Though the crown and roll of the cap were of different colors, both were decorated with narrow bands set at regular intervals. Properly worn, it was pulled down over the ears, only the lobes being visible, and the hair was completely hidden. Parasols, mirrors of polished metal, gold and silver ornaments, perfumes and scents were also well known to these women of Gaul.

The ancient Egyptian custom of carrying crystal and amber balls for cooling the hands, was evidently passed on by the Romans to the women of Gaul. Little gold and silver nets containing the balls were carried to the theater or festival and when the hands became heated the warmth was allayed by pressing and twisting first the crystal ball and then the amber, the latter giving forth a delightful odor.

The extravagant love of the Gallo-Roman woman for jewels and ornamentation rivaled even that of the Roman

A   B   C   D   E   F

PLATE X—COSTUME OF THE MIDDLE AGES—600-1100

A—752—A Merovingian woman wearing the long, simple garment with the fitted neckline.

B—600—A Gallo-Roman woman. The women of Gaul adopted the dress of the influential Roman women—the stola, girded at the waist, and the palla.

C—1000—A type of costume worn by Carlovingian women. The girdle of this day was a luxury, studded with jewels and gold.

D—1000—The costume of a man of rank showing the lingering influence of Roman dress.

E—1100—A nobleman wearing the embroidered tunic over an undertunic with long sleeves.

F—1100—Capetian woman wearing the long flowing tunic over an undertunic of contrasting color.

75

matrons. The goldsmiths of the East furnished the richest
of ornaments for the head, neck, and arms. Handsome
necklaces made of disks of gold inlaid with heavy pastes,
enameled in color, and encrusted with pearls; rings, bracelets, and earrings set with stones cut *en cabochon* and the
metal enriched with filigree and encrustations. The emerald,
amethyst, sapphire, and engraved stones of great value
were profusely used. An ornamental anklet or garter was
also worn about the leg to confine a trouser of fine linen.

After the invasion of the Franks under the young Prince
Merowig, other changes in costume took place. This period
of Frankish rule is known as the Merovingian period (428
A. D.-752 A. D.)

The Frankish women were large and coarsely built, and
their taste in dress was of a corresponding character. During the earlier period of the Merovingian monarchy both
men and women wore garments of felt, and of a coarse
cloth made of camel's hair and called "camlet." Later this
was woven with a silk warp. Narrow silk mantles of red
and scarlet were also favored in these early centuries. As
the Franks became firmly established their rusticity began
to blend with Latin refinement and produce a new type.
These Merovingian women no doubt appropriated many
of the features they admired in the Gallo-Roman dress.
They, too, continued to wear head draperies often confined
by a jeweled band. They continued to wear the long flowing tunic and ample mantle. The loose, flowing garment
required a belt or girdle; consequently, large, heavy buckles
and clasps of intricate design were in general use. (Photo
C.) Belts were sometimes made of leather and studded with
bosses of gold. Placques of gold, each elaborately chased
or set with stones, were often hinged together or sewed
upon a strip of material, making a very flexible belt or
girdle. Large brooches heavy with stones, encrustations,
or enamel work also held a very important place in the
dress of the period. Queen Clotilde is frequently represented as wearing a tunic confined about the waist by a
band of some precious material, and a mantle laced across

PLATE XI—COSTUME OF THE MIDDLE AGES—1100-1350

A—A knight wearing the chain armor with surcoat emblazoned with
heraldic device.

B—A costume showing the influence of the Crusades upon dress. The
simple, straight tunic and the mantle hanging straight from the
shoulder together with the little chin-banded cap produced a marked
severity in the trend of costume at this time.

C—A Capetian lady wearing the two-tunic dress with the mantle fastened
with a jeweled clasp.

D—A knight of the First Crusade wearing the chain coat of mail.

E—A gentleman of rank wearing the long, tight hose and doublet which
succeeded the loose robes of earlier times.

the breast, over which fell her long plaits of hair. The Merovingians favored many-colored tunics, and bright and showy colors. Gregory of Tours, bishop and historian, who from his position was well acquainted with the customs of the Merovingian court, speaks of the "silken robes," which he describes as "splendid." There were tunics, gowns with long trains, mantles, hoods, and veils.

The Merovingians were forbidden to cut their hair, and consequently it often grew to great length. They usually arranged it in two thick plaits, intertwined with ribbon and flowers; falling over the shoulders it often reached to the knees. (*A*, Plate X.)

As usual, every woman of wealth loaded herself with jewels, necklaces, bracelets, and rings. Costumes worn on festive occasions sparkled with gold and jewels. This love for ornament, for girdles of gold, and gilded embroideries with which they later enriched the borders of tunics and cloaks, savors of the East; it attests the influence of the Imperial Court, which had been removed in the third century from Rome to Byzantium, later called Constantinople in honor of the Emperor Constantine. It was here at the court of Constantine that a new influence was developed, which was to play a mighty part in the shaping of costumes during the succeeding centuries. Here the Emperor gradually gathered artisans from the centers of Europe, and under the zeal of the new religious awakening they produced designs which expressed in many ways the early Christian ideas. The new emblems of Christianity were combined with the traditional form of the Greek and Roman period, producing a type of design and ornament characteristic of the age, and known as Byzantine. The geometric form of this design was combined with the pictorial. For instance, an entire surface of cloth was laid out in connected squares or circles, and within these were pictured scenes and figures from the Gospels. Those of beasts, inclosed in geometric form were also frequent. Many times all manner of conventional floral patterns were used in this geometric background. Rare tapestries were

PHOTO C—COUNT EKKEHARD AND COUNTESS UTA
From Naumberg Cathedral. Twelfth century

Typical figures of the early Middle Ages. Both wear the enveloping mantle. On each mantle appears the left half of a handsome clasp which held the mantle in place about the shoulders. Note the ornate belt and breast ornament of the count. The countess wears the chin strap, introduced during the twelfth century. Note ring on forefinger.

made with inwoven design. Sometimes the warp and woof
were both of linen, again of linen and wool, and still again
of silk. These were used as hangings in the churches. The
designs used in dresses and mantles were similar. The
entire surface of fabrics was covered with conventional

Fig. 24. Byzantine ornament

floral patterns. These were inwoven, printed, and embroidered. Both the men and women of the Franks adopted
these rich materials from the Eastern Roman Empire into
their costume.

The Christian symbols used in Byzantine design were
full of peculiar significance. The cross, the vine, the lamb,
the dove, the square, and the circle was each a reminder
to the early Christian of his new faith. The circle was the
emblem of eternity; the square, of the city that "lieth four-
square." The lamb was a symbol of the Christ; the dove
suggested the Holy Spirit; and the cross, though used in
the classic period, changed under the Byzantine influence,
and was the distinct symbol of Christianity. As in the
familiar Latin cross, the lower limb is the longest, but the
top and arms expand rather than continue straight.
(Fig. 24.)

Not only did the design assume and express the mind
of the period, but soon the colors in use took on a religious
significance. White was the symbol of purity; blue, of heav-
enly trust and sanctification; red, the love of God; purple,
of dignity; green, of eternal youth; gold, of virtue; bright
yellow, of fertility; violet, of humility. The Byzantine contribution to costume, combining pagan and Christian

elements, produced a magnificence in dress rivaling that of any later period.

Under the reign of Charlemagne there was no marked difference in the fashionable costume. The rich stuffs from the East still continued to furnish materials for costume,

Fig. 25. Head-drapery of the early Middle Ages

even after the art of embroidery, tapestry weaving, and appliqué work was carried on in Europe. It is recorded that the daughters of Charlemagne did silk weaving in 800 A. D., but the trade in fine fabrics was practically monopolized by the East. The long tunic still continued the vogue. The most elegant ladies of the period inclined toward two close-fitting tunics of different colors. (*F,* Plate X; *C,* Plate XI.) The neck, sleeve, the lower edge of the tunics, and the mantles were often trimmed with wide bands of embroidery. Transparent and somewhat clinging materials, which revealed the lines of the figure, were frequently used for the tunics. Later, however, the delicate tissues were replaced by heavier materials, and the dresses became much more ample. The girdle was placed just above the hips, and was often of great value, being ornamented with jewels and gold studs. Splendidly embroidered veils were worn upon the head, and frequently secured by a diadem or band. The ladies of noble birth continued to wear their hair long, plaited, and intertwined with ribbons and purple bands, and reaching below the waist. About the eighth century the fashion of concealing the hair, which was in marked contrast to the earlier styles, began to have a following among the leaders of fashion. Squares of white linen and colored stuffs over white linen, which were formerly used to drape the head and shoulders, were now used for framing in the face and hiding the hair. Various kinds of hoods were also worn, known as *chaperon* or *amusse*. (Fig. 25.) The drapery covering the hair and neck is frequently referred to as the *couvrechef* (head covering.) The walking-stick was a fashionable caprice among the Carlovingian women. (*C*, Plate X.) These were usually cut from apple wood, and ornamented with a bird, flower or other device at the top. Gold was lavishly used both in jewels and in ornamentation; jewels were much appreciated, and were worn fastened to the costume of which they seemed to be a part. "Among the admirable miniatures in the Mazarine Library, one shows a queen wearing an under tunic of black, and the upper one in the style of a mantle is purple. Both are edged with bands of yellow, which probably is gold. The shoes also are yellow, with gold ornamentation."[1]

We know much more about the costumes of ladies of rank than about those of the great mass of people. History is almost silent on this point, telling us only that they wore their skirts extremely long, and that their veils were quite thick and almost enveloped the figure.

Like the Greek and Roman women, those of the early Middle Ages were skilled in the art of embroidering. In this way each was able to supply herself with beautiful bits of trimming and ornamentation. Bags, scarves, sleeves, and belts were among the articles of dress favored with the personal touch. It is said that Empress Judith, mother of Charles the Bold, who was unusually skilled in the art of embroidering, presented to the Queen of Denmark a gown richly ornamented with gems and gold, which was the work of her own hands.

The usual mourning costume of the early Middle Ages was quite different from that of the classic world, and resembled somewhat the nun's dress of today. A mantle

---

[1] Augustin Challamel, *History of Fashion in France* (translation, New York, 1882), p. 26.

was worn over a wide-sleeved tunic; under the tunic was a second gown with long close-fitting sleeves buttoning at the wrist. A guimpe of fine material covered the upper part of the bust, encircled the throat, and then joined the veil, which was banded across the forehead and arranged in two large folds over the ears. It was also customary to have the instep of the hose cut open as a sign of mourning.

With the accession of the Capet family (987-1328), the nationality of France became gradually more pronounced. The Gallo-Roman, Frankish, and German women merged into the French women of feudal times. Though the mediæval period is commonly called the "Dark Ages," it is one of the most interesting periods in the world's history. During this stretch of time the foundations were laid for the great forward movements in religion and social life, and for the advancement of the arts, of music, and of literature.

It was an age of adventure and romance—of noble ladies and knights in armour. The life of the young woman of this day was one of freedom when compared with the restricted existence of earlier times. She roamed at will about the castle of her father, sat in the great banqueting hall, took part in the merry conversation and listened to the tales of adventure related by the knights. Her serious moments were spent in religious study under the guidance of the nuns. Together with other young girls of her class she was taught to embroider, and later spent much of her time embroidering the family coat of arms, or in weaving fine silken trophies for a gift to her favorite knight. To be skilled in horsemanship was an ambitious accomplishment of the period. Having attained this, her pet diversion was to join a company of noble knights and ladies as they went hawking.

The crusaders exerted a marked influence on dress for a brief time, and a tendency toward severity set in. In the eleventh century men and women both adopted the *bliaud*—a long straight garment with large loose sleeves, resembling the present-day kimono sleeve. The knights frequently wore this over their armor, and since women's costume was influenced by that of the crusaders, it is not surprising that they adopted the same garment. The modern blouse has preserved the name of this early *bliaud*. It is this garment, no doubt, which in the thirteenth century changed into the surcoat. One of the quaint customs introduced by the crusaders was the fashion of wearing purses attached to the girdle. They were called *amônières sarrasinoises,* or Saracen almsbags, but usually carried other things besides coin for the poor. The little purse, or *amônière,* remained in fashion all through the Middle Ages, and reappeared throughout the century as one of the indispensable adjuncts of costume. (*B,* Plate XI; *A,* Plate XIV.) In this early period they were remarkable either for the material or for the needlework bestowed upon them.

The simple and severe costume effects which came in during the period of the Crusades proved to be only temporary. (*B,* Plate XI.) Soon the Crusaders were returning from the East, bringing with them the habits they had acquired there; before long the mass of the people were vying with one another in imitating the rich and powerful nobles and their consorts. Further, the extensive commercial relations existing between France and the East did much to refine French taste in matters of dress, and from the eleventh century on, the expression became more artistic. Greater attention was given to dress by both men and women. The Roman influence was still seen in the costumes of men as late as the eleventh century, but the knight in armor is the outstanding personage of the Middle Ages. And what a statuesque figure he is! He wore no loose folds of costume as in the classic days but instead, the metal armor, highly polished, which defined the figure and gave an impression of great strength. Under the armor a padded garment was worn to protect the body. In warm weather when the armour became unbearably hot, the silken robe (*bliaud* or surcoat), with heraldic designs, was worn over it. A similar cover was used over the shield when not in use. This decoration was the beginning of heraldry, which played so important a part in the art of the Middle Ages, and greatly influenced architectural ornament, furniture, and interior decorations.

Heraldry is a science. It treats of blazoning or describing armorial bearings in which every line or part has a specific meaning. The use of these designs no doubt originated with those who took part in the tournaments, and they were worn as marks of distinction. In no other way could the Lady of the Tournament recognize her knight, for his features were concealed by the helmet.

The armored knight occupies the stage of the Middle Ages, but the long easy tunic of the earlier period lingered, gradually becoming shortened to the knees. This was girded at the belt, and the long sleeve closed at the wrist. Over this was worn the very ample cape or mantle. (*D*, Plate X.)

It was following the Crusades that the demands of fashion were so exacting that great numbers of artisans and working women found profitable employment in producing all kinds of luxurious wearing apparel. There were innumerable makers of head-dresses, trimmers, dress cutters and makers, ribbon makers, dyers, makers of buckles and delicate clasps, furriers who possessed the most delicate and costly furs, makers of brass, copper, and wire buttons, hosiers, shoemakers, glove makers, and hosts of others.

This age is memorable for a new division of the people, and the appearance of the "middle class." Heretofore there had been but two classes, the rich and the poor, the lord and the serf. The coming of the craftsmen created an entirely new order of society. This class did the work which required both a high order of intelligence and manual skill. These qualities, developed at this time, brought forward in the next century the great artists and men of letters of the Renaissance.

Soon the great trade fraternities and trade guilds sprang up, and became a very positive influence in the life of the time. Great credit came to the tradesman who made an article of such refined and superior workmanship that it brought recognition. To influence, in even a small way, the design or decoration of objects in common use brought an added dignity to the craft worker. The carving of a

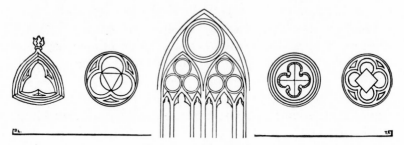

Fig. 26.   Gothic tracery

piece of wood, the fashioning of a bit of gold or silver, or the weaving of a length of embroidery were not looked upon as tasks, but as real opportunities to excel in intelligent design and finished execution. Sincere pride and pleasure in one's work was the key-note of craftsmanship.

The dress of the craftsman was a combination of smock, the regulation dress of the poor, with the richer dress of the nobles. While these garments were simple and practical, their artistic color and touches of added ornament made them distinctive.

The return of the Crusaders also marks a period of pronounced departure in architecture and ornament. These early Christians saw many beautiful temples in the East, and returned with unbounded enthusiasm to erect houses of worship. Not wishing to imitate the heathen nations, they evolved and in less than a hundred years perfected a type of architecture different from anything that had existed before—the Gothic cathedral. All classes helped to build the churches; nobles and peasants worked side by side, such service being regarded as a form of religious worship. The Gothic lines are "infinitely perpendicular." The vertical masses and the leading lines of windows, arches, and

towers "lift the thought and feeling ever and ever upward."
(Fig. 26.) Before the close of the fourteenth century the
towering spires of the cathedrals had contributed their
influence to the fashion of the day.

Fig. 27. Handsome net arrangements or *cauls* worn during the late Middle
Ages, 1300-1480

The twelfth century is a period which defines many
changes in the dress and customs of the people. At this
time the beard appeared in France. It passed through various degrees of change. First, there was the full beard;
then the little pointed beard covering only the point of the
chin; and bye and bye it became the fashion to wear it to
join the mustaches. At the close of the century, all chins
were shaven.

This same period marks an interesting departure in the
coiffure of women. Up to this time the hair had been covered by various hoods which concealed it. Even when visible, it was without ornamentation of any kind. Consequently the history of head-dressing proper may be said to
begin with the late twelfth century. Now the rolls of hair,
sometimes plaited, are arranged at the sides of the head
over the ears, and confined in a net called a crispine, cres-
pine, or crespinette. Among women of wealth these were
of gold thread enriched by a band or coronet of gold and
jewels. (Fig. 27.) The veil and wimple were frequently
worn over this very elaborate headdress; this style endured
for something like three hundred years. The wimple was
used to encircle the face, neck, and head. (Fig. 25.)

A kerchief of linen was brought up tightly around the face and caught at the top of the head, while another piece was pinned close to the brows and fell loose to the shoulders (1000-1200). A hundred years later came the fashion of the chinband and headstrap (1100-1300). (Photo C.) A century later the *gorget* found its way to popularity. This was a piece of linen wrapped about the head and neck, half way framing the face (1200). Later came the head-dresses of the fifteenth century (1400).

Gloves made their appearance as part of the costume about the twelfth century, and naturally were worn only by ladies of the highest rank. During the preceding century there are rare instances of persons of the most exalted rank wearing gloves. One old manuscript of the tenth century pictures a lady wearing something like a glove. It has a thumb but no fingers, resembling the modern mitten. It was during the twelfth century, however, that gloves as we know them were accepted as fashion. It was not long before glove makers were meeting all the demands of the trade. There were long buttoned and scented gloves, "gloves made of kid and prepared with violet powder." Sheepskin, doeskin, and hareskin were much in favor.

> Some of chicken skin for night,
> To keep her hands plump, soft, and white.

Silk and linen gloves, beautifully embroidered, were also made. Frequently the very long sleeves of the gown, falling over the hand, supplied the place of gloves, (*E*, Plate XII), and at times the long mantle served the same purpose. In this day it was not enough to be able to buy gloves, but a lady was supposed to display her taste by knowing just how and when to wear her gloves.

In woman's costume, the twelfth century is designated as that of the "fitted garment." (Fig. 28.) At this time lacing was introduced. This practice reached its most outrageous form during the following centuries. As early as the thirteenth and fourteenth centuries, however, the wasp-like waist of the ladies was admired. Romances of this early period teem with allusions to and praise of the diminutive waist. Chaucer, describing the Carpenter's wife, says her body was "gentyll and small as a weasel." In Calthrop's history of English Costumes we read, "Not that the lacing was very tight, but it commenced the habit, and the habit begat the harm, and the thing grew until it arrived finally at the buckram, square-built, cardboard and tissue figure which titters and totters thru the Elizabethan era."

Fig. 28. The twelfth-century fitted garment (After Viollet-le-Duc)

Though the twelfth-century dress does not go to the extreme of the later centuries, it shows the long waist defining the figure. The skirt gathered full hangs from the hips. The sleeves are large and flowing, disclosing the fitted sleeve of the undertunic. A large mantle, and a little veil, confined with a circlet or crown, complete the costume.

During the following century the fitted tunic continued to be worn over the undertunic. This fitted tunic was called a *cote* or cotta, and was held by a girdle placed just above the hips. A sleeveless garment either long or short, called the *surcot,* or surcoat, was worn over the fitted cotta. (Fig. 29.) Many have been the transformations of the *cote* and the surcoat through the succeeding centuries. The *cote* became the *cottahardie*—a tunic either long or short, fitting the figure closely, the lower part, if long, made voluminous by gores (*E,* Plate XII); the surcoat merged into the jacket (*B,* Plate XII.) The dress of this period is an important departure in clothes. The surcoat was sleeveless; the armscye was so large that the front and back of the surcoat proper were reduced to a few inches. (Fig. 29.) With these large openings at the side, the girdle worn below the waist and the tunic or cotta were easily seen. The surcoat and cotta were of contrasting material and color,—an important feature of costume at this time. The coat was the richest part of the attire, being made of velvets and silks, elaborately trimmed with ermine. Frequently in walking, the ladies, when wearing long-skirted surcoats, held them up showing the cotta beneath. This was the same color as the sleeves, and made a pleasing contrast with the surcoat.

The thirteenth and fourteenth centuries witnessed a great increase in materials appropriate for garments. There was *samite,* a thick silk in white, green, and red; *cendal,* resembling our silk of the present day; *pers,* a blue cloth; *camelin,* a fabric made from camel's hair; *isambrun,* a cloth dyed brown; "moleskin," a linen cloth; *fustaine,* a strong stuff manufactured from cotton; and finally *serge,* woven of wool, and occasionally mixed with thread. The progress of the arts of weaving and dyeing was extraordinary, and the great supply of fine materials developed a taste for the beautiful in all ranks of society.

Mantles of silk, edged or lined with ermine, surcoats richly embroidered in gold, and jewels of exquisite workmanship, were the common extravagances of the day. Not only was the lady of rank privileged to wear this finery, but the wealthy *bourgeoises* as well adopted the latest decrees of fashion. All ranks affected the leading styles, until it was impossible to distinguish the classes by their dress. Men were arrayed in scarlet, and women in cloth of gold. The limit of income was the only check on the follies of fashion.

The preachers of the day attacked these extravagances. One, Maillard, sketched the portrait of a lawyer's wife dressed like a princess, and others drew comparisons between the poverty of the masses and the indulgence of the wealthy. "The poor," said one of them "are dying of cold, while you, Madame Pompous, Madame Boastful, you have seven or eight gowns in your coffer that you do not put on thrice in a year.'' In fact, luxury knew no bounds. Fortunes were consumed in the desire for finery. Louis IX, known as Saint Louis, admonished his courtiers: ''You should dress yourselves well in order that your wives may love you more, and your people will esteem you the higher for it.''

During the fourteenth century (about 1395) the demand for colorful embroideries increased. The art so captivated the noblewomen of this day that they soon devised a plan for distinguishing themselves from lesser folk. They began to embroider the family coat-of-arms upon the dress! The arms of the husband's family were emblazoned upon the right side and that of the lady's own family upon the left. The fashion grew so popular that soon fleur-de-lis, birds, fishes, ramping lions, and leopards were embroidered on the costume. Wives and daughters employed all their leisure hours in the fine art of embroidering. The fascinating variations made by colored threads and interesting stitchery was a delightful pastime. Not only were their dresses more distinctive, but their belts, bags, gloves, and shoes as well.

Fig. 29. The surcoat—a fashionable feature in the dress of the thirteenth and fourteenth centuries (After Viollet-le-Duc)

Out of this fashion for heraldic display on the dress there developed an interesting phase of historic costume. This was the parti-colored gown! It now became the mode to have one's gown fashioned half of one color, and half of another. (*B*, Plate XII.) One noble lady of Provence is described as wearing a gown, the left side and left sleeve being white, while the opposite side was blue. All through the

A   B   C   D   E

PLATE XII—COSTUME OF THE MIDDLE AGES—1395-1495

A—1495—A lady of rank wearing the fitted garment and the two-horned
head-dress of starched lawn.

B—1395—A parti-colored dress. This fashion followed the vogue for
heraldic designs in dress. The close-fitting, long-sleeved jacket is
the late development of the surcoat.

C—1483—A lady of rank wearing a fitted costume.

D—1422—A lady of rank wearing the great hennin. The collar effect of
revers passing from the center of the waistline in front to the center
of waistline in the back succeeded the surcoat.

E—1495—A fashionable costume of this period—the voluminous skirt,
flowing fur-edged sleeves, close bodice and the escoffion, or two-
horned head-dress, which vied with the hennin for first place.

century wealth and display marked the costume. Gold, silver, and rich materials were worn. The large pattern brocades were much in favor, and the gowns continued to be very long. One side of the skirt was often held up by a clasp attached to a chain which hung from the girdle. This clasp and chain served as an ornament, and was known as the *tussoire*. Often as a finishing touch to the costume the rosary or paternoster of coral or gold was added. Ornament was added to ornament to attract attention. Finally handsome prayerbooks became a part of the general costume. These were often of artistic workmanship, and were carried in cases which hung from the girdle.

> My book of hours, those of Notre Dame, I must have;
> And it should be, as becometh noble dame of high lineage,
> Of subtle workmanship, gold and azure, rich and rare,
> Well ordered and well shapen;
> Covered in fine cloth or in wrought gold;
> And when it is opened to be closed again
> With two golden clasps.
> —*From the French of Augustin Challamel.*

During the latter half of the century a new style in dress was born. The voluminous houppelande became the fashion. This was a one-piece dress in which women are said to have discovered the normal waistline. (See Photo D.) The diminutive bodice was tight-fitting, with a deep V-shaped neck and large revers very wide at the shoulders; the sleeves were long and close, and the skirt enormous. It was usually made of material resembling tapestry in design. The skirt was frequently carried in huge folds over the arm. (See dedication page). Isabelle of Bavaria, queen of Charles VI, set the fashion of having the long trail carried by a lady's maid or pages—a custom much in vogue in court circles during the following centuries. The tapestries of the fifteenth century picture the ladies of this day in voluminous houppelande and towering head-dress. It was at this period, when the bodice was very tightly laced, that the extreme décolleté became fashionable. Isabelle was, moreover, the first to wear linen undergarments. This

PHOTO D—DETAIL, FRANCO-FLEMISH TAPESTRY, *Romance of the Rose.*
(About 1435-1445)

The voluminous houppelande is here pictured with the high headdress
of the period. Note the handsome cauls and the veil. The courtiers wear
the typically masculine dress, including the *roundlet,* usually worn over a
cap as shown, and with the long streamer, a vestige of the peak of the
early hood, worn as a scarf.

fashion was also readily adopted by the ladies of the period. The linen chemise was regarded as a luxury, and called *robe-linge*. In order to allow a glimpse of the underlinens, the ladies of the court cut slashes in the sleeves of their gowns and also in the hips of their skirts. This vanity finally led to a deception. Only that part of the chemise which could be seen was made of linen, and the remainder of the old-time woolen material.

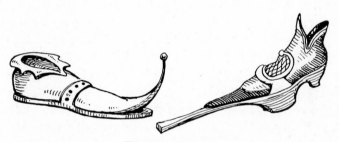

Fig. 30.   Pattens

In men's clothes the long tight hose and doublet were adopted, and being such a decided change after centuries of long robes which concealed the figure, they were stigmatized for their "horrible inordinate scantiness." (*A, C,* Plate XIII.) The long tight hose were made of rich materials, and were often parti-colored. Frequently one hose was decorated in a style quite different from the other, rendering "uncertain the fellowship of the legs." The long hose was connected with the doublet by means of points, which were ties or laces with a metal tag at the end, and used to fasten garments together. They were in general use until the seventeenth century both for armor and for civilian dress.

> Their points being broken, down fell their hose.
> —SHAKESPEARE.

Buttons are believed to have been used in a very limited way in the late thirteenth century, and during the vogue of the tight-fitting gown of the fourteenth century. Laces and points seem to have superceded buttons in the fourteenth and fifteenth centuries, but in the sixteenth they came again into their kingdom, and great were their variety and magnificance. Buttons of diamonds and other precious stones are mentioned; buttons of gold, silver, brass, and other metals; of horn, mother-of-pearl, ivory, bone, jet, glass, and wood, covered with silk and velvet. Paste buttons, which rivaled in brilliancy the finest precious stones, were also made. At this time (1600-1700) thousands of men, women, and children were employed in making buttons.

The curious shoes of the late Middle Ages called *poulaine,* by the French, were made with an exaggerated point to the toe which was inclined to turn up resembling the prow of a boat. (Fig. 30.) The fashion had come from Cracow, in Poland; in England the same shoes became known as "Crackowes." These were made of soft, pliable material and were only ankle high. Sometimes the tops were turned back to display the gay-colored lining. The toes of men's shoes gradually grew to an exaggerated length and had to be stuffed with moss, tow, or hay to keep them in shape. By-and-by they became needlelike points that had to be pinned back in order for the wearer to get about. Finally the long point became so difficult to manage that one end of a chain was caught in the toe and this was then drawn up to the correct angle and the chain permanently adjusted about the leg.

Shoes were a mark of distinction, the various materials and particularly the length of the shoe indicating the wealth and dignity of the wearer.

It is not surprising that women, in particular, soon found a protection for the flimsy footwear of their day. A wooden sole with the same drawn-out toe and probably an inch or two in thickness was adjusted by means of straps over the long-toed crackow. This set milady high above the mud and filth of medieval cities.

It is a curious fact that the most depressing period of French life, the Hundred Years War (1400-1450), has become known historically for the remarkable splendor of its fashions. This period is famed for its unusual head-

A   B   C   D   E

PLATE XIII—COSTUME OF THE MIDDLE AGES—1386-1498

A—1498—A man of rank wearing the long, tight hose and the doublet. The hose were often in gay color and frequently each of a different color.

B—1498—A lady of rank wearing an elaborate gown. The bodice is snug and the skirt voluminous.

C—1498—A man of rank wearing parti-colored trunk-hose. Insignia— Order of the Golden Fleece.

D—1395—The short-waisted garment followed the long-waisted costume. The hood, in stiffened form, was made of parchment and covered with silk or cloth.

E—1386—A lady of rank wearing the fitted tunic. The hood is a variation of the Phrygian bonnet. Gloves were more generally worn at this time than in the earlier centuries.

97

dresses, which grew to such an exaggerated height that the ceilings in the castle of Vincennes were raised to permit the ladies of the court to move about in comfort.

It is to the rich tapestries produced by our mediaeval ancestors that we turn to find these dames of high degree pictured in all the splendor of their rich materials and towering head-dresses. These woven chronicles invite us to study not only the costume of the period, but the love of color and color harmony which these ladies of the long-ago carried into their gowns and all their belongings. "Never perhaps," writes Viollet-le-Duc, "did extravagance in head gear reach such a pitch with the fair sex as during those melancholy days from 1400 to 1450. The hair itself formed but a small part of the head-dress; hoods, covrechefs, chapels, fremillets, and chains were built up into the most extraordinary edifices."

The styles of head-dresses were various, but the hennin took the lead, and became the *ne plus ultra* of fashion. (*D*, Plate XII.) This particular type of head-dress was a tall conical cap, probably a yard high, fitting close to the head. From the peak of this towering edifice a veil of finest texture fell over the shoulders. This style was termed the great hennin; of course there were various heights, each woman adopting that which appealed to her.

The escoffion was a second distinct type which is believed to have been introduced into France by Isabelle of Bavaria. Naturally all the ladies were anxious to copy the fashion. (*E*, Plate XII.) Thus the new head-dress vied with the hennin for first place. The escoffion was a two-horned arrangement, being about a yard high, made of fine lawn, and stiffly starched and wired to keep its horns in place. From the tips of the horns flags, fringes, and other materials fell to the shoulders. Besides these two distinct types there were others: the turban, the heart-shaped cap, and the little hennin.

Again the philosophers and moralists organized a deadly warfare against these extravagances of fashion. They compared the women who wore these head-dresses to horned beasts and to pictures of Satan. The cry was: "War to the hennins! War to the hennins!" One Carmelite monk, Brother Thomas Connecte, traveled from place to place denouncing the extravagances of dress, and hurling all sorts of invectives against the women who desired to be fashionable, even threatening them with the divine wrath. Not only did he preach against these whims, but he fared forth one day and massacred without mercy all the hennins he encountered. All the preaching against the style, however, only stimulated the taste for hennins, and they continued as high as ever. "The ladies," wrote Guillaume Paradin, the historian, "imitate the snails, who draw in their horns, and when danger is over peep them out farther than ever; in like manner the hennins were never more extravagant than after the departure of Brother Connecte." The headdress continued, and was given up only when a caprice for change decided it.

As we of today read of the attacks of the church fathers upon the extravagances of dress, we are inclined to be amused. We should not forget, however, that it was the church, the religious life of the period, that gave to the world the beautiful in art and ornament,—gave it permanence and bequeathed it to the coming ages. The great cathedrals scattered over the land, with their colored glass windows, mosaics, and rich tapestries are among the world's greatest treasures. The most beautiful embroideries and tapestries of any age were made by the nuns of the church. In these are recognized all the stitches in popular use today; the chain stitch, the tapestry stitch, cross stitch, couching stitch, appliqué, and the origin of crochet. The monks lettered and illuminated books, tooled and embossed the leather covers, and finished them with delicately wrought clasps.

The influence of the East is felt in the early designs and ornament of the Middle Ages; the originality, however, which developed through the years is remarkable. Heraldic designs, decorative lettering, and Gothic tracery are the types of ornament always associated with the period. The thought of the designer combined with the spirit of the craftsman made the art of the period an inspiration for all future time.

The relation existing between fashion and architecture is keenly appreciated at this period of the Middle Ages, when the Gothic turrets of castle and cathedral echoed the towering head-dress of the lady of fashion. The bright coloring of the Gothic period is seen alike in cathedral and in milady's trailing and emblazoned gowns. Looking back to the Egyptian days the same similarity exists between the massive and heavy temples and the simple and severe costumes of the Egyptian people. The love of color is seen alike in the dresses of these primitive artists, and upon the walls of their marvelous temples. Simplicity and grace were the distinguishing charm of Greek dress and Greek architecture. The Roman Empire appropriated much of Greek refinement in both building and dress; in the later period, however, the decline in taste is suggested by many of the portraits—figures ornamented "from head to foot with pearls and precious stones intermixed with cameos."

It was in the closing years of the fourteenth century that beautiful dolls dressed in the very latest mode were used as models of fashion, being passed from France to other European countries. The charming Isabelle is said to have sent a number of dolls, dressed in the very latest French fashion, as a gift to the Queen of England. Venice annually imported a French doll, which was exhibited on Ascension Day in the Piazza of St. Mark, the fashionable quarter of the city, as "the toilette of the year." During the seventeenth and eighteenth centuries these fashion dolls became more and more indispensable for supplying the latest word in French fashion.

The depressing period toward the close of the reign of Charles VI caused a lull in the fashion world. This, however, was only temporary. When Charles VII ascended the throne he set an example of such luxury to his people, that the devotee of fashion again plunged into the greatest extravagance of dress.

Agnes Sorel, famous both for her wit and beauty, now takes the place of Isabelle of Bavaria as the fashion leader of the court. She was dubbed "the Lady of Beauty" of the period, and the fashion world eagerly awaited her every decree. The fashions set by this fair creature, no matter how extreme or indecorous, became the rage. She introduced the fashion of leaving the bosom uncovered to the waist, and was the first to wear diamonds in her hair. Her portrait, painted by an artist of the period, hangs in the famous gallery at Versailles. Trailing gowns, high head-dresses, laces, gloves, mittens, rings, and necklaces were the order of the day. Walking-sticks made of valuable wood with ornamented tops again came into vogue. Toward the end of the fifteenth century (1495) gold and silver embroidery was added to the backs of gloves, which still continued to be violet scented. Fans, usually made of feathers, were carried to church by these ladies, and used to disperse the flies.

On one point, that of the color of the hair, the taste of the Middle Ages was similar to that of the classical world. Fair hair was still considered the most beautiful. The French maidens who were not fortunate enough to be fair-haired by nature became so in spite of nature's edict. This preference for light hair led to the manufacture of great quantities of false hair.

Toward the dawn of the Renaissance a sudden change took place in the whole character of costume.

When Charles VIII and his army made their famous expedition into Italy they incidentally captured lords and ladies alike by their agreeable manners and French finery. The Italians made haste to adopt many details of the French costume; likewise many pleasing features in the dress of Italy were appropriated by the French nobles. Later when the King of France and his retinue returned to his court, the French ladies in turn were fascinated by the Italian coloring, materials, and many of the styles which were entirely new. This enthusiasm was expressed in the fashions of the day, and many Italian ideas were assimilated in French dress. Tight-fitting bodices, many colored fringes trimming the gown, and a black veil, were especially novel. Bright colors were the vogue, and the great demand led to the importation of rich Milanese and Venetian merchandise.

The hennin was at last declared passé, and the long-toed shoes became a matter of history. The round toes called *sollerets,* such as were worn by Italian women, and which fitted the foot, were substituted. High heels were as yet unknown, but they gradually grew out of a kind of slipper with several soles placed one above the other. Hose or stockings were made of pieces of material sewed together. The word "stocking" as applied to hose does not appear until the fifteenth century.

Later in the period, sleeves became a curious novelty. In the outside garment they remained long and flowing, while those of the underdress were frequently made of different colors fastened together by ribbons. Sleeves were large, long, wide, or close-fitting; sometimes they were buttoned from the shoulder to the wrist; sometimes puffs were worn at the shoulder and elbow. (Plate XII.) Sleeves which took the form of mittens were called *mitons;* then there were the sleeves like wings, with edges cut like oak leaves and edged with fur. The poet and chronicler of the fifteenth century, Olivier de la Marche in his *Le Parchment des Dames* speaks of slippers, shoes, boots, hose, garters, stomachers, stay laces, chemises, pin holders, *amônières,* mirrors, coifs, combs, and ribbons, all of which were to be found in the wardrobe of these women of the long ago.

With the beginning of the Renaissance (1500), foreign materials of the finest manufacture began to pour into France. The linen from Holland was especially fine; Bourges was famous also for its rare cloth. French gentlemen usually stipulated that the tailor use "fine Bourges cloth.'' Fine wools came from Spain; gold and silver from Italy.

Although the fashions of the Middle Ages reached an extreme which was considered excessive for that period, it is in the following century that the most luxurious extravagance finds expression.

REVIEW

1. What is the outstanding contribution of the Middle Ages to costume?
2. Discuss the various influences which brought about the change from classic to modern dress.
3. What century marks the introduction of the fitted garment?
4. What conspicuous practice marked the coming of the fitted garment? Has this been a permanent influence in dress? Discuss.
5. Contrast woman's dress of the early Middle Ages with that worn later.
6. What materials were in popular demand in the early period? Name new materials introduced during later centuries.
7. Give a list of popular accessories first introduced into the western world during the Middle Ages.
8. Discuss trade guilds—their introduction and aim.
9. Describe men's dress of the early period. What change in the dress of men followed the crusades?
10. Describe the shoes worn during this period. Describe the patten and tell something of its use.
11. Name and discuss the conspicuous types of head-dress fashionable during this period.
12. Define: *bliaud, surcoat, cottahardie, chaperon, couvrechef, wimple, amônière, houppelande, robe-linge, points.*
13. How and when were fashions first introduced from France into other countries?

CHAPTER SEVEN

The RENAISSANCE in France
(1500)

THE Renaissance opened under the dazzling splendor of the court of Francis I. The king was always in elegant attire, and set the fashions for the gentlemen of the period, which were no less magnificent than those of the ladies.

It is interesting to note that the decided change in costume, which set in during the previous century and which marked the break between the costumes of the ancients and those of the modern world, continued to grow and become more general. The long tight-fitting hose extending from the waist to the foot became known as the "trunk-hose"; the doublets began to have close-fitting and large sleeves; hats with brims, and shoes and boots were adopted. Women too had everywhere adopted the tight-fitting gown, an entirely different type of dress from that of antiquity, and the common type upon which fashion has played in varying strains ever since.

In the earliest years of the Renaissance the general style of costume continued similar to that of the previous century, at least, until that great innovation of the Renaissance—the farthingale (*vertugale, vertugade, vertugadin.*) This new feature in dress, which was destined to play a role so important, was ushered into France from Spain in 1530. It was a contrivance unheard of before, and upset and changed all the lines of costume. The farthingale remained the vogue for about three hundred years under various names,—the hoop, crinoline, panier, pouf, and bustle.

The initial appearance of the farthingale was the stiffened pad stretched upon wire frame. This was attached to the waist giving width to the hips. It was then known as the "shakefold." The name, shakefold, grew out of the appearance of the skirt as it fell in great flute-like folds over the extension and swayed gently to and fro as milady moved about. Later the stiffened pad was made of whalebone or cane and bell-shaped in form, suggesting a cage-like petticoat. Afterward the name farthingale was applied to petticoats mounted on hoop, iron, wood, cane, or bone. As usual, women vied with one another in the width of their hips and fullness of their skirts, until, forsooth, again came the edicts against the new mode. These were many and severe, but the more numerous the edicts, the more general and daring the fashion. In the *Discours sur la Mode,* published in 1613, we read as follows:

> The large vertugadin is common to all French women;
> The bourgeoises wear it freely now,
> Just the same as the great ladies, if it be not
> That the bourgeoise is content with a smaller one;
> For the great ladies are not satisfied
> With a vertugadin less than five yards round.

It is recorded that a young widow wearing a hoop of extraordinary width was accused before the court. There she gave her word of honor to the counselors that the "exaggerated size of her hips, which was the cause of the complaint, was simply a gift of nature." The judges, of course, acquitted the widow.

The boned bodice, called the basquine, and resembling a corset, also made its appearance during the reign of Francis I. This was usually worn over a chemise of fine material.

The materials in use were very elegant—silk, satin, damask, serge, camlot, and velvets of blue, crimson, violet, green, grey, and orange. In winter the gowns were often lined with the richest of furs.

The style of dress varied but little as the years passed by. The costume *la mode* was made with a deep-pointed bodice, to which was attached the skirt, which opened all the way down the front, showing a handsome underskirt harmonizing in color and material with the gown. (*D, E,* Plate XV; *A,* Plate XVI.) The sleeves were often narrow to the elbow, where they widened into great hanging cuffs of fur or silk. (*C, D,* Plate XIV.) These great hanging sleeves are those seen in the famous portraits of Queen Jane Seymour, Anne of Cleves, and other fashion leaders of this early period. Later large puffs were raised on the shoulders and were followed by a succession of puffs down the sleeve. These were sometimes cut or slashed showing puffings of different colored silks. During the century the leg-o-mutton sleeve which had been worn formerly was revived for a short period. (*B,* Plate XV.)

The same slashing of garments was carried out in men's dress, and was also applied to the soft pliable shoes of the period. There was little change in the material for shoes. They were still made of soft leathers, velvet, silk, and brocades and were always without a heel. The conspicuous change, however, was in the shape of the shoe. As the long, pointed crackowes faded from the scene, all toes began to round. The former exaggeration in length now changed to an exaggeration in width. No one was considered fashionable unless his shoe measured a foot across the toe! Then, as in the past, the law was invoked, this time to regulate the width of the shoe! At times the broad toes were filled with moss, making them appear as stuffed rolls. At other times they were slashed or cut, carrying out the same decoration seen in the dress.

The patten with its thick sole, sometimes divided, forming two elevations, one in front and one at the back, helped to bring in the heel. One of the earliest shoes with a heel is said to have been worn by Catherine de' Medici (1519-1589). The heel of this shoe, however, had a curious connection with the ball of the foot by a kind of second sole to which it was attached. A shoe belonging to Queen Elizabeth and one of Mary, Queen of Scots, both of which are preserved in museum collections, are said to be the first shoes with a heel.

The towering headdresses of the late Middle Ages now gave way to the opposite extreme—a little nunlike hood. So it is that, with the introduction of the full skirt, the broad shoes, and the low headdress, the tall, slender lines of

A   B   C   D   E

PLATE XIV—THE RENAISSANCE IN FRANCE—1500

A—1515—A lady of rank.

B—1550—A nobleman wearing the long trunk-hose, the doublet and jacket. The embroidered doublet was gradually transformed into the waistcoat.

C—1545—A lady of rank wearing the fitted garment with the great, hanging sleeves. A small cap of velvet takes the place of the exaggerated head-dress. The girdle, with pendant set with jewels, was indispensable.

D—1520—A fashionable dress showing the pointed and boned bodice to which the open skirt was attached.

E—1558—A lady of rank wearing a variation of the prevailing style. The slashed bodice and sleeves show the underdress of contrasting material.

the Gothic period gave way to the curved lines of the Renaissance.

Hoods were fashionable in France, England, Italy, Spain, Flanders, and Germany. Each differed, however, according to the taste of the nation adopting it. The first little hoods fell free to the shoulders but soon variations began to appear. First, the sides were cut upward, forming lappets, which hung at each side of the face. Next, the lappets were pinned up to the crown, and shortly all sorts of fanciful arrangements were invented by the women themselves. Usually the hair was first covered with a white coif or with a close covering of silk, gold tissue, or brocade and the hood set over this. In England the hood became famous as the "gabled headdress" because the front edge was wired to give a pointed effect. Bye and bye the hood grew very diminutive with, at times, a little flaring brim. It was set back on the head and often tied under the chin. A long veil usually hung from the back. This was known as the "French hood" and remained popular for many years.

In men's dress the low, broad beret was the fashionable head covering. It is seen in many portraits of the period, the flat crown often encircled with a feather. This low beret gradually changed its form and came to have a high fulled crown usually set off with the tips of plumes, etc.

Women still retained their necklaces, bracelets, and rings. Rosaries and handsome chains were suspended from the center front of the girdle, and from this hung pretty trifles—scent boxes, fans, the silk purse, or a jeweled ornament. (*D, E,* Plate XV.) (*C, D, E,* Plate XIV.)

With the coming of Henry II to the throne in 1547, troublesome times were brewing. The extreme splendor of the fashion of the previous period changed to one of gloom. Bright and gay colors became more somber in tone, and were for a time succeeded by black, which alternated with the brilliant and showy. The great fulness of skirts and the enormous sleeves were characteristic of this period.

The ruff, a new fashion, and one which became extremely popular, was introduced from Italy by Catherine

A B C   D E   F

PLATE XV—THE RENAISSANCE IN FRANCE—1500

A—1547—Costume worn by Francis I. The long hose with the puffed
 trousers of silk and velvet; the fitted doublet with huge sleeves;
 broad-toed shoes and little hat with a feather picture the dress of
 this leader of fashion.

B—1558—This costume pictures the leg-o-mutton sleeve which was revived
 at this time, and the Marie Stuart cap.

C—1589—The costume worn by Henry III The king wears the corset,
 the fitted doublet with peplum, the short breeches, and the velvet cape.

D—1560—A lady of rank wearing the fashionable dress of the day—the
 boned bodice and open skirt.

E—1559—A fashionable lady wearing the pointed bodice and hoop-skirt.

F—1575—A costume showing the prevailing fashion.

de' Medici, the wife of Henry II. This novel accessory of dress was destined to run the whole gamut of extravagance. In its early days the ruff was usually of plaited lawn or other fine material, encircling the throat and extending to the ears. (*B, D, E, F,* Plate XV.) Later, however, it was made of the most exquisite laces and extended not only to the top of the ears, a very modest height (*A, D,* Plate XVI; Photo E), but to the top of the head, and the ultrafashionable did not hesitate to raise it beyond the top of the headdress.

An amusing incident about the ruff is told by Brantome, the historian. On one occasion a gentleman of the court was in conversation with Queen Catherine. The subject was ruffs. The gentleman expressed his surprise that women should care to wear such deep ruffs, and his doubt of their ability to take their soup without soiling them. The next moment a valet handed the Queen a *bouilli* for refreshment. The queen sipped the *bouilli* without embarrassment and then said, "You see, Monsieur de Tresnes, that with a little intelligence one can manage anything."

After a brief space of dark colors, the women of France were again seized with a boundless caprice for refinery. Silks, velvets, cloth of gold, and handsome embroideries were the fashionable requirements of the day. Again the edicts came forth! Laws were passed regulating the colors and quality of materials according to rank. Only a princess was privileged to wear a crimson gown, while other women of high degree might have only a part of a costume of the royal color. Silk was forbidden to working women, except for trimmings, and other discriminations were made that constantly maintained class barriers.

Notwithstanding the edicts, however, the entire century is conspicuous for its elegant materials and handsome embroideries. With the use of gold thread and pearls the rich effects were unparalleled. Men's dress did not escape. Black velvet with gold and silver threads touched here and there with colored embroidery was much in evidence. At the same time many women of rank were decorating their cos-

A   B   C   D   E

PLATE XVI—THE RENAISSANCE IN FRANCE—1500

A—1574—A lady of rank. The open overdress displays the handsome
underskirt of a harmonizing color. The jeweled *cordelière* was always
worn with dresses of this type. The Medici ruff and Marie Stuart
cap picture the vogue at this period.

B—1545—Costume worn by Francis I. He wears the trunk-hose and
the open jacket, displaying the elaborate doublet.

C—1590—A lady of rank wearing the barrel-shaped hoop. The pointed
bodice and puffed sleeves continue.

D—1586—A costume of the same period.

E—1598—A nobleman. The long boots of Russia leather were introduced by Henry IV. The mancheron, or false sleeve is seen in the
costumes of both men and women.

tumes with *fers* (E, Plate XIV), an ornamentation resembling metal buttons. Laces too, imported from Venice, Brussels, and Genoa, added a pleasing decorative note to the costume.

In many of the costumes of this and later periods the curious custom of wearing the *mancherons* came into vogue, and was adopted by both men and women. (*E,* Plate XVI.) These were false sleeves which hung from the shoulder at the back, or from the epaulette, and extended below the hip. The general lines of the gowns continued similar to those of preceding reigns. The slashed and embroidered costumes, the close bodice, the puffed sleeve, and the ruff remained in vogue. Usually necklaces were discarded when the ruff was worn though occasionally, in court circles, the two were seen together.

The general head-dress was a little cap, pointed in the center, coming down to the edge of the forehead, making the face look heart shaped. This is the particular style known as the "Marie Stuart." (*B, F,* Plate XV.) Black velvet and silk hoods were also much in vogue. (*D,* Plate XIV.) This was the favorite head-dress of Catharine de' Medici. They were often padded, and a square of stuff was fastened to the string of the hood which could be drawn like a veil over the lower part of the face. This type was usual in cold weather. The charming little toque or cap with soft crown and narrow brim was exceedingly popular with both men and women. A little feather was always worn at one side, giving a piquant charm to the wearer. (*E,* Plate XIV; *C,* Plate XV.) Hats were less generally worn, and were usually oval-shaped with wide brims and made of fine materials of fine felt.

The curious innovation in head decoration was the wearing of a mask, called *loup,* meaning wolf. This name arose from the fact that when first worn it had a tendency to frighten the children. It was considered very bad form indeed for any lady of quality to go upon the streets without the *loup.* These masks were made of black velvet and at first were quite short, allowing the lower part of the face to

PHOTO E—MARIE DE MEDICI—*Frans Pourbus, the Younger* (1573-1642)

The queen wears an unusual ruff cut in deep scallops, and matching cuffs. The extravagantly extended skirt suggests the farthingale or barrel hoop. This, with the stiffly boned bodice and puffed sleeves, was the very height of the mode.

113

be seen. Later they were made longer, coming to the edge of the chin. The short ones were kept in place by being fastened behind the ears; the longer ones were secured in a more elegant way—by a glass button held between the teeth. The object of the mask was presumably one of protection. It preserved from sunburn the French complexion, which was usually made up with white paint and rouge.

Paint had been introduced into France by Catharine de' Medici, and the faces of the fashionable and the wealthy bourgeoisie were literally coated with patches of white paint and vermilion. Pomades and drugs reigned galore! Strange and weird were the concoctions destined to outdo nature herself in promoting beauty. The wings and claws of pigeons, pulverized and mixed with fresh eggs, lilies, Venetian turpentine, shells, ground mother of pearl, and camphor, the whole distilled with musk, was the witching pomade of the period. All of this vanity created another indispensable trinket, the dainty little hand-mirror, which must ever be ready. Consequently it hung from the girdle, and thus milady was never in doubt as to her correct appearance.

The religious wars overshadowed France at this period (1560-1574), and had a gloomy effect upon all matters of dress. Charles IX openly professed his contempt for over-attention to dress, and during the first year of his reign sent out the royal edict: "We forbid our subjects, whether men, women or children, to use on their clothes, whether silken or not, any bands of embroidery, stitchings or pipings of silk, guimp, etc., with which their garments or part thereof might be covered or embellished, excepting only a bordering of velvet or silk of the width of a finger, or at the most two borderings, chain stitchings or back stitchings at the edge of their garments." He also forbade farthingales of more than one and one-half yards in width, gold chains, buttons, and all devices for ornamentation.

As usual, however, Fashion continued to wield her scepter. The king might pass edict after edict, but it was of no avail. The great arts and crafts movement of the Middle

Ages had taught the people the use of their hands. This, combined with a knowledge of pattern, enabled a woman of the middle class to embroider her gown at no expense to herself, and to make it as finished and beautiful as that of the great lady who spent immense sums on her clothes. The fine laces of Brussels and Venice were also imitated by the craftswomen of the period, and ornaments of the finest workmanship, made by their own hands, were used as rich accessories to their costume. Towards the end of the reign of Charles IX (1560-1574) we find an interesting account of costume given by the Venetian ambassador, who was evidently a close observer of fashion. In this account he says:

> French women have inconceivably slender waists; they swell out their gowns from the waist downwards by stiffened stuffs and vertugadins, the which increases the elegance of their figure. They are very fanciful about their shoes, whether low slippers or escarpins. The cotillon (underskirt), which in Venice we call *carpetta*, is always very handsome and elegant, whether worn by a bourgeoise or a lady. As for the upper dress, provided it is made of serge or *escot*, little attention is paid to it, because the women, when they go to church, kneel and even sit on it. Over the chemise they wear a *buste* or bodice, that they call a *corps piqué*, to give them support; it is fastened behind, which is good for the chest. The shoulders are covered with the finest tissue or network; the head, neck, and arms are adorned with jewels. The hair is arranged quite differently from the Italian fashion; they use circlets of wire and *tampons* over which the hair is drawn in order to give greater width to the forehead. For the most part their hair is black, which contrasts with their pale complexions; for in France, pallor, if not from ill health, is considered a beauty.

When Henry III came to the throne in 1574 the gloom in France had by no means been lifted. Religious strife and bloodshed still made the atmosphere of Paris heavy. One would think that under such conditions fashion would step aside and give place to thoughts of more serious import. Generally speaking the national mood is reflected in the dress of the period; but at times extreme frivolity will flaunt itself in the face of disaster. Just such a condition in France attended the accession of Henry III.

Instead of the simplicity which Charles IX tried to sustain, Henry of Valois set the pace for his nobles in the most eccentric extravagance of dress. Great was the luxury and license of the French nobility. The men and women vied with each other in the elegance of their dress to such an extent that the gentlemen became as feminine as possible in their attire, and their whims and absurdities were unbounded. They imitated the ladies in wearing not only necklaces, rings, and ear-rings, but also ruffs and rolls of artificial hair. They adopted the corset to give them slim waists, and the busked doublet (the doublet with boned front coming down to a point), which gradually evolved into the padded front, forming a pouch-like protuberance which imparted a grotesque appearance to the wearer. This fashion, however, did not last, possibly because it was clumsy, or still more likely, because it created a great deal of ridicule. It was in the latter part of this century that pockets were introduced in the trunk-hose, thus doing away with the pouch which had been in common use for six hundred years. The doublets, also called pourpoints, were usually open, revealing the most exquisite Venetian point. Fans were carried by these "curled darlings" of society, and as a vanity of vanities they wore at night masks and gloves saturated with oils and pomades.

Henry himself wore the little plumed toque, the aigrette of diamonds, and the ruff. (*C*, Plate XV.)

At one time he appeared in a ruff made of fifteen breadths of cambric a half-yard in depth. "To see his head against that ruff," said Pierre de l'Estoile, "put one in mind of St. John the Baptist's head on a charger."

The serious minds of the time were aghast over the king's eccentricities. D'Aubigné exclaimed:

> So that at a first glance each comer was at a loss
> To know whether he beheld a king-woman or a man-queen.

Worse than all this, however, was the king's love for paint, powder, and perfume. Perfumes were the rage. Everything was bathed in amber, musk, ambergris, and other scents. With all this foppishness in gentlemen's attire, certainly feminine extravagances may be condoned.

The whalebone bodice, worn as tight as could be endured became the vogue. "When the princess or duchess," says Montaigne, "had not whale-bone bodies, they tightened their waists with wooden splints; for, above all, it was necessary to astonish the world with a slender waist." Fig. 31 shows a type of steel corset worn by Catharine de' Medici.

Fig. 31. Steel corset worn by Catharine de' Medici

The bodices were loaded with beads, embroidery, or gold and jewels. Pearls were arranged in design on both the bodices and skirts. The girdles were often the work of artists in goldsmithing, and the mirror which continued to be a part of feminine attire was richly set with jewels. Ruffs assumed fantastic proportions; in fact the one note in women's attire was the exaggeration of former styles and the over adornment of their gowns. The farthingale was not to be overlooked, and it grew apace.

As Isabelle of Bavaria and Agnes Sorrel each had her day as a leader of fashion, so at this period of the Renaissance Marguerite of Valois, the king's sister, became the social arbiter for her sex. She was very beautiful and very charming, but with all her beauty and engaging manners she is said to have degraded the fashions of the period. It was she who lengthened the waist to an excessive degree; who puffed the sleeves at the shoulders and tightened them at the wrist; and lastly tried to replace the farthingale with masses of padding on the hips. (*C*, Plate XVI.) Thus the days of the Renaissance wore on in unbridled extravagance.

Not until the close of the century did the change come.   In 1583 the murder of the Duke of Guise created a period of extreme depression.   Deep mourning prevailed and fashion in dress became intolerable.   Feeling ran so high that offenders in dress, whether they wore the obnoxious ruff, the over-puffed sleeve, or superfluous ornament, were attacked and the hated object torn into shreds.

So deep was the gloom and so great the depression that the few remaining years under Henry IV were largely years of recuperation.   Those who would be fashionable began to adopt brilliant colors and to initiate high hair-dressing, which gave rise to enormous quantities of false hair and powdered wigs.

Thus the first century of the Renaissance ended. Although the late Renaissance was destined to become the brightest period in the world of art and letters, its opening century contributed little but extravagance and gloom to the world of dress.

REVIEW

1. What outstanding feature in woman's dress is always associated with this century?   (1500.)
2. Describe its earliest form.   Trace its later development.
3. Describe the new form of bodice adopted by women.   How was this feature adapted to men's costume?
4. Give a description, naming materials, of the dress *a la mode.*
5. Compare the shoes of the period with those of the Middle Ages.   Compare head-dresses.
6. What novel accessory in neckwear appeared for the first time? Describe fully.   Trace its evolving forms.
7. Name various ways in which the costume was enriched.
8. Tell something of the use of ornament.   Of cosmetics.
9. What famous beauty set the fashions for women at this time?   Who led in the fashions for men?
10. What one word expresses the keynote of dress in this century?

CHAPTER EIGHT

The RENAISSANCE In France (1600)

W ITH the opening days of the new century, Paris begins to breathe more easily and gradually to emerge from the stifling atmosphere of the past into the bright Parisian sunshine. The love of change, the love of admiration, and the love of elegance are so largely a part of the French temperament that once the spirit revives, it goes on to free if not extravagant expression.

Henry IV, one of the greatest statesmen and soldiers of the period, occupied the French throne during the first ten years of the century. Giving himself wholeheartedly to the stupendous task of reconstruction after the religious strife and bloodshed of the preceding period, he was naturally less interested in matters of dress than were the foppish puppets whom he succeeded in the royal office. The position of arbiter of fashion for the kingdom did not appeal to him; whenever he deigned to don elegant attire, it was always from a sense of duty rather than from taste. Toward the close of the century, however, one fashion entirely new to the period was set by the king,—the high boots of Russia leather, which were worn on all occasions, even for dancing. (*E,* Plate XVI.) It is said that the king introduced the fashion in compliment to one of his equerries. The few who did not wear boots were barred from polite society unless they wore silk stockings. Even in winter anything but silk was tabooed by the elite; but in order to secure a little warmth several pairs were worn, one over the other.

The general style of dress remained quite similar to that of the previous century. The long-waisted doublet and the quilted stuffed-out trunk-hose or breeches met no change

until the successors of Henry IV came to the throne.
(*D*, Plate VIII.)   The name "breeches" as applied to
trousers is first used in the opening years of this century.

> With woole, with flax, with hair also,
> To make their breeches wyde.
>
> —*From an old ballad.*

During the court festivities of these early years the pen-
dulum began to swing gradually, very gradually, toward
greater and greater luxury.

In the reigns of Louis XIII and XIV we hear again the
words of disapproval, and the edicts go forth, only, however, to be smiled upon and to vanish!

The boots introduced by Henry IV were worn by men
of fashion throughout the period, but in 1625 they were reduced in height and the top increased to a great width,
falling over the middle of the leg, displaying the silk stocking or boot-hose.   (*A, F*, Plate XVII.)

Men's dress of this period had its origin no doubt in
Flanders, and flourished about the time of the marriage of
Louis XIII to Anne of Austria, a daughter of Phillip III
of Spain.   With the bringing of this new Spanish influence
into France, the Italian styles introduced by Catharine de'
Medici and Marguerite of Valois in the preceding century
gave way to the *mode espagnole.*

The trunk-hose of the past were now replaced by
trousers.   The word is rather obscurely derived from the
old French *trousser,* which meant to tie up, to tuck, or to
gird.   The coming of the short trousers marked a distinct
departure in the garments of men.   Usually they extended
to the knee or a little below.   They were made of linen,
batiste, or well starched Holland cloth, and were often
trimmed with edgings of lace, ruffles, and ribbon.   These
short trousers have passed into the annals of costume under
the name of "rhingraves."   (*A, F*, Plate XVII.)   The name
owes its origin to the Count of Salm, who bore the title
of Rhingrave, and who introduced the short trousers into
fashionable society in Paris.

With the fanciful short trouser, the hose became of great importance. Silk knitted hose had been introduced in the previous century and now, with the "rhingraves," they were indispensable. Green, gray, russet, black, and white were worn. White, however, took the lead, especially with those who had adopted the high boot. When the great tops of the boots began to turn down, displaying the hose, white silk hose were in demand. A cotton hose was frequently worn as a kind of protection between the silk hose and the boot. This was often edged with lace and ruffles and sometimes was turned down over the boot top. This hose came to be known as "boot-hose." So effective was this decoration that the gallants of the day dispensed with the foot of the hose and wore only the fluffy tops which spread out in imposing style over the turned-down boot top. Garters had been transformed into sashes with fringed and lace-trimmed ends. These were carried around the leg below the knee and tied in fanciful loops and bows.

The characteristic hat of the period had also come by way of Flanders. This was the high-crowned, broad-brimmed beaver set off with plumes. With the passing of the years the crown grew lower and rounded, but the tilted brim with its sweeping plume never failed to give an enviable "dash" to the wearer. With the fanciful trousers, the great top boots, the broad-brimmed beaver, and the sword dangling at his side, the cavalier costume of that day was complete.

The beard, which was worn pointed at this time, was shortly reduced to a small tuft on the chin, and called the "imperial." (*A, F,* Plate XVII.) It is said that the style was inaugurated by the king who, in one of his eccentric moods, had his principal gentleman attendant shaved, leaving the little tuft on the chin. Immediately the "royal beard" became the fashion.

In women's dress the farthingale still continued the fashion, though not in the extreme style of the preceding century. Now it resembled a huge bell as it fell over the roundly padded hips. (*B, C,* Plate XVIII.) Three petti-

A   B   C   D   F
                                            E

PLATE XVII—THE RENAISSANCE IN FRANCE—1600

A—1600—A lord of the court. Rhingraves or short trousers of fine linen, batiste or Holland cloth succeed the trunk-hose. The wide-topped boots, the cape of rich material and the plumed hat complete the costume of the dashing gallant of the day.

B—1694—A lady of the court wearing a gown of rich fabrics, trimmed with bands of gold lace, and the Fontange head-dress.

C, D—1668—Ladies of fashion carrying the long train of the overdress.

E—1600—This early dress resemb'es the types of 1595. The overdress is open in front displaying the beautiful underskirt.

F—1600—Cavalier wearing short, lace-trimmed trousers, turned-down boots, shoulder cape and plumed hat. The beard, the Imperial, was the popular fashion set by the king.

122

coats, each of a different color, were usually worn beneath the gown, and the lady, by assuming queer but elegant mannerisms in walking, managed to display all three. The rigid corset still remained indispensable, and the heavily boned bodice was carried down to a deep point at the waistline. Possibly to relieve the discomfort caused by the corset, the neck and shoulders were bared most liberally—in fact, to a degree termed "indecorous" by the clergy. Finally, His Holiness, the Pope, interfered. The threat of excommunication, however, had little effect. Fashion still continued to wield her scepter as she chose.

During the previous century, fans had attained great popularity and now they were everywhere adopted as both a fashionable accessory and a graceful way of relieving the discomfort caused by the tortuous stays. The folding fan held undisputed sway. Indeed, a lady was seldom seen without her fan!

The English traveler, Thomas Coryat, writing in 1609, tells of the early use of the fan as he had witnessed it during extended visits on the continent:

> Men and women carry fans to refresh themselves in the heat and often fan their faces. Almost all are pretty and elegant. The mounting is composed of a piece of painted paper which is pasted on it on both sides, very curiously ornamented with excellent paintings either of love scenes with Italian verses written below or of some famous city with a short description.

During the passing of the years the fan came to be one of the most beautiful of dress accessories. Many were mounted in wood, mother-of-pearl, gold, and silver. In the late century the first all-lace fan appeared, having come from Flanders. Handsome needlepoints now gave priceless value to the lace fan. The importance of the fan in costume is set forth in this letter written at a later period by Mme. de Staël to a friend:

> Let us picture to ourselves a most charming woman, splendidly dressed, graceful and gracious to the highest degree; yet if with all these advantages she manages her fan in a bourgeoise way, she may at any moment become a laughing stock. There are so many ways of playing with that precious appendage that by a mere movement

A   B   C   D   E   F

PLATE XVIII—THE RENAISSANCE IN FRANCE—1600

A—1695—A courtier carrying the muff. The long coat succeeded the
doublet and the cravat took the place of the ruff and broad collar.

B—1650—A lady of the court. The falling collar and turned-back cuffs
continued through the century.

C—1614—A lady of rank. The boned bodice with slashed peplum was
fashionable in the garments of both men and women.

D—1600—Costume worn by Henry IV. The short-waisted doublet with
peplum corresponds with the fashion in women's dress.

E—1600—A citizen wearing the knee-breeches fastened with points, and
the short jacket with ruff and cuffs.

F—1600—A woman wearing the simple flowing gown with the little
shoulder cape, which gradually grew into the modern tippet.

124

of the fan one can tell a princess from a countess, a marchioness from a plebeian. And then it imparts such gracefulness to those who know how to manage it; twirling, closing, spreading, rising, or falling according to circumstances.

Sleeves were large, and were confined at the wrists with cuffs. Over the sleeve proper a second sleeve, caught at the shoulder and cuff, but remaining open and showing the real sleeve, was sometimes worn. The second sleeve was often decorated with rows of buttons, but only as ornament; they served no useful purpose.

Fig. 32. Chopines. They were adopted by fashionable women to make them appear taller.

Venetian and Florentine laces were much admired at this period. The wired ruffs and collars of these exquisite laces emphasized the line and whiteness of the shoulders and neck, as well as the delicately beautiful work of the needle. So great was the demand for these foreign laces and so much French gold was going into the coffers of other nations that their importation was forbidden.

Then it was that quantities of ribbon, in lieu of lace, profusely adorned the skirts, bodice, sleeves, and hair of the women, as well as ornamented the dress of the gay cavalier. Loops of ribbon, rosettes of ribbon, yes, garlands of ribbon bedecked the costume.

Added to this extravagant use of ribbon was a great love of jewelry. Necklaces of diamonds, strings of pearls, and colored glass mounted as jewels, which were made by a clever French artisan, were in great demand. The queen is said to have worn on one occasion a gown with thirty-two thousand pearls and three thousand diamonds, and of course the queen's example was followed by all the lesser lights of the court and by those just outside the charmed circle. Added to this was the taste for the richest kinds of materials, garments of brocade, satin, and exquisite damask. Though the long flowing gowns largely concealed

the shoes and stockings, still a love of bright color displayed itself even here. Silk stockings of scarlet, apple-
green, and light blue were the common quest. The shoes
or slippers were equally gay, being of blue, red, violet, or
yellow satin, with very high heels. In fact, heels of eight
centimeters were considered quite ordinary. This extreme
brought forth much lively comment.

> Tall Lise *will* be, despite her nature.
>
> —REGNARD.

For outdoor wear velvet clogs or pattens with thick
cork soles were slipped on over the high-heeled shoes. The
chopines, introduced into Italy and thence into France from
Turkey, and eagerly adopted by the fashionable, no doubt
called forth much similar satire. (Fig. 32.)

> You will have clumsy actresses,
> Half woman and half patten.
>
> —VOLTAIRE.

> But just think of their pattens,
> Which raise them half a foot.
>
> FRANÇOIS COLETET, *Les Traces de Paris.*

There were gloves for all occasions, the various styles
being named after the perfumes with which they were
scented, or after the royal lady whose fine skill invented
the perfume. There were *gants de Neroli,* after the Princess
Neroli whose perfume was in high favor; *gants à la
Frangipaire,* after a Roman nobleman whose similar invention had won him distinction; then there were the gloves
à l'occasion, à la nécessité, and *à la Phyllis.* Many of
these were very elegant, the back and gauntlets often ornamented with embroidery.

Perhaps the most expensive article which demanded a
real sacrifice to do without and to which very few were
equal was the girdle or sash of silk, which was decorated
with silver plates or discs, chased or designed in enamel.
To these belts were often hung keys, purses, and various
gewgaws.

Of all the frailties of feminine vanity, one of the most unusual made its appearance during the reign of Louis XIII. The wearing of patches certainly was a novelty! A patch was simply a bit of black silk court plaster given an advantageous position near the mouth, upon the chin, or near the eye to increase its luster. The dark patch was believed to enhance, by contrast, the fairness of the skin. It is said that patches were first prescribed as a remedy for headache, but retained as an aid to beauty. (*B,* Plate XVII.) Every lady carried the little patch-box, which was also supplied with a mirror; and indeed it was no unusual sight to see a fair damsel upon the public promenade calmly adjust a patch or two.

Again the masks were in vogue and their popularity had greatly increased. To conceal one's features behind a mask may hide beauty or it may not, but the element of mystery has its charm.

A caprice new to the period, however, was the affection bestowed upon the muff and the little muff-dog. The muff was small, and the dog, even more diminutive, was carried within its cozy depths. The lap-dog was indispensable to the correct appearance of the fashionable lady. To caress the little head protruding from the muff, feed it dainty bits of cake and sweets and lavish upon it endearing phrases, constituted the lofty aim of the fashionable lady. The grace and artful manner in which these marks of affection were bestowed established the degree of refinement and taste of this fair daughter of Eve. In the *Book of Addresses* for 1692, the Demoiselle Guérin, Rue de Bac, Paris, is given as the approved shop for the making of muffs especially for this purpose.

The first muff bearing any resemblance to that now familiar to us is seen in a satirical engraving by Jasper Isac, entitled *L'Ecuyer à la Mode,* and signed 1634. This is a cylinder of silk or some other material, not fur, trimmed on each end with bands of thick white fur. It is in the precious engravings of Hollar, Abraham Bosse, Arnoult,

Sandraft, Bounar, and Trouvain, that we may readily note the authentic birth of the muff.

Middle class women who could not spend more than fifteen or twenty francs for this luxury used muffs made of cat skin or dog skin. In the latter part of the century sable was the favorite fur among the court belles.

It is not surprising that with all these frailties and follies becoming so pronounced another storm of disapproval was heard. The stern edicts of Richelieu came forth about 1638. The ban was placed on all the elegancies of fashion. Gold lace, fringes, lace work enriched with gold or silver, were prohibited throughout the country.

The lack of these rich materials necessarily made a change in the dress. There was now no overloading with ornaments or laces; in fact, nothing to suggest the extreme. The skirt began to fall in large simple folds to the floor; the farthingale became passé; the large ruff was succeeded by a band or collar fitting under the chin. In fact, the dress became serious, almost to the point of severity, but not for long.

France ever smiles and shrugs her shoulders over edicts. The fair ladies of France now take this modest costume "according to edict" and transform it into one more elegant and more charming than any their artful hands had yet devised, and one which, with slight changes, was destined to play a distinguished role in the brilliant court of Louis XIV.

With the advent of Louis XIV fashion evolved into a point of etiquette, with the king as sole arbiter. Paris became the acknowledged center and home of fashion and taste. Several influences conspired to bring this about at this time. Chief among these was the understanding and appreciation of the importance of industry on the part of Colbert, the able Prime Minister of Louis XIV. Through his influence a great forward movement took place in all the industries. It was at this time that lace-making in France reached its highest development. The discovery of a route to the East around the Cape of Good Hope was a

RENAISSANCE COSTUMES, CHIEFLY, 15TH CENTURY

A—Italian man wearing a full cape-coat. Sleeves were thrust through cape armholes.

B—The young Florentine woman, 15th century, wore a long fitted bodice joining a full skirt.

C—Flemish girl with cloak and bonnet. From a drawing by Bruegel, 1558.

D—Flemish woman wearing a fur trimmed, slit-sleeved gown. From a painting by Jan Van Eyck, 1434.

E—British boy's costume with cutaway sleeves, 1485.

F—The Englishman's bell-shaped sleeves turned back to the shoulders.

G—The little girl's long dress has a peplum at the waist.

H—Puffed sleeves and a tight bodice with a long full skirt mark this English woman's gown. The headgear was netted and draped.

128A

16TH CENTURY COSTUMES

A—Spanish couple, 16th century. The man's broadcoat was slashed and furred, his breeches short and padded.

B—The woman's costume, elegantly lavish in line, was rich in ruffs, puffs, embroidery, and metals.

C—A Swiss gentleman congratulating a young German scholar, 1577. (*D*) The scholar's attire continues into the present for educational and clerical robes.

E—Long skirt, puffed sleeves, and ruff are parts of this 16th-century English girl's dress.

F—An English noblewoman wearing a ruff, pointed waistline, and a farthingale, with a velvet and figured silk gown of 1558. Her hair was brushed upwards over a wire foundation.

G—English youth as swordsman, 1570.

128B

second direct cause. The French trade in silks, no longer
dominated by Italian merchants, now dealt directly with
Asiatic ports. Consequently Italian taste, which had for-
ked influence on the dress of France,
ignored in French design. The beau-
tiful gardens which were being built, supplying motifs of
design, were of far reaching importance. The high position
of artists was an inspiration to excellence. All of these
factors, combined with the taste of Louis and the court
queens, had a share in the establishment of Paris as the
acknowledged fashion center. The court followed every
dictate, and the bourgeoisie followed the example set higher
up. Each endeavored to outshine the other in the richness
of his dress or in the individual eccentricities which might
be added to complete the costume. One fashion was
scarcely born when another appeared upon its heels. Never
in the past had fashion reached such unlimited extravagance. Of course the king issued edicts, but on the other
hand encouraged extravagance by his own example.

It was some ten years previous to this (1660) that the
periwig, which has since claimed a place for itself in the
history of costume, made its initial bow to the Parisian
world.

A very pretty story is told of its origin. When Louis
XIV was a child his beautiful and abundant locks of hair,
which hung in great waving masses over his shoulders,
won the admiration of all. One day his courtiers, by way
of compliment, had heads of false hair made to resemble
the king's natural locks. When the king grew to manhood,
as a return compliment he adopted the peruke, and by so
doing set the mode for some years to come.

Now the simple costume worn at the close of the previous reign takes on unbounded elegance. The full straight
skirt is made of richest materials, either silk or satin,
trimmed with bands of plaiting or puffs of gold lace; over
this is a voluminous second skirt, open in front and trailing
in great folds behind. (*B, C, D, E,* Plate XVII.) The
length of the train was decided entirely by the prestige of

the wearer. The queen's train measured nine ells;[1] those of the king's daughters, seven; other princesses', five; and that of a duchess, three. The imposing train was usually carried in graceful style over the left arm.

The bodice was fitted and quite snug, and the front ended as before in the long point, which, however, gradually grew shorter. Dainty bits of gimp, chenille, and ribbon adorned the bodice, and these bits of trimming when placed in tiers at each side of the bodice were called "ladders." The sleeves became close-fitting, and were finished with ruffles of fine lace or other dainty material.

Men tailors were patronized in this century, as in the past, by these leaders of fashion.

At this period the silk worm was introduced into France, and silk of all kinds was manufactured at Lyons.

The taste for fine laces also led to the establishment of home manufactories. The very ordinary kinds which were produced in Lyons, Normandy, and Auvergne no longer satisfied the popular taste, and manufactories of the finer sorts were established at Valenciennes, Havre, Lille, Dieppe, LePuy, and the Bois de Boulogne. The most exquisite of the laces naturally could be purchased only by the women of wealth; those of lesser means were quite content with a lace called *gueuse* or *neigeuse*.

Later "transparents" became the fashion. These were dresses of the finest gold or azure brocade, worn under a transparent black gown of lace. The shimmer of gold and black was the desired effect at this period of French elegance. "Have you heard of transparents?" writes Mme. de Sevigne. "They are complete dresses of the very finest gold or azure brocade, and over them is worn a transparent black gown of beautiful English lace, or of chenille velvet, like that winter lace that you saw. They form a "transparent," which is a black dress with a gold, silver, or colored dress just as one likes, and this is fashion."

The present Jardin des Plantes is the outgrowth of the

---

[1]Ell—About 1½ yds.

work of a clever horticulturist who here cultivated all sorts of foreign as well as domestic plants with the view of supplying designers with ideas for these embroidered and brocaded materials.

During the early years of the century the arrangement of the hair led to the innovation of many pretty styles. In one, *à la Ninon,* the hair was parted in the middle and allowed to fall in loose ringlets to the shoulders, sometimes partly concealed by a transparent white veil. (*C,* Plate XVII.) When the hair was arranged *à la garcon,* a horizontal parting was made along the forehead and a few loose curls fell over the brow. (Photo F.) Later, the hair was cut short and curled. Long ringlets, called *moustaches des dames,* were adjusted by pin or ribbon to the sides of the head, and fell over the ears to the shoulders and even below. This style developed into a taste for wigs and curls and whatnots of the wig-maker's art.

Soon after the year 1645 a rather venturesome Frenchman contrived to establish a reputation as a lady's hairdresser. Previous to this a lady's hair had usually been dressed by her own maid. He was successful, however, only for a time; his daring getting the better of his wisdom, his clientele became gradually less. His successor, one Mme. Martin, brought into being the popular fashion of wearing the hair in several rows of short curls. This style was immediately adopted by Mme. Maintenon, and became the popular mode—*à la Maintenon.*

Later a mere chance precipitated a new style of head-dress which was destined to play a conspicuous part in the closing days of the century. During one of the royal hunting parties at which the Duchess of Fontanges, a favorite of the king, was present, the fair lady displayed her rare ingenuity. A gust of wind suddenly and without warning carried off the Duchess' hat; but, nothing daunted, she gathered up her disordered locks and confined them by tying her ribbon garter around her head. The entire party was enchanted with the result, and the next day every one appeared with the head-dress arranged *à la Fontanges.*

PHOTO F—HENRIETTA MARIE, QUEEN OF CHARLES I (1609-1669)—*Van Dyck*

The handsome, white silk gown shows a very ample skirt but without farthingale or hoop. The bodice is low cut and the full sleeves, elbow length, are edged with lace. A simple string of pearls takes the place of the former elaborate jewelry. Note the fashionable hairdress, *a la garçon.*

The inspiration of the Duchess had become the aspiration of the followers of fashion, and the *à la Fontanges* prevailed for years with many variations. (*B*, Plate XVII.) In the end it became an intricate structure of wire about two feet high, upon which were mounted in successive tiers ribbons, laces, and flowers, each part of the unusual conceit having a distinctive name.

> A stockade of wire
> Supports the superb structure
> Of the lofty head-dress;
> Even as in time of calm upon the sea
> A vessel bears its mast.
> —*From the French.*

The king frowned upon all these eccentricities, and continued to frown, for they were not given up until the early part of the next century.

The various arrangements of the hair kept coming and going, and since the hair itself was much lower, high ruffs went out and were succeeded by large flat collars of lace and embroidery, which fell very low over the shoulders and arms. (*B, C*, Plate XVIII; *F*, Plate XVII.) The cuffs which matched the collars were very large, sometimes extending from the wrist to the elbow. This fashion of the large flat collar and cuffs lasted until 1672, when it entirely disappeared.

The little shoulder cape or palattrie (called pelerine by the English, but in fact the very modern tippet) was introduced at this time. (*F*, Plate XVIII.) The extremely low-cut bodice, which was worn during court functions and for full dress, caused the Princess Palatine, Charlotte of Bavaria, daughter of the Elector Palatine, to introduce the fashion to avoid the immodest exposure of the shoulders. The short capes were usually made of gauze or lace in summer, and of fur in winter.

About this time, 1670, a decided change is noticeable in the costume of the French gentleman—a change which subsequently took place in all countries looking to France as the center of fashion. The doublet gave way to the coat and waistcoat, each descending to the knees and fastened all the way down. (*A*, Plate XVIII.) Silver brocade was now used only for the waistcoat, while the coat proper was made of less costly stuffs—cloth, poplin, and camlet. The only decoration of the coat was a large bunch of ribbon on the right shoulder. Further, the cravat of lace or linen, tied at the neck with a bow of ribbon, took the place of the large falling collar.

This new cravat was inaugurated after the battle of Steinkirk, which took place in 1697. It is said that the French officers, taken by surprise had no time to prepare an elaborate toilette, but simply threw their cravats about their necks and rushed out to meet the English. After that the "Steinkirk" tie was adopted by both men and women of the fashionable world. (*A*, Plate XVIII.)

Swords were now worn only by those who were properly qualified; they were carried in broad baldricks fringed with silk. The baldricks were partly covered by scarves or sashes which were worn about the waist.

During 1668 the muff made its appearance in the costume of gentlemen, being suspended by a ribbon about the neck. (*A*, Plate XVIII.) In the priceless old prints of St. Jean and Bonnard we have preserved to us the French gentleman under Louis XIV carrying his huge muff with all the graceful languor befitting a leader of fashion. Never before in history had the taste for furs been so lavishly displayed as in this and the succeeding century. It was in this century that the art and craft movement of the Middle Ages attained its highest development. Designers of jewelry and textiles abounded. Manufactured articles from the various countries were being sent over all the world. It became easy for the craftsman of this day to execute many and new designs, since he had access to the silks and ornaments of the Orient, the laces of Brussels and Venice, the textiles from Spain, and the well made articles from England and Germany. Ideas from all these sources were combined and elaborated. The use of vases, crowns and animals became common. Cupids, the horn of plenty, and garlands of flowers were combined with many streamers and bows of ribbon. Wreaths, and festoons of foliage looped with cord and tassel, were among the interesting details of design.

Toward the end of the century, besides the reigning belles of Versailles, Mme. de Fontanges, Mme. Maintenon, and Mlle. de la Vallière, the stars of the Paris stage were becoming an influence in the fashion world. Little eccentricities of the popular singers of the day were quickly caught and copied. At one time the king presented Mlle. de Brie and Mme. Molière with mantles which they wore in the comedy *Sicilien*. This recognition by the king was an added reason for the popularity of the belles of the stage.

The long clinging robe, without the suggestion of a plait, a style designed by Mme. Molière, and one which revealed the lines of the figure to advantage, was looked upon with high approval by the leaders of fashion.

Thus the seventeenth century wore on in a pomp and splendor which was not confined to the limited circle of court leaders and those of distinguished rank, but extended to that of lesser folk as well. In fact, dress was scarcely any longer an index of rank; the cook wore her laces with the dignity of a countess, and the tailor donned the attire of the gentleman of the court. It is further said that in going to church these gentle dames borrowed a lackey to carry the train of their gowns. A poet of the day voiced his satire in the following lines:

> No longer are our ladies to be distinguished
> From the women of the people;
> Since a person of honor
> Wears a colored petticoat
> Or changes the fashion of her clothes,
> In short, since she dresses herself
> In a gaudy manner.
> A bourgeoise does as much as that;
> She, too, will put on plumes
> And stick in moustaches,
> False hair and pads,
> "Tours," plaits and knots;

White and yellow coifs,
With ells of lawn in them,
And those fine striped silks
Which are sometimes not paid for;
For often such bravery of dress
Hides much roguery.

—From the French.

The Renaissance (1500-1700) is known as the age of
extreme styles. It must be admitted that the costumes
lacked the grace of the long flowing line of the classic period, and that the figure, hampered in steel and bone, had
little opportunity to display its natural artistic proportion
and line. Nevertheless the beautiful textiles of rare color,
heavy brocades, satins, and velvets, the fine linens, the
rarest of laces, and strings of pearls and ornament produced a mass of richness and color imparting to the costume
an air of grandeur unequaled in any other age.

REVIEW

1. What conspicuous change took place in men's boots, trousers, and hats
   during the early part of the century? (1600.)
2. Contrast the femine silhouette of 1600 with that of 1500.
3. What two modern accessories became very important at this time?
4. When did the muff first appear? The mask? Patches? When were
   muffs carried by gentlemen? Discuss.
5. Describe the fashionable shoe of 1600. How were stockings made?
   Give fashionable colors.
6. Give the exact period when coat and waistcoat took the place of
   doublet. At the same time what succeeded falling collars? Describe
   the "Steinkirk."
7. What particular industry in the field of the arts became famous during
   this century? Under what French king did this occur? Who was
   prime minister?
8. When did lace dresses become the vogue? What were "transparents"?
9. When was the silk worm introduced into France? What city led in the
   manufacture of silk?
10. What is the outstanding contribution of the century in materials, lace,
    and ornament to the field of dress?

CHAPTER NINE

FRENCH Costume (1700)

RNK

IN THE opening years of the new century, the brilliant reign of Louis XIV takes on a strangely somber hue. In marked contrast to the gaiety of former years, the tone becomes heavy and dull. The king repented of the follies of his youth, and now resigned himself to the spiritual direction of Mme. Maintenon, whom he secretly married in 1685.

Extravagance in all lines was given up. Stuffs were of one color; lace was restricted to the cravat and ruffles; buttons succeeded points; and ribbon, which was now limited to shoulder knots and cockades, finally disappeared altogether. The trouser was superceded by short tight breeches; in fact everything was reduced in size except coat sleeves, coat skirts, and wigs. The skirts of the coats were stiffened with wire or other material to make them sufficiently bouffant, being a fit companion for the monstrous panier. (*A,* Plate XIX.) The wig had immensely increased in length and descended almost to the waist. In 1705 the wig was powdered white, and not only the wig but the shoulders as well. The long queue was turned under and tied, and known as the "club."

The making of a wig, or peruke, demanded the greatest skill and moreover a fine artistic sense. Those who excelled in this particular line were called *perruquiers*. They had their academy and were considered artists. The wigs they produced were marvelous and of great value.

Colbert, the French statesman and financier, was highly indignant over such extravagance and tried to initiate a change of fashion. Fashion, however, was not quite ready to follow the dictate of a mere statesman.

Things wore on thus until, toward the close of his reign, Louis suddenly tired of his own moroseness and the melancholy tone of his court and urged the fine ladies and gentlemen to restore the gaiety of former years. The response was instantaneous. Immediately the beautiful gowns reappeared, the *fontange* was again the mode, the fan attained its most elegant form, laces developed into rich, filmy creations, and the muff turned into an object of great beauty. All these accessories added richness and a distinct charm to the dress of the period.

The beautiful gowns which appeared were elaborately trimmed, and even the lineal descendant of the farthingale peeped its head above the opening years of the century in the guise of the hoop. The new hoop was constructed of whalebone and was much lighter. Over this the skirt was properly extended. Many times the skirt was slightly puffed and fastened to the hoop by means of ribbon bows. Bodices were long and pointed, with square, open necks and usually a succession of ribbon bows down the front. The sleeves were elbow length and finished with flounces of beautiful lace, for lace held first place in the hearts of women of the period.

The new trimmings for the skirt were called *pretintailles* and *falbalas* (anglicised "furbelows"). The *pretintailles* were cutout patterns laid on the gown making it resemble a piece of upholstery. The style led to a revival of brocade stuffs of gold and silk. The *falbalas,* though known in ancient times, were flounces of silk and lace, a style invented by a son of the waiting maid to the queen. He later gave the style the more modern name. This youth, through the queen's favoritism, became the oracle of fashion to the French world.

A woman in *pretintaille* and *fontange*
Thinks herself as beautiful as an angel;
But this vain *falbala* by its vast size,
Makes her as big as a tower;
And all this set-out inflates and stuffs her up,
Until she resembles a fat turkey.
—Lines printed under a caricature of the period.

A   B   C   D   E

PLATE XIX—FRENCH COSTUME—1700

A—1750—A man of rank wearing the fitted coat with extended coat-skirt. The hat, cravat and buckled shoes are characteristic of the century.

B—1760—The watteau sacque worn over the hoop.

C—1760—A variation of the hooped costume showing the draped panier and boned bodice.

D—1720—The hooped costume showing a popular trimming of the period. The little wired hood and diminutive muff were favorite accessories of dress.

E—1700—A citizen of France wearing the long coat, the waistcoat and ruffled cravat. The knee-trousers, hose and buckled shoes were worn well on toward the end of the century.

139

The outer skirt, cotillon, of previous years was now trussed up behind, and a shaped form of gummed material was placed under the skirt to give it greater amplitude. The noise made by the stiffened linen in walking or when touched ever so lightly gave them the name of *criarde.** The criarde, as did the farthingale, gave the appearance of added slimness to the waist. Above all else, the waist must be diminutive! (Plate XX.) Consequently, it is not surprising that the hoop or panier soon made its bow to the French world.

With the passing of Louis XIV in 1715, Mme. Maintenon retired to St. Cyr, where she founded a school for the education of poor girls of good family. Thus the influence which had caused the temporary lull in the brilliancy of court life passed away. Now Paris was again fully astir, and the most lavish display reigned not only in the palaces of the king, but in the salons of the bourgeoisie as well. Thus the regency ended under the Duke of Orleans.

The fashions during the regency and the reign of Louis XV are so similar that it is almost impossible to mark the point of transition (1715-1774). Both lived under the motto "All for pleasure"; the realm of fashion was ruled entirely by the ladies of the court. Mme. Pompadour and Mme. du Barry were the favorites of Louis XV. They wielded the scepter of fashion this way and that, following the dictates of their own capricious fancy. All materials used were lighter and softer. It was Pompadour who set the fashion for pronounced stripes and the gaily flowered silks known as "Pompadour." During the reign of Louis XIV, who detested scents, the use of perfume disappeared completely. Now, however, "Pompadour and du Barry spent fabulous sums upon both perfumes and cosmetics. Pompadour's favorite astringent is said to have been crushed strawberries, and after a strawberry bath she was massaged with sponges of fine silk saturated with violet-scented milk. Du Barry is said to have preserved her beauty by the use of a receipt given her by an Italian perfumer.

---

*Criarde—noisy fellow.

| A | B | C | D | E |

PLATE XX—FRENCH COSTUME—1700

A—1790—A lady of rank, wearing the fitted jacket, the shoulder scarf and the tall crowned hat—a costume brought in by the approaching Revolution and termed "masculine" or "British."

B—1780—A lady of the court. The short hooped skirt, the trailing over-dress and the towering head-dress mark the reign of Marie Antoinette.

C—1789—The days of the Revolution brought in more simple styles. The waist became short, and the long scarf was invariably worn about the shoulders.

D—1780—A type of short dress made fashionable by Marie Antoinette during her days of farming at the Petit Trianon. A crook was often carried with this costume.

E—1760—An elaborate panier costume with stiffly boned bodice.

The farthingale had made its reappearance in the new guise of hoop and panier in 1711. (Plates XIX, XX.) The panier derived its name from its resemblance to a large basket, being a framework constructed of hoop, reed, or whalebone, held together with cord and tape. The real origin of the panier is quite obscure. It is believed by some that the farthingale had probably survived in some obscure German village, and was carried to England in the time of Queen Anne; here it was adopted by the English ladies, who in turn introduced it into France. M. Quicherat tells an amusing incident relative to the popularity of the hoop-skirt in France:

> Some unusually stout women had ordered petticoats made for them mounted on hoops. These were intended for the privacy of the ladies' own apartments. One summer evening, however, without a change of attire they were led to risk a stroll in the gardens of the Tuilleries. As soon as the pair approached, they were surrounded by the curious crowd. Both men and women, eager in their curiosity, pressed upon them from all sides, until the venturesome dames were rescued by a gallant officer of the court. The women reached home, deeply humiliated and believing they had been hopelessly scandalized by the incident. On the morrow, however, they were amazed to discover that they had set a new fashion, not only to the court but to the city as well!

The first paniers were simply the large hoops bound together with tape, and known as *paniers à guéridon*. (*B, D,* Plate XIX.) Those of a second style were given the form of arches springing from the waist, and were called *paniers à coudes* because the wearer could rest her elbows upon them. (Fig. 33; *B, D, E,* Plate XX.) This is the type with which our modern idea of panier is always associated. Its outstanding feature is the width of the sides and the flatness of the front and back. The wide swinging paniers became the last word in fashion and attained the most extravagant dimensions. They continued to grow until they reached a breadth of six feet, their circumference being eighteen. The largest boxes at the theater could accommodate only three ladies; as they rode through the avenues of Paris, their skirts extended from each side of the carriage.

The unprecedented demand for whalebone in the construction of paniers became a source of great revenue to Holland. Coopers and basket-makers alike undertook the manufacture of paniers; their prices became the ruin of homes, and their use the misery of pedestrians.

RNK

Fig. 33. *Paniers à coudes*

The story is told of a French youth who saw two ladies approaching, dressed in the latest breadth of panier. He understood the situation at a glance; it was necessary for him either to turn back or leave the path, neither of which he cared to do. When the ladies drew nearer and were within a few feet of him, he deftly turned a handspring which landed him over and beyond them. He then nonchalantly pursued his way.

Throughout the history of French fashions such extremes have always led to the same end. War is declared against the panier! The anathemas of the clergy were hurled against paniers, the venom of the press assailed them, and the ridicule of the scholarly world was heaped upon them. Churchly authority, argument, and ridicule were alike powerless. Again Paris smiled and shrugged her shoulders.

A pamphlet published in Paris in 1725, entitled *Indignité et Extravagance des Paniers pour des Femmes Sensées et Chrétiennes,* contained the following:

> But I wish to know, ladies, by what evil genius you are possessed, and what can be your opinion of us, that you endeavor when in such deplorable case to pass yourselves off to us and to the eyes of the Christian world as spiritual and devout persons, while you are laden with an immense and superb panier, that takes up the room of at least six persons, and is the miserable cause of the inconvenience you experience in passing along, having to hold your panier in both hands and displaying wooden hoops under an arrogant and splendid skirt. Is it not the said panier that makes your carriages groan and that bulges through them like the sails of a ship, while you are holding your noble wooden heap in both hands, and displaying it beneath a costume that is a scandal to the church and a laughing stock to the whole world, and that insults the magnificence of our altars by its audacious splendor?

Voltaire's disapproval was voiced in the following satirical lines:

> After dinner, the indolent Glycera
> Goes out, just for the sake of going out, having nothing to do.
> Her insipidity is deposited in a chariot
> Wherein her tightened body groans under the trammels
> Of a heavy panier which protrudes from the two windows.

The charming and graceful fashion which we have named "watteau" after the painter of French gallantry was now combined with the panier (1730). (*B*, Plate XIX.) The gown sometimes fitted to the waist only in the front, and the back hung from the shoulders over the wide-spreading panier, falling to the floor in easy folds. For the watteau costumes, silks and brocades were used; also many of the lighter materials—lawn, dimity, muslin, and flowered stuffs of bouquet pattern and vines. The sleeves were close-fitting and finished with billows of lace.

The leading actresses of the day did their part in making the panier popular. Mlle. Jancourt played the part of Galatea in *Pygmalion* and wore a costume which had been presented to her by Mme. Pompadour—a polonaise

16TH AND 17TH CENTURY COSTUMES

A—Dutch Group, mother, daughter, and son, from paintings by Pieter de Hooch (1629–1677). The little girl wears a white bodice and folded back skirt. B—The mother wears a furred velvet jacket with collar, and a red skirt. C—The boy's school clothing features a wide pair of knickerbockers and a broad hat.

D—The elegant 16th century Venetian gentleman wears a slit doublet, with shoulder pieces and a cape.

E—English girl, 1630, with lace-edged collar and cuffs, and a tabbed bodice.

F—English cavalier, 1638, wearing a sleeveless leather jerkin, feathered hat, bucket-top boots, and cape.

G—English lady with side curls, high waistline, and tucked-up outer skirt, 1655.

144A

EIGHTEENTH CENTURY COSTUMES

A—English group, 1710. The woman wears an off-shoulder full skirted gown.

B—The baby's garments were long and cumbersome.

C—Young English woman with hat, 1740.

D—Lad's attire, similar to a man's 1735—curled hair, tab trimmed velvet coat, breeches, knit hose, slippers, and tricorn hat.

E—French woman's flowered silk costume with bow and lace head covering. Painted fans were fashionable, 1731.

F—German man with long coat, suspenders, furred hat, long trousers, and bows on shoes, 1795.

G—Little French girl's two-piece costume. From a painting by Jean Chardin (1699–1779).

H—The first governor of Louisiana, Spanish Antonio de Ulloa, 1766, wears lavish gold braid on his dark brown velvet coat.

144B

with paniers, satin slippers, and a huge pouf ornamented
with green leaves and surmounted with three ostrich
feathers.

It is to the French actresses, Mlles. Clarin and Hus of
the *Comédie Française,* that the press and the clergy are
both indebted for the disappearance of the panier. Shortly
after this a little book was published entitled *Les Paniers
supprimes au Théâtre.* The ladies of high rank began to
follow the example set by the two actresses and the hoops
became passé.

Then it was that we heard more of the corset, and the
women gave up the one folly for the other.

> Is there anything more beautiful than a corset,
> Which naturally defines the figure,
> And shows how one is made
> In the mould of nature?
>
> —*From the French.*

Toward the middle of the century the daintily colored
cambrics which had been imported from India and Persia
became fashionable. In fact the cambric gown took precedence over the gown of silk. At this same period, (1759) a
print manufactory had been established at Jouy just outside Versailles. Soon this industry was putting out cambric
prints quite as beautiful as those imported from the East.
When this was discovered by the court leaders, Jouy prints
immediately became the fashion. They were soon adopted
by the great mass of the people and continued to be worn
for many years.

The scarf or mantilla, (borrowed from the Spanish *mantilla*), of silk or satin, was worn about the shoulders or
thrown over the head and the ends tied loosely in front.
This was a continuation of the formal style of head-dress
set by Mme. Maintenon. In winter a full mantle or cape
was worn, sometimes lined with fur and buttoned all the
way down the front. The hood, *bagnolette,* was held out
from the face by means of wire. Later the little wired hood
became the fashionable all-season head-dress. (*D,* Plate
XIX.)

Again head-dresses began to grow high. They were raised about the forehead, arranged in bows and rolls mingled with ribbon, feathers, and jewels, and finally given the supreme finish, a thick covering of powder. Mme. de Graffigny, a French writer, protested against these high head-dresses, and preferred to wear her own hair close to the head, powdered and covered with a small cap. This little cap was adopted by many leaders of fashion and was worn for years by all French women.

The great ambition of the ladies of this period was to have not only small waists, but the smallest possible shoes. The heels were still very high and the jeweled and enameled buckles were in popular favor.

Among the small necessities of the complete toilette were necklaces, tablets set in chased gold, crosses of gold filigree, and the little bags or reticules.

Patches, paint, and powder were still the final touch to the *toilette française*. The patches were of various shapes, and given as many different names. The "coquette" was placed on the lips, the "gallant" in the middle of the cheek, the "impassioned" patch at the corner of the eye, and the "rougish" on the nose. Sharp criticism arose over the wide-spread fashion of patches, and the great court preacher, Massillon, delivered sermon after sermon in which he vehemently anathematized patches. Strangely, however, more patches than ever were worn, and further they were now dignified by the name *mouches de Massillon,* (spots of Massillon). Could it be that the ladies themselves were indulging in sarcasm!

Powder, a starch pulverized and scented, was used until 1760, when it disappeared for a time. It returned, however, in 1780, and after the Revolution it reappeared under the Directory in 1795.

Lady Mary Wortley Montague who visited Paris at this time gives an interesting impression of the French leaders of fashion:

> Their woolly white hair and fiery faces make them look more like skinned sheep than human beings.

From the time of Louis XIV fans were indispensable. With their mounts beautifully carved in mother-of-pearl and ivory, they still continued to rule the feminine world.

Toward the end of the reign of Louis XV the first Indian or Cashmere shawl was imported into France.

In 1725-1775 the same general lines of the gown continued. The best period of the Louis Quinze costume was between the exaggeration of the Regency and the accession of Louis XVI, in 1774—the reign of the beautiful and artistic Mme. Pompadour.

To appreciate the charm of the period we have only to call to mind the canvases of the French painters of the day.

With the accession of Louis XVI a new Queen of Fashion, Marie Antoinette, rules in the realm of dress. Thus each goddess has her little day only to be succeeded by the next.

Fig. 34.   Head-dress *à la Belle Poule* (After Robida)

The watteau and panier continued with slight variations. The new queen did not venture to make a decided change in the mode of dress, but directed all the energy of her artistic nature to that marvelous invention of the eighteenth century, the head-dress, with which the name of Marie Antoinette is inseparably connected. The mere whim of the artful queen turned the head of a fair lady into the most wonderful landscapes, into sea pieces, and into towering pyramids. Little cardboard figures of men, women, and children were added to complete this absurdity, and women were proud to wear the freakish novelties devised at court.

Mlle. Rose Bertin, who next to the queen was arbiter of taste at the French court, became famous throughout Europe for her marvelous constructions in head-gear. Her name, as well as that of the queen, is historically associated with these monstrosities of the eighteenth century.

Imagine a hedgehog lying upon the head! And more, considered beautiful! The *herisson,* or hedgehog style as it was called, consisted in frizzing and tangling the hair from the tips to the roots. This was carried up very high and was encircled by a ribbon to keep it in place. Later it was reduced to a *demi-herisson,* or half-hedgehog.

Fig. 35.   *Pouf au sentiment*
(After Robida)

One of the most amazing of all these fantastic creations was the coiffure *à la Belle Poule,* which became fashionable at the time the frigate "La Belle Poule" was victorious over the English ship the "Arethusa." Upon the sea of waving hair rested the ship in full sail—all its masts, guns, and sailors complete. (Fig. 34.)

Ridiculous names were given to these inventions of the queen and of others who strove to surpass her. There was the "English Garden," "The Forest," "Enameled Meadows," "Spaniel's Ear," "The Ingenuous Maiden," "The Councilor's Wife," "The Royal Bird," "Mad Dog," and many others. The comet of 1773 was the suggestion for a new head-dress. Contemporary with its appearance, the "Comet" became the rage, with flame colored ribbons the conspicuous feature. The mother of Louis Philippe, the Duchess of Chartres, wore in her hair a most marvelous combination of designs made from the hair of her departed relatives. Moreover, by way of added ornament were little images of her son in his nurse's arms, a little negro, and a parrot nibbling a cherry. No doubt these figures were mementoes of significant events in the life of the lady. The *pouf au sentiment* (Fig. 35) was the favorite court style, and consisted of various ornaments fastened in the hair,— branches of trees representing a garden, birds, butterflies, cardboard cupids flying about, and even vegetables. As a finishing touch a thick coating of powder was added to the towering mass.

These great scaffoldings of gauze and feathers reached such a height that it was quite impossible for the ladies to

Fig. 35, a. Caricature of period

sit in their carriages, and it became necessary for them to kneel upon the floor of the coach to protect the fragile beauty of the towering head-dress. The caricatures of the period show these French belles in their Sedan chairs with the roof taken off to permit the top of the snow-covered edifice to come through. (Fig. 35, a.) It was Marie Antoinette who set the fashion of wearing plumes in the hair and carried it to the greatest extravagance. French literature refers many times to this one caprice of the queen. In Soulavie's *Memoires* we read: "When Marie Antoinette passed through the gallery of Versailles, one could see nothing but a forest of waving plumes a foot and a half higher than the ladies' heads." A lady of the court declared: "It was a fine sight to see that forest of plumes in the Versailles gallery, moving with the least breath of air. It looked like a moving garden of bright flowers, gently caressed by the zephyrs." (Photo G.)

One day the queen appeared in a gown of chestnut brown which pleased the king so much that he commented on its beauty, calling it "flea color." Thereafter, flea color became the fashion. "Old flea," "young flea," and "flea back," were so much in demand that the dyers were unable to meet the needs of the trade.

The names given to the colors of this period are quite as ludicrous as those given to the head-dresses. There was "Paris mud," "rash tears," "canary's tail," "agitated nymph's thigh," "newly arrived people," "stifled sigh"; and after the burning of the Opera House in 1763 the fine ladies would have nothing but "burnt opera house," described as a shade of flame color. As for ribbons, the most exclusive were "conviction," "the sigh of Venus," "a sunken eye," "an instant," "attention."

Trimmings were "indiscreet complaints," "great reputation," "vapors," "agitation," "regrets," "sweet smile," etc. Shoes were long and narrow, with emeralds set in the seam of the heel. These were given the trade name *venez-y-voir* (come and see).

The costume of one of the belles of the period is described by a French writer as follows:

> Her gown was a "stifled sigh" trimmed with "superfluous regrets," with a bow at the waist of "perfect innocence," ribbons of "marked attention," and shoes of "the queen's hair" embroidered in diamonds with *venez-y-voir* in emeralds. Her hair was curled in "sustained sentiments," a cap of "assured conquest" trimmed with waving feathers or ribbon of "sunken eye," a "cat" or pelatine of swan's-down on her shoulders of color called "newly arrived people," a Medici arranged as befitting, a "despair" in opals, and a muff of "momentary agitation."

Under Louis XVI the designers drew from all sources. Foliage, flowers, landscape, allegories, Chinese ornament, and Arabesque composition appear in all the design of the period. Stripes in fabrics were revived by Marie Antoinette. So fashionable did they become that in 1788 it was said that "Everybody in the king's cabinet looks like a zebra." The Antoinette stripes, unlike those of Mme. Pompadour, were broken with flowers, medallions, and

Photo G—Marie Antoinette, Queen of France—*Callet*

In Marie Antoinette (1755-1793) was the complete fulfillment of the most extravagant fashions of the century. Paniers, ribbons, laces, plumes —all contributed to the dazzling effect of the fashion queen.

151

ornament. Her taste is everywhere seen in the entwined ribbons and garlands of the time.

In 1780 the fires of the revolution were smoldering, and about to break forth into the Terror. Still the old

Fig. 36. a, shoe of 1780; b, shoe of 1790

regime continued; French society was still brilliant, though lowering clouds foretold the coming storm.

This year witnessed the birth of the modern hat as we understand it in the twentieth century. The new straws imported from Italy took the popular fancy. Shapes were as whimsical as the minds that conceived them. (Plate XX.) Some were tall and straight, with little if any brim, and adorned with a bit of ribbon, lace, or feather; some were funnel-shaped and equally elaborate in trimming, while others resembled parasols, their wide brims almost hiding the face.

For the sake of variety many were made of silk and trimmed with ribbons, ruches, and tufts of cock's feathers.

The theater continued to exert a marked influence over the fashions, and nearly every popular actress of the day found herself famous, at least for a time, in the craze for the latest hat.

About 1780 the high heels of the fashionable shoe were thrust farther beneath the foot. (Fig. 36, a.) Toward 1790 the opposite extreme, the low flat heel, became the vogue. (Fig. 36, b.)

Gowns with full skirt and drawn-in waist continued to be worn. The novelty of the period was the fichu of gauze which filled the low-cut neck of the bodice, giving the chest an ill-proportioned prominence. (*F*, Plate XXI.) All kinds of materials were in vogue,—satins, silks, and cloth, either plain or striped. However, as conditions changed, materials grew more simple. Cottons, India prints, and lawns were increasingly popular.

Both men and women at this time wore their watches with short fobs. Indeed, watches were considered an essential detail of correct masculine dress, and many men, not content with one, wore two, with fobs attached, tucked in opposite pockets of the waistcoat.

As the years wore on, the old world of frivolity and luxury grows more blasé, seemingly ripe for destruction as it is engulfed in the catastrophe of the Revolution. The monarchy that has endured for centuries is about to fall. As the horizon darkens, the tone of Paris grows serious.

By 1792 all is changed. The salons of Paris are closed; the king, the queen, as well as France's greatest and fairest, face the guillotine; Paris crouches in deadly fear of the Terror—the tremendous upheaval of the Revolution.

No more brocade, tissues, and gold lace! No more jewels, feathers, and furbelows! No more perfumes, scents, and cosmetics! Changed conditions were so reflected in dress that the appearance of French women was strangely altered. Clothes became extremely simple. Skirts were plain. Bodices were without ribbon or lace, and sleeves were either long or short and close-fitting. The neck of the bodice was filled in with a generous fichu of soft mull or a similar material. The high headdress of the preceding years practically vanished and now women's hair was dressed low with soft curls falling to the shoulders. (Photo H.) Many began to drape the head with scarves of silk, crepe, or gauze arranged in turban fashion, while others adopted a high helmet-shaped hat with red, white, and blue feathers and worn with the costume *à la Constitution*. (*C*, Plate XXI.) The only ornament was some small symbol of the Revolution, military or naval trophies, or perhaps the national colors. All classes were leveled, even the very wealthy adopting great simplicity of dress.

English fashions came into favor for a time. Close-fitting jackets with large lapels were adopted by women of

PLATE XXI—FRENCH COSTUME—1700

A—1785—A gentleman of France wearing the long topcoat with revers.

B—1795—The costume worn during the Directory.

C—1790—A costume of the Republic called *à la Constitution*. This was of fine lawn or muslin striped in red, white and blue. The helmet-shaped hat was adorned with red, white and blue feathers.

D—1785—A gentleman wearing the knee-trousers, undervest and coat with cutaway front.

E—1795—A costume of the Directory. While the gowns of the period were simple, many were trimmed with borders and revers.

F—1795—A lady of rank wearing the novelty of the period, a fichu of gauze which filled the low-cut neck of the bodice.

fashion, and with these waistcoats and cravats were frequently worn. They also adopted the long plaited hair and "club" of the men, and carried the cane as gracefully as their brothers had formerly sported the muff. London became and remained for some years the center of fashion. Paris, concerned with matters other than fashion, willingly accepted the styles from across the channel.

Perhaps the most marvelous miracle of the Revolution was the total disappearance in France of the powder-puff and the rouge-pot. No wonder the chronicles record: "Our way of living is being purified; extravagance and luxury are diminishing."

Though the mind of France was serious in the extreme, striking public events were likely to give rise to a new mode; be it a trinket in jewelry or a bit of millinery. When Charlotte Corday focused attention by the assassination of Marat, the large hats gave way to caps *à la Charlotte Corday*. (Fig. 37.) On the taking of the Bastille, fragments of its stones were polished, set in gold, and worn by patriots who thrilled at the name *Liberté*.

Jewels, *à la constitution*, were also much in favor. The Constitution jewelry bore the word "Patrie." The costume *à la constitution* was of fine lawn or muslin in red, white, and blue stripes or flowers; the cambric neckerchief, the vermilion sash, and the helmet-shaped cap, with possibly a spray of feathers or a red, white, and blue cockade at the side. (*C*, Plate XXI.) In 1793 the wearing of a tricolor cockade was obligatory for women, under penalty of seven days' imprisonment.

Thus fashion responded, in a measure, to the great events of the period.

After the passing of the Terror, chastened and blood-stained France lifted her head and tried again to be merry. Then appeared the *incroyables* and the *merveilleuses*—those freaks of fashion, the natural outcome from so vast an upheaval. (*C, D, E,* Plate XXII.)

Looking back upon them from today they appear as caricatures of figures from the ancient world. As the

PHOTO H—MLLE. CHARLOTTE DU VAL D'OGNES—*David*

Following the Revolution, the extravagance of former fashions vanished, and in their place came the simple and charming style of the Directoire Period (1795-1799).

156

statesmen of the Revolution, Danton, Marat, Robespierre, chose for their models the patriot-martyrs of the Greek and Roman democracies, Demosthenes and Brutus; so the women of the period harked back to antiquity for the popular fashions. The *merveilleuses* were the feminine exaggerations, devoted to the worship of the antique. (*C*, Plate XXII.) There were no more Parisians; the craze for antiquity seemed universal. Gowns became long, straight, diaphanous tunics, short in front and trailing behind, confined by a girdle worn high. Usually the long train was lifted and carried in grotesque fashion in front. (*C*, Plate XXII.)

Fig. 37. Charlotte Corday cap (After Robida)

The leaders of fashion often wore the tunic slashed from the hip to the foot, displaying flesh colored tights and a golden garter. The cold winters of France affected the ladies not at all. They still continued to go lightly clad, and the furs of the previous century having been discarded, only a mantle, wrap, or large circular cloak, *rotonde*, shielded them from the wintry blasts, the ice and snow. The arms were usually bare, laden with bracelets or covered with long kid gloves. Hats were various, but the more modish among the *merveilleuses* preferred the small hat elaborately trimmed with ribbon or tall feathers. (*E*, Plate XXII.)

And what shall we say of wigs! With the tunics *à la Diane, à la Flore, à la Galatine,* or *à la Minerva,* the wigs naturally aspired to *à la Sappho, à la Venus,* or *à l'Aspasia.* The various arrangements of the hair were borrowed from the types seen in the closely curled hair of the Greek statues.

The little reticule was a very necessary part of the costume for the gauzy materials of the day were too flimsy to support a pocket, and the handkerchief and purse were still the necessary adjuncts of the toilette. (*E*, Plate XXII.)

Reticules seem to have been a revival of the little bags carried by women of ancient Greece. Many resemble in shape the old Etruscan vase forms. They were invariably supported by long strings. This was a distinguishing feature of the reticule. Every lady of fashion carried her reticule, which contained her "handkerchief, fan, card-money, and essence bottle."

The shoes resembled the old-time sandal, being a light sole held in place by ribbons laced about the ankle and leg. Not every *merveilleuse,* however, was willing to disfigure the foot with a sandal; some preferred to go unshod, wearing little rings of gold upon the toes. Another type of *merveilleuse* wore a high cravat which was folded several times about the bared neck in a clumsy and awkward manner. This, with the disordered locks of hair streaming over the ears and about the face, and the huge hat all astir with ribbons, presents a picture in perfect accord with the mental tone of France. (*E,* Plate XXII.)

While the *merveilleuses* adopted the gowns "antique," the *incroyables* simply brought theirs from across the Channel. The high-collared coats, the fashionable cravat which swathed the neck and muffled the chin, the twisted walking-stick, the high boots, and the cocked hat were all decidedly English. (*D,* Plate XXII.) In fact, at this time in France, a costume not displaying a touch of "English" was considered decidedly bourgeois.

With this great change in clothes, the hairdress could not escape. Suddenly the Titus coiffure became the fashion. This, too, was an aftermath of the Terror, suggesting the lingering influence of the guillotine. The hair was cut very close at the back; the front, somewhat longer, was arranged in loose, flowing ringlets softening the brow. (Fig. 38.) To complete the suggestion, a red necklace was worn, and often a red shawl was draped about the shoulders. Other popular styles suggesting the same period were given such names as *à la victime* and *à la sacrifice.* Many details of the eccentric dress of these years are recognized in the charming modes of the succeeding period.

A   B   C   D   E

PLATE XXII—FRENCH COSTUME—1800-1814

A—1804, *B*—1814—Women of rank wearing the costume of the Empire. The finest of materials were popular. The turban of the Orient was adopted and with the poke-bonnet became the leader in fashionable headgear.

C, E—1800—The *Merveilleuses,* or "Impossibles," the feminine product of the Terror. They adopted the antique in dress, copying that of Greece and Rome. Jewels bedecked both fingers and toes. (After Robida.)

D—1800—The *Incroyable,* or "Unimaginable," the masculine product of the Terror. These men wore exaggerated copies of the English fashion. The high-collared coats, huge cravats and twisted walking-sticks reflect the spirit of the time.

159

The Directory (1795-1804) followed the Revolution. The antique costumes became more and more restrained, the waist short, and the skirt long and clinging. At this time,

following the Egyptian campaign, the India shawl with Persian design was introduced. It became so popular that it led to imitation by the French, and later to the Paisley copy made in Paisley, Scotland.

Under the Empire, the costume became simple and beautiful. The celebrated portraits of Mme. Récamier and Josephine de Beauharnais by Jacques Louis David, the court painter of Napoleon, show the

Fig. 38. Titus coiffure
(After Robida)

charm, beauty, and grace attained by these costumes in the opening years of the new century.

REVIEW

1. What conspicuous fashion in woman's dress do you always associate with this century? (1700.)
2. Describe two types of this accessory. Describe the appearance of the costume worn over the device.
3. Describe the general types of materials worn during the century.
4. In men's dress what succeeded the trousers of 1600? What succeeded *points?* Why were coat-skirts wired?
5. What famous fashion leader devised the built-up "heads" for women? Describe many of these.
6. Compare women's shoes of the early half of the century with those of the late century.
7. Discuss the use of "make-up" during the century. Of ornament.
8. How did the Revolution affect dress, "make-up," and ornament?
9. Why did fashions at this time revert to those of ancient Greece? Describe the silhouette of the period.
10. What particular name is given this period in French history?

CHAPTER TEN

COLONIAL Costume In America (1620-1781)

D URING the wonderful seventeenth century new vistas were opened. The English, Dutch, and French were setting sail for the new land beyond the sea. Many were seeking the religious freedom denied them in the Old World, others were in quest of adventure and wealth, and still others were lured by the opportunity for larger living.

The greater number of colonists came to America through stress of circumstance. They found a wide gulf between the European manner of living and that found necessary as dwellers in the New World. Looking back from the highly developed living of the twentieth century, one is wont to believe that these earliest settlers, so occupied in finding a new home, and adjusting themselves to new conditions, were not concerned with dress, and the exacting demands of fashion. However, drawing our knowledge from old records, it is evident that these early New Englanders had an inborn regard for the niceties of dress, that even in this early day the "moral effect" of clothes was appreciated.

The various groups of settlers in the New World brought with them certain habits of dress, and ideas concerning dress which were particularly characteristic of the group itself.

The first settlers in Massachusetts, the Pilgrims or Separatists, came to Plymouth in 1620, having previously lived for a time in Holland after leaving England. Their garments followed the general lines and fashions of those of the English court under James I (1603-1625), in which the doublet and hose were the outstanding features. This col-

ony was poor, and their condition did not improve until
the second and third generations.

Following the Pilgrims came the Puritans of the Massachusetts Bay Company. They were Puritans but not Separatists and their condition was much different. This
colony was not poor but had the advantage in wealth and
aristocratic connections. Many of their number held degrees from English universities. It is said they brought
property aggregating in value a million dollars. Charles I
was on the throne of England at this time (1625-1649), and
the dress of the Puritan fathers followed the lines of this
luxurious period with one exception—all extravagance was
eliminated.

Many of the Virginians and neighboring colonists were
Cavaliers, sympathizers with the Royalist faction in England, and with them fine dress was a hobby.

The colony in Manhattan was made up of both Dutch
and English elements. The Dutch brought with them their
characteristic thrift and optimism. Their customs and the
details of their dress were similar to those of the homeland.

A knowledge of the relative social and financial state
of the different colonies leads to a clearer understanding
of certain conditions and surprises in dress. Though the
dress of all these early settlers bore the stamp of that
center of fashion—the French capital, in each instance the
individuality and taste of the homeland was seen, possibly
in a change of color, an added ornament or a difference in
material. However, in the dress of the Pilgrim and Puritan
there were other significant differences, of far greater
import. Though the dress followed the type of the period,
all extravagance had been omitted and all color subdued.
The rich laces, ribbons, feathers and other gay trimmings
were conspicuously absent—an evidence of revolt against
the extremes of English court dress. Not only had those
of Puritan faith expressed their feeling by a change of
dress, but many did likewise who still remained with the
Church of England. Further, this change toward more
simple dress had been made previous to their departure for

the new land. No doubt the materials were heavier, the shoes more substantial; and still other changes, advisable under the new conditions of living, were also made.

The dress of the early settler in America, particularly of the Pilgrim and Puritan, has always been associated with the word "dull," "drab," and "sad-colored." These words picture to the mind a group of gloomy, sober-hued individuals. This, however, was by no means the dress that these early Puritans presented. The colors were dark, to be sure, but by no means dull. They were warm tones of brown, varying from dark rich hues to orange and presented a picture of far more warmth than is commonly associated with the period. Other colors worn and classified in the old records as "sad-colours" are purple, deere-colour, and French green.

Early historical data furnish reliable sources of knowledge on this dress of the first New Englanders. The various lists of the Colonization Company of London, furnishing apparel to the different groups, are still preserved. Here each article is named and frequently described, even the color being given. Many of the old wills bequeathing various articles of apparel are still on record, as are also private letters in which extensive wardrobes ordered from London, are listed with full descriptions. There remain, besides, personal letters, diaries, and last, but by no means least, the portraits of famous folk dressed in the costume of the period.

Looking through the inventories of the Colonization Company we find that the distinguishing characteristic of all clothes coming to America, is their wearing quality. Doublets and jerkins were of leather or heavy woolens; the cassock, a garment similar to a coat, was of canvas and fastened with hooks and eyes, for "buttons were a vanity." Heavy shoes and stockings were also listed, and the mandillion, a loose cloak, is described as of "strong durable stuff."

As prosperity became more general, however, the drift was toward finer and costlier dress. The leather doublets

and breeches were replaced by others of fine wool, and it
is said that even damask and velvet were ventured.
Women's dress, too, tended to become more elaborate and
costly until the inevitable laws were passed to prohibit such
luxury and regulate the dress. As early as 1634 the
Massachusetts court forbade the purchase of

> —any apparell either Woolen, or Silk, or Linen, with any lace on
> it, Silver, Gold or Thread, under the penalty of forfeiture of such
> clothes. Also that no person, either man or woman, shall make
> or buy any Slashed Clothes, other than one Slash in each sleeve
> and another in the back. Also that Cut-works, embroideries, or
> Needlework Caps, Bands, or Rails,[1] are forbidden hereafter to be
> made and worn under the aforesaid penalty.[2]

In 1634 all use of lace, except a small edging on linen
was forbidden. From 1620 to 1640 the usual costume of a
well-to-do Puritan colonist of Massachusetts Bay consisted
of a cloth doublet and breeches, stockings or hose of dark
gray or green wool, fastened to the knee-breeches by points
of black galloon or ribbon. (*A*, Plate XXIII.) The tall
broad brimmed hat was of black felt. The beaver hats
which were so popular in England were also worn. These
were very expensive, and of course could not be purchased
except by the very wealthy.

> Of all the felts that may be felt
> Give me the English beaver.
> From *Merry Drolleries*, 1661.

The large white collar or "playne band," which superceded ruffs, and the turned-back cuffs of Holland linen were
indispensable to the Puritan costume. The change from
the standing ruff to the falling band took place in the seventeenth century in France, and was simply the turning down
of the high ruff. This falling band gradually became known
as simply the "fall," and was worn by both men and
women.

---

[1] Rail, or Rayl—A woman's loose gown or sack worn during the day.
[2] Alice Morse Earle, *Two Centuries of Costume in America* (New York:
The Macmillan Company, 1903), p. 61.

WHY WOMEN WEAR A FALL

A Question 'tis why women wear a fall?
And Truth it is to Pride they're given all;
And *Pride,* the Proverb says, *will have a fall.*

All Puritans took great pride in the nicety of this
"playne band." The doublets, waistcoats and cloaks of
the colonists were usually fastened by hooks and eyes, but
buttons must have been worn, for records show that
buttons were used for traffic with
the Indians. They were sometimes
made of coins, often Spanish dollars; pewter buttons were also
made, and doubtless worn on men's
clothes from earliest colonial days.
Buttonholes were a matter of ornament as well as use, being often
embroidered in silver or gold thread or bound in gay colors.

Fig. 39.   A clog

The Puritan woman wore gowns of cloth in purple, russet or gray. The skirt of the gown was turned under and
looped back, showing the petticoats of homespun and linsey-
woolsey. (*B,* Plate XXIII.) Over this was worn the large
apron of white linen. Every woman of consequence had
a white apron in her wardrobe. The large kerchief was put
about the shoulders on going out-of-doors. The hood was
a necessary part of the outdoor costume, and was made
of dark colored silk or camlet.[3]

The hood is plainly a development from the custom of
throwing a strip of linen over the head and tying it under
the chin. Throughout the colonies hoods were worn by
women of every station. In very cold weather the cloak
and hood were of heavier material or fur, sometimes fur-
trimmed. Many of the early engravings of the Puritan
woman picture her a statuesque figure in voluminous
skirts, the outer one gathered up and carried, displaying
the under petticoat. The tall beaver hat, similar to that
worn by the men was quite as commonly worn as the hood.

[3]Camlet—a material of hair, silk or wool, or all these materials combined, in general use in colonial days for cloaks and petticoats.

Woolen stockings and stout shoes with wooden heels completed this substantial costume. In rainy or inclement weather clogs were worn. (Fig. 39.) These were somewhat similar to the pattens of the French women. Though all served the same purpose, types varied. In general they were simply thick wooden soles, raised by means of rings of iron fastened underneath. Straps adjusted about the instep kept them in place.

In the colony of Manhattan the dress of England mingled with that of the Hollanders. The handsome silks, velvets, and brocades were seen side by side with the more simple attire of the Dutch. Both English and Dutch dress were cut on the same lines; that is, full skirts and pointed bodice. Sometimes, however, a second skirt was worn over the first. This was left open in front, and if trailing, was carried over the arm. Materials of the Dutch differed in that they were more durable and practical and often self-made. The Dutch women were wonderfully skilled in lace-making and embroidering. In fact, lace-making had already became a lay industry in Holland for which her women were famous. They also understood the making and mixing of dyes, which they used in coloring their garments. They understood carding and weaving. The woolen materials worn by the family as well as the household linens were made at home. The coarse cloth called ''linsey-woolsey,'' the warp being linen and the woof, wool. was made throughout the colony.

The fashionable lady of New Amsterdam about the year 1660 wore the loose jacket, or samare, edged with fur, and a full skirt over an equally ample petticoat. (*E*, Plate XXIII.) The portraits of the period show the hair arranged by turning the side locks under and tying with ribbon, while the remainder was fastened at the back in a coil into which ribbon was frequently twisted.

The appearance of these dames of New Amsterdam is accurately pictured by Washington Irving:

> Their hair, untortured by the abominations of art, was scrupulously pomatumed back from their foreheads with a candle, and

A   B   C   D   E

PLATE XXIII—COLONIAL COSTUME IN AMERICA—1620-1725

A—1620-1640—A Puritan colonist. The costume was usually of black cloth. The broad-brimmed hat, the "playne band" and turned-back cuffs, heavy shoes and mantle completed the typically Puritan dress.

B—1620-1640—A Puritan woman wearing a characteristic type of dress. The kerchief about the shoulders, the apron of white Holland linen and the turned-back cuffs were indispensable.

C—1682—The Quaker dress was a survival of the French dress of 1660-1680, with all the extravagances eliminated.

D—1682—The dress worn by Quaker women. The dress was usually of soft-colored silk.

E—1725—The dress worn by women of New Amsterdam. The full skirt and the loose jacket, or samare, edged with fur are frequently seen in the paintings of the Dutch masters.

167

covered with a little cap of quilted calico, which fitted exactly to
their heads. Their petticoats of linsey-woolsey were striped with a
variety of gorgeous dyes, though I must confess these gallant garments were rather short, scarce reaching below the knee; but then
they made up in the number, which generally equalled that of the
gentlemen's small clothes; and what is still more praiseworthy they
were all of their own manufacture, of which circumstance, as may
well be supposed, they were not a little vain.

Those were the honest days in which every woman stayed at home,
read the Bible, and wore pockets—aye, and that too of a goodly
size fashioned with patchwork into many curious devices and osten-
tatiously worn on the outside. These, in fact, were convenient
receptacles where all good housewives carefully stored away such
things as they wished to have at hand; by which means they often
came to be incredibly crammed. Besides these notable pockets they
also wore scissors and pincushions suspended from their girdles
by red ribbons, or, among the more opulent and showy classes, by
brass and even silver chains, indubitable tokens of thrifty housewives and industrious spinsters. I cannot say much in vindication
of the shortness of the petticoats; it doubtless was introduced for
giving the stockings a chance to be seen, which were generally of
blue worsted with magnificent clocks; or perhaps to display a well
turned ankle and a neat though serviceable foot, set off by a high-
heeled leathern shoe, with a large and splendid buckle.

There was a secret charm in these petticoats, which no doubt
entered into the consideration of the prudent gallant. The wardrobe of the lady was in those days her only fortune; and she who
had a good stock of petticoats was as absolutely an heiress as is the
Kamtschatka damsel with a store of bear-skins or a Lapland belle
with plenty of reindeer.

The dress of settlers in Connecticut and Maine followed
the same general lines as those of the Puritans. Many of
the Southern colonists were Cavaliers. They had no particular feeling against fine dress. The great tobacco crops
of the South yielded rich returns and the ready funds, together with the taste of these settlers, expressed itself in
a luxuriousness of dress quite comparable to that of the
fashion circles of London and Paris.

In 1660, as in France and England, the doublet was
gradually transformed into the coat, which became the
general style of men's attire. With the coat came the vest,
the cravat, wigs, garters and buckles. All these came in
about the same period, between 1660 and 1666. The cravat,
or neckcloth, as it was frequently called, was a scarf of

white linen, quite sheer and over two yards in length. It was passed twice about the neck and lapped in front after the manner of the French Steinkirks.

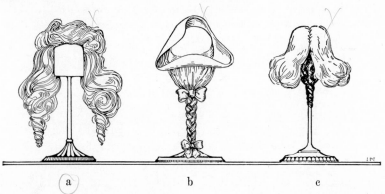

Fig. 40. Wigs. a, campaign wig; b, Ramilie tail; c, periwig

Wigs were not in general use in England when Plymouth and Boston were settled, and had not been adopted for general wear before 1670. Numerous references to wigs are made in the diaries of famous folk both in England and in the colonies. From this it is evident that wigs had a tremendous run. They were worn by governors, ministers, magistrates and "plain people," as well. Many of the portraits of this early day picture the great black thickly curled wigs of the colonists. In 1673 the legislature of Massachusetts took up the matter, and the clergy hurled denunciations from the pulpit. They were hotly termed "Bushes of Vanity," "Artificially deformed Maypowles fit to furnish her that in a Stag play should represent some Hagge of Hell." "Monstrous periwigs such as some of our church members indulge in make them resemble locusts that come out of the bottomless pit." The Puritans resolved that "Ye wearing of extravagant superfluous wigs is altogether contrary to truth." However this matter of wig-wearing was a most difficult one to solve, for among those who had adopted the wig were the most prominent members of the colonies. By 1716 the fashion was general. Wigs were called by various names which passed from the

French court to England. The peruke and periwig were the distinctly formal wigs. (Fig. 40, c.) In May, 1706, the great victory of Marlborough on the battlefield of Ramillies gave the name to the new style of wig. The "Ramilie" wig was puffed out at the sides and had a long queue, called the "Ramilie tail." It was tied with a large bow at the top and a smaller one at the bottom. (Fig. 40, b.) This style of wig was worn for many years; finally the length of the braid was reduced to seven inches and later cut off altogether. The Campaign wig was curled and had long side pieces twisted at the ends. (Fig. 40, a.) Later, in the reign of George II, bob wigs came in, aiming to represent the natural hair. These were sent to New England in great quantities and eagerly purchased by the colonists. (Photo I.)

About the same time that wigs became popular, muffs were introduced for gentlemen's wear. It is a severe strain on the imagination to see our colonial fathers adopting that novel French vanity, the muff. It is nevertheless true that they, as well as the French and English of the period, were enthusiastic over this whim of Dame Fashion. It was believed to lend an air of importance and dignity to the wearer. *The Boston News Letter,* of March 5, 1715, announces: "Any Man that took up a Man's muff drop't on the Lord's Day between old meeting house and the South are desired to bring it to the Printer's office and shall be rewarded." The first muffs were made of rich materials, not always fur, and trimmed with laces and ribbon. It was some time after this that fur muffs became fashionable.

While the dress of men was taking on new vanities, women were adding strange eccentricities to their toillette. Patches were in vogue as early as 1650, and were widely worn by the belles of the day. At the same period in France the following appeared:

> Our ladies have lately entertained a vain custom of spotting their faces out of affectation of a mole, to set off their beauty such as

PHOTO I—CALEB HEATHCOTE (1665-1721)

The elaborately curled wig raised in the fashionable double peak was a favored style during the early years of the eighteenth century. The early cravat was simply lapped and drawn up under the chin, the ends falling free.

171

Venus had; and it is well if one black patch will serve to make their faces remarkable for some fill their faces full of them, varied into all manner of shapes.

Perhaps the extreme of patch-wearing as described in Bulwer's satirical lines was not seen on this side of the Atlantic:

> Her patches are of every cut,
> For pimples and for scars;
> Here's all the wondering planets' signs,
> And some of the fixed stars,
> Already gummed to make them stick
> They need no other sky.

The patches were usually carried in very costly patch-boxes of silver, ivory and tortoise shell.

About 1701 hoops became the fashion. Though at first they were considered as "trenching on morality," by 1713 the reign of the hoop had begun in earnest. Even though they were condemned by the press and the clergy as against the "Light of Nature and the Laws of God," they still prevailed. They reached their most extreme form about 1745. Many and varied were the types of hoop, and the hoop and petticoat combination. Even the children were hooped as modishly as their fashionable mothers. The hooped petticoat is seen in many of the charming costumes of the period.

With the adoption of all these luxuries of fashion the dress became more and more extravagant. This love of dress so evident throughout the colonies affected also the simple Quaker folk. At the time the Quakers came to Pennsylvania with William Penn, no distinctive style of dress had been adopted. It had not, at this time become necessary to formulate any strict rules of dress. It is true that the color and style of dress among the Quakers was serious when compared with the fashionable dress of that day. However, it would indeed be a gala dress for our gentleman of the twentieth century. The Quaker dress was a survival of the English fashion worn during the reign

of Charles II (1660-1685), similar to the **French of 1660.**
(*C*, Plate XXIII.) It was dark brown or plum in color
and without trimming of any kind. The full shirt sleeves
ended in ruffles which fell over the hand, and the neckcloth
was of the finest linen but always untrimmed. Though
the hats were similar in style to those of the French period,
they were never adorned with a feather. They were set
straight upon the head, and never "doffed in deference to
either rank or sex." The hair was cut with a short bang
across the forehead, and fell to the shoulder. Occasionally
it was powdered; moreover periwigs are said to have been
worn by these "genteel Friends." With slight modifications in material and color the general style of Quaker dress
remained the same for years.

The dress of Quaker women followed in its general lines
the prevailing mode; full skirts, pointed bodices, kerchief
and hood. (*D*, Plate XXIII.) However, the manner of adjustment and the lack of ornamentation produced an effect
of severe plainness. The gown was usually of some soft colored silk; the fine white kerchief was an indispensable
nicety of the costume; the long full apron was also of silk,
and usually of a dark green color. In 1698, at Aberdeen,
the following was resolved: "Let none want aprons at all,
and that either green or blue or other grave colors, and
not white upon the street or in public at all; not any spangled or speckled silk or cloth or any silk apron at all."
The report at Lincolnshire in 1721 says: "We think Green
aprons are Decent and Becoming to us as a People."[4] The
black hoods were worn by Quaker women for a long time.
Late in the century they adopted the beaver hat, and in
the nineteenth century, the poke-bonnet. Like all other
items of colonial dress the hood may be traced directly to
the French court, and to Mme. Maintenon's preference for
this particular type. It was undoubtedly chosen by the
followers of Fox because, historically, it suggested godli-
ness of mind.

---

[4]Earle, *Two Centuries of Costume in America*, p. 601.

> The black silk hood with formal pride
> First rolled beneath the chin was tied
> So close, so very trim and neat,
> So round, so formal, so complete,
> That not one jag of wicked lace
> Or rag of linen white had place
> Betwixt the black hood and the face,
> Which peeped from out the sable hood
> Like Luna from a sullen cloud.

Under the black hood which was put on for outdoor wear was worn the little ruffled cap of sheer lace. The hair was parted in front and arranged in a coil at the back.

In William Penn's book, *Some Fruits of Solitude,* we read a message of counsel to his people, whose welfare was ever his first concern:

> Choose thy clothes by thine own eye, not another's. The more simple and plain they are, the better. Neither unshapely, or fantastical and for use and decency, not for Pride.

In 1726 when the love of dress was becoming excessive, the "women ffriends" at the quarterly meeting at Burlington sent the following message to their fellow women-workers:

> At first, That Indescent ffashion of hooped Pettycoats, or ye imitation of them, Either by Something put into their pettycoats to make you set full, Wearing more than is necessary, or any imitation whatever, which we take to be but a Branch Springing from ye said corrupt root of Pride.
>
> And Also that none of sd ffriends Accustom themselves to wear their Gowns with Superfluous ffolds behind, but plain and Decent. Nor to go without Aprons. Nor to wear Superfluous Gathers or Plaits in their Capps, or Pinners, Nor to wear their heads drest high behind; Neither to cut or lay their hair on ye fforehead or Temples.
>
> And that ffriends are careful to avoid Wearing Striped Shoes or Red and White heel'd shoes, or Clogs or Shoes trimmed with gaudy colors. And also that no ffriends Use ye Irreverent practice of taking Snuff or handing a Snuff box one to Another in Meetings, lest it Divert ye mind from ye more inward spiritual exercises which all ought to be Concerned in.[5]

However, notwithstanding all this precaution, it was not long before Philadelphia, Penn's own city, was taking the lead in matters of dress.

[5]Earle, *Two Centuries of Costume in America,* p. 609.

During the early years of the new century times were thriving and costume was gradually growing more and more elaborate. However, in Massachusetts the everyday dress still continued to show the same tendencies as in early years. All materials had wearing quality. Women wore dresses of camlet or moire camlet (watered camlet) over stiffened petticoats made of durant, a close-grained woolen material. The "falling whisk," or "whisk," of fine linen or lace suggests the French period of 1666-1700. The whisk was probably another name for the "fall"; both no doubt refer to the turned-down ruff of the previous century. At this time the dresses were cut low and the whisk used to cover the neck. The popular style of wearing the hat over the little ruffled cap has been made familiar in the pictures of Hogarth.

The close commercial relations between England, France and the colonies made it possible to keep up with all the latest decrees of fashion. In order to publish abroad the most recent modes, jointed dolls dressed in the latest fashion were sent from Paris to London and thence to America. These fashion dolls date back to a former period. In 1391, according to French records, a doll was sent to the Queen of France; one hundred years later another was sent to the Queen of Spain. Later they were sent to the larger cities as forecasts of fashion. In 1764 these dolls were made the size of a full-grown person, dressed in the latest mode, and called *grand courrier de la mode* (guide to the fashions). The inventions in millinery and coiffure were likewise illustrated in these traveling dolls.

At regular intervals of from four to five months came the fashion dolls to the colonies, and all the mantua-makers made haste to copy the latest ideas for their wealthy patrons. The *New England Weekly Journal,* of July 2, 1733, contains the following announcement:

> To be seen in at Mrs. Hannah Teatt's, Mantua-maker at the head of Summer Street, Boston, a baby dressed after the newest fashion of Mantuas and Nightgowns, everything belonging to Dress Latilly arrived on Captain White from London. Any ladies that desire to

see it may either come or send, she will be ready to wait on 'em; if they come to the house it is two shillings, if she waits on 'em it is seven shillings.[6]

In 1757 two fashionable mantua-makers of Boston announced that they had

just arrived from the kingdom of Ireland, and have furnished themselves from London in patterns of the following kinds of wear for Ladies and Gentlemen and have fixed a correspondence to have from thence the earliest fashions in miniature.[7]

Thus the fashion dolls of the day published abroad the latest dictates in dress quite as effectively as the modern fashion periodical.

Going on with the century, times were indeed prosperous, and greater richness and extravagance in dress was indulged. Boston became a center of fashion and display. This in part was inspired by the extravagance of political leaders who endeavored to follow the styles of the English court which in turn drew its inspiration from the court of France. The wealthy took on an extreme richness of attire which set the wheels of rivalry in motion. One English traveler wrote in 1740: "Both the ladies and gentlemen dress and appear as gay in common as courtiers in England on a coronation or birthday."[8] Hawthorne looking back to the period wrote: "There are tokens everywhere of a style of luxury and magnificence we had not associated with our notion of the time. The gaudiest dress permissible by modern taste fades into Quaker-like sobriety compared with the rich, glaring splendor of our ancestors."

During these early years of the century the dress of New York was rich in materials and lavishly ornamented with jewels. Imported brocades, taffetas, poplins, silks and satins were generally worn. The ladies adorned themselves with necklaces, flowers, aigrettes, handkerchiefs, silk gloves and mitts, satin shoes and silk hose and in winter donned the richest furs. Indeed the love of dress on the part of

---

[6]Earle, *Two Centuries of Costume in America*, p. 661.

[7]*Ibid.*, p. 666.

[8]Earle, *Costume of Colonial Times* (New York: Charles Scribner's Sons, 1894), p. 24.

COLONIAL AMERICAN COSTUMES

A and *B*—A Puritan couple, 1630. In line with their religious beliefs, the
Puritans simplified their clothing.

C, *D*, and *E*—A Dutch family that came to New York state in 1649.

F—Costume of William Penn, founder of Pennsylvania, 1682. The long waistline, outer coat, and other articles of his English clothing were later modified
to the simpler ones of the colonists.

G and *H*—Young girl and her mother of the Middle Atlantic states. Most
clothing in 1700 was still fashioned after foreign styles. Necessity and lack
of merchandise, however, created new uses for native materials.

176A

AMERICAN COSTUMES, 1700–1804

A and *B*—Couple dancing the minuet. For the man the costume included a
powdered wig, flaring coat, breeches, and buckled slippers. The attire of the
woman was gay wth paniers, a tight bodice, ruffled skirt, and powdered hair.

C and *D*—Little girl and housewife, 1785. Copied from the woman's, the girl's
dress was long. Clean white caps, fichus, and aprons freshened the marketing
attire.

E and *F*—Couple, 1804. The man's attire—velvet collar, tail coat, and jersey
trousers—created the "dandy" appearance. The woman's high waistline
and long skirt were consistent with the Empire period. Ribbon band and
ostrich plume added richness to the coiffure.

G—Town crier, New England, 1776.

176B

the colonial dames of New York caused lively comment by travelers of the period. One, Chevalier de Crève Cœur, declared: "If there is a town on the American continent where English luxury displays its follies, it is New York."

Philadelphia completed the trio of large centers that were becoming famed for their extravagance in dress. The colonial gentlemen of the period wore the fashionable dress adapted from the French of 1700. The style of coat was not changed. It was still straight and full-skirted, and the tails stiffened with buckram or wadding. (*B,* Plate XXIV.) Thus our gentlemen's dress of the day vied with the hoop and the panier of the ladies. Waistcoats were of heavy silks and satins often elaborately embroidered. Colored silks, threads of gold and silver, and these combined with narrow, flat braids are responsible for the delicate designs which enriched the fronts, played about the buttonholes, and bordered the pockets. Shoes with square toes and silver buckles were gradually giving way to the rounded toe and strings, but the red heels still continued the vogue.

The colonial dames wore rustling gowns of silk, satin, and brocade, with bodices cut low. (Photo J.) In the National Museum in Independence Hall, Philadelphia, is a charming costume of this period. It is of yellow damask silk. The overdress is looped back with narrow braid and ribbons, showing the French tendency of the eighteenth century. The bodice and edges of the overdress are finished with ruchings of pinked material. The dainty slippers worn with the costume are of white satin with the semi-pointed toe and medium heel.

It was about 1750 that powdered hair invaded the ranks of the colonists, and every colonial dame wore her hair thickly dusted with fine white powder. All early powders were chiefly pulverized starch or wheat flour, heavily scented. Though the origin of hair powder is obscure, it is well known that the fashion dates back to the ancient Assyrians and Persians, who dusted their elaborately dressed hair and beards with a yellow powder resembling gold dust. The modern world accepted the fashion when it was introduced

A   B   C   D   E   F

PLATE XXIV—COLONIAL COSTUME IN AMERICA—1710-1777

A—1770—The quilted petticoat, the watteau overdress and little cap are characteristic of the period.

B—1710—A colonial gentleman, wearing the fashionable dress of the French of 1700. The long skirt of the coat is stiffened with buckram.

C—1777—The fashionable watteau of colonial days.

D—1727—A colonial costume. The long-skirted coat is worn with a waistcoat elaborately trimmed with lace and embroidery.

E—1725—A colonial dame in the hooped skirt and the boned and pointed bodice, wearing the pompadour with a curl.

F—1725—A dress of the same period with the overdress looped in panier effect.

into France by Marie de' Medici, about 1600; however, it is known to have been used at a much earlier date. At this time the pompadour style of hair-dressing ranged to various heights and continued for many years. This fashionable style was attained by drawing the hair back from the face and over a roll or cushion of hair. These rolls grew from one of small size to those of much greater dimensions. After reaching an exaggerated height a change gradually took place and the roll descended to about two inches in height, and the hair was roughed and pulled high in the center. This was named the "macaroni roll." The term originated in 1770 in London with a group of Englishmen who had just returned from a town in Italy and had formed themselves into a club called the "Macaroni Club." In matters of dress it stood for all things that were eccentric and extreme.

Fig. 41.   The calash

During the reign of the high head-dress, the calash, often called the "bashful bonnet," was fashionable. (Fig. 41.) It is said to be the novel invention of the Duchess of Bradford. It was of great size, usually of brown or green silk, or dainty white material. It was extended by whalebone run through shirrings, which were usually about three inches apart. The neck line was drawn in and fitted with a little cape. The resemblance to the extension top of a light form of carriage called *calèche,* which was commonly used in France, is striking. No doubt it was due to this resemblance that the bonnet received its name. The use of the term "bashful" arose from the arrangement of the ribbon streamer at the top edge. This permitted it to be drawn over the face, if the fair wearer wished, or pushed

PHOTO J—MARGARET SYLVESTER CHESEBOROUGH—*Blackburn*

A handsome gown of the mid-century showing the low-cut and boned bodice, and the full, extended skirt. Note the style of sleeve, and the use of lace about the neck and sleeves. Painted about 1754.

back of the head. This bonnet was worn well on toward the end of the century and continued to be in use by old-fashioned ladies even to a later day.

Toward 1755 the charming watteau was in high favor. (*C*, Plate XXIV.) The watteau is often called the French sacque, though it was usually long, falling to the floor. Frequently, however, it was looped in polonaise fashion, thus showing to more advantage the costly petticoat. (*A*, Plate XXIV.) These costumes were often of flowered silk and brocade; quite as frequently of muslins, dimities and other dainty fabrics. Many variations of the watteau were played upon until the nineteenth century, when the Empire became the leading mode. The flounces, plaited, pinked and lace-edged, which were the *falbalas* of the French, were often festooned about the petticoat, and frequently trimmed the sacque. The *pretintailles* of France were also introduced in the form of appliqués. These were large designs in color, cut out from one material and sewed upon another. Other trimmings of the century were pinking, ruching and narrow plaited ruffles set on in semi-circular or wave pattern.

Between 1770 and 1776 the quilted petticoats were as much in favor as were the hooped petticoats of earlier years. (*A*, Plate XXIV.) These fashionable petticoats were usually made of dainty colored materials, filled with a layer of cotton or wadding, and then run with stitches, quilt fashion, to keep the wadding in place. Often the stitches were so arranged as to form a pleasing border or design at the lower edge. Much of the value of these garments was in the handwork, for they were often elaborately quilted. The handsomest petticoats were of quilted silk or satin, and no design was too elaborate for the skillful needlewoman of the period. Over this the watteau sacque of dimity or chintz was worn. It was looped back somewhat after the French fashion of the same century.

The little cap so fashionable in the early years of the Washington administration dates back to colonial times. (*A*, Plate XXIV.) It was made of laces and the finest gauze and remained the fashion for nearly half a century. This quaint head-dress was no doubt the direct descendent of the French cap, which was worn generally in England and then carried to America. The portraits of Martha Washington and others of the period have familiarized us with this dainty head-dress of colonial times. The long pointed bodice was the very acme of fashion during the greater part of the century, and it seems, with the hooped petticoat, the fichu and the little cap, to be a distinguishing characteristic of colonial dress.

The early painters, Copley and Stuart, have left to posterity a rich heritage of costume in their portraits of American men and women of this early period. (Photo K.)

With the oncoming days of the Revolution, one is wont to believe that all thought of fashion must vanish. Quite to the contrary, however, historical records assert that much gaiety and style in dress continued in the larger centers— Philadelphia, New York, and Boston. This love of dress, so manifest in these later days of colonial history, soon blossomed afresh and became the distinguishing characteristic of the early years of our national life.

REVIEW

1. Who were the first settlers in Massachusetts? Date? Whence did they come? Their clothes followed the fashion of what period? Describe.
2. When did the Puritans arrive? Who sat upon the English throne at this time? Describe dress.
3. Describe the dress of Puritan women—their hood, stockings, shoes.
4. Contrast the Pilgrims and Puritans in point of wealth and learning. In point of dress.
5. Whence came the colonists of Manhattan? What were their tendencies in dress?
6. Discuss the Virginians and their ideas about dress.
7. How did the Quaker folk regard dress? Describe Quaker dress.
8. What was the general quality of clothes coming to America in the early days? At what period did simplicity in dress give way to luxury?
9. What three cities became leading fashion centers?
10. Name two American painters who have preserved in their portraits the fashions of this early day.

PHOTO K—DETAIL, WASHINGTON AND LA FAYETTE AT MT. VERNON, 1776—*Rossiter and Mignot*

The typical American dress of 1776 shows the long coat with curved front, waistcoat shorter than previously worn, and trousers buttoned below the knee. With the low shoes, hose was given careful attention. The lawn or lace jabot, and frills about the hands, are still in evidence.

CHAPTER ELEVEN
American Costume (1781-1900)

THE opening years of American life are strangely colored with gaiety and extravagance—an unusual hue after so depressing a period. Victory and independence had come to the colonies. The future was bright. Spirits were high. At the same time conditions were unsettled. Political institutions were as yet unorganized. The relation of the state to the national government was under debate; the people had not yet adjusted themselves to any well defined national life. Naturally all these influences, combined, were tonal in shaping the expression of dress in these first years of independence.

Abounding extravagance, clearly the mental tone of the new republic, was the striking feature in the costume of the period. This was largely independent of foreign influences, for both France and England were soberly clad. Paris, under the lowering clouds of the Revolution, had become serious-minded. This was reflected in the dress of the day. In conservative England, restraint in the use of frills and furbelows tended to produce a quiet and unostentatious type of dress. In contrast with these two world centers, America, so young, so buoyant, presented an appearance quite compatible with her youth.

Quoting from an account of the inauguration ball written by one Colonel Stone, a clear idea of the love of dress in these early days may be gleaned:

Few jewels were then worn in the United States, but in other respects the dresses were rich and beautiful, according to the fashion of the day. One favorite dress was a plain celestial blue satin gown with a white satin petticoat. On the neck was worn a very large Italian gauze handkerchief, with border stripes of satin. The headdress was a pouf of gauze, in the form of a globe,

the creneau, or headpiece which was composed of white satin having a double wing, in large plaits, and trimmed with a wealth of
artificial roses, falling from the left at the top to the right at
the bottom, in front, and the reserve behind. The hair was dressed
all over in detached curls, four of which in two ranks, fall on
each side of the neck and were relieved behind by a floating chignon.
Another beautiful dress was a perriot, made of gray Indian taffeta
with the dark stripes of the same color—having two collars, the
one yellow, and the other white, both trimmed with blue silk fringe,
and a reverse trimmed in the same manner. Under the perriot was
worn a yellow corset or bodice, with large cross stripes of blue.
Some of the ladies with this dress wore hats à l'Espagnole, of white
satin, with a band of the same material placed on the crown, like
the wreath of flowers on the headdress above mentioned. This hat,
which, with the plume, was a very popular article of dress, was
relieved on the left side, having the handsome cockades—one of
which was at the top, and the other at the bottom. On the neck
was worn a very large plain gauze handkerchief, the ends of which
were hid under the bodice.[1]

Other instances of recorded extravagances are preserved. One French economist declared that the wives of
bankers and merchants were clad alike in the very height
of French fashion. He adds: "At Mr. Griffin's house, at
dinner, I saw seven or eight women all dressed in great
hats, plumes, etc. It was with pain that I remarked much
of pretention in some of these women; one acted the giddy,
vivacious; another, the woman of sentiment. This last had
many pruderies and grimaces. Two of them had their bosoms very naked. I was scandalized at this indecency among
republicans."[2]

Among the many personal letters of famous folk por-
traying the dress of these early years are those of
Mrs. John Adams, the wife of our first minister to England.
In writing from London to one of her friends in America,
she says:

I am a little surprised to find dress, unless on public occasion,
so little regarded here. The gentlemen are very plainly dressed,
and the ladies much less so than with us. 'Tis true you must put
a hoop on and have your hair dressed; but a common straw hat,
no cap, with only a ribbon on the crown is thought sufficient dress

---

[1] Earle, *Two Centuries of Costume in America,* p. 735.
[2] *Ibid.,* p. 735

to go into company. I have seen many ladies but not many elegant ones since I came. There is not that neatness which you see in our ladies.[3]

The extravagances in American dress soon attracted the attention of the national leaders, chief among whom was Benjamin Franklin. Franklin himself was always considered a model of dignity and simplicity in dress. He, with other leaders, discussed publicly the offending extravagances. Display and show were condemned and the public urged to exercise restraint in matters of dress.

The lines of costume in these early days followed in the main the dress of the French Directory. They were long and clinging. Waists were short and necks were low. The buffont, or puffed-out fichu, so popular in France at this period, became a part of every woman's costume.

Hat styles also followed the lines of the Directory. At this time many new types of hats were evolved. The little toque, which was an outgrowth of the French turban, was one of the popular hats of the period. (*C*, Plate XXV.)

Especially noticeable at this time (1790) is a change which took place in the attire of gentlemen. The knee-buckles were discarded and the trousers buttoned or tied below the knee. These were similar to those worn by the gentlemen of France. Naturally with the short breeches, stockings were still in evidence and received much careful attention. The lines of the coat also changed, the fronts formed a long curve downward and back, meeting the long tails. This was the typical costume worn during the Washington and Adams administration. (*B*, Plate XXV.)

With the beginning of the new century, Americans began to adopt the strange costume seen in the French capital. As Paris dresses, the world dresses. Thus it has always been, century after century, since Paris established herself as the world's fashion center. The source of the wide-collared coats and swathing neckbands in America is plainly evident. The *incroyables* called themselves the Republicans of France; the Republicans of America adopted the

[3]Earle, *Two Centuries of Costume in America*, p. 733.

same dress. All the eccentricities of the French Republican were seen in the American dress, the tight trousers, high boots, short-waisted coat with long narrow tails, the cocked hat, and tangled hair.

Not only the *incroyables* but the *mervielleuses* also were reflected in a small way in the new land. The lightest and thinnest of materials were adopted and worn throughout the severe winters. Muslin, crepe, and organdy gowns were the order of the day. Necks were low and sleeves were short. Velvet, silk, and cloth shoes alternated with those of kid. For outdoor wear little shawls and cloth capes were thrown about the shoulders. At this time the pelisse was an indispensable item in every wardrobe. Every woman possessed a pelisse! In its original form it resembled a modern three-quarter jacket with close sleeves. The neck and sleeves were edged with fur, for it was decidedly a winter garment. In France, however, it resembled a cape with large openings for the arms. The pelisse remained a very popular form of wrap for many years. Fur had gained great popularity during the preceding century, and this only increased with the years. Fox, sable, and squirrel were the favorite pelts, and those who could not afford the luxury of real fur contented themselves with cloth and velvet combined with fur. Muffs were now barrel-shape and sufficiently large to hide the arms to the elbows.

Fans still continued to play an important role in fashionable life. Both black and white lace and painted fans were the vogue. These were usually mounted in handsome ivory or mother-of-pearl sticks. Never has the fan held so enviable a place in costume as it did during the seventeenth and eighteenth centuries.

The French Empire was proclaimed in 1804 and with it the dress of the period, the Empire. This fashion had evolved in France under the Republic, the Directory, and the Consulate. The outstanding feature of the new style was the long, clinging skirt and the short waist. Consequently, the Empire style is distinguished from all others by the long, flowing line, the short waist, and the absence

A   B   C   D   E   F

PLATE XXV—AMERICAN COSTUME—1790-1824

A—1804—The American adaptation of the costume worn during the French Empire and known as the "Empire."

B—1790—The costume of an American gentleman. The long coat is similar to that worn during the Washington administration.

C—1790—The American dress of this period echoes the fashion of the French Directory.

D—1824—The shortened flaring skirt and short waist succeeded the Empire. Breadth of shoulder began to appear about this time.

E—1811—A pantalet costume which appeared in a fashion plate of this date. The poke, the scarf and the fan echo the French fashion of the period.

F—1816—The costume of this period was incomplete without the huge muff and towering poke.

188

of pressure on any part of the costume. (*A*, Plate XXV;
Photo L.) This was indeed a contrast to the tightly laced
and boned bodice of previous centuries, and marks one of
the great changes in the costume of women. Corsets were
now completely out of the picture. The waist was so short
that it was scarcely a waist at all. The flowing gown hung
in long, easy lines to the floor. The popular materials were
mulls, lawns, and batistes; the richer fabrics, however, such
as velvet and silk, were sometimes worn. By 1810 the
dresses grew shorter, just escaping the floor, and were often
trimmed around the lower edge with a running border of
self-material combined with net and beads, or one embroidered on the material. In the early years of the Empire
Period the sleeves were short puffs at the shoulder, and
later extended almost to the elbow. By 1813 these gradually
changed into the long, close-fitting sleeve, sometimes extending well over the hand. By 1818 an increase in the
number of petticoats to be worn under the short-waisted
Empire gave the figure a wide, clumsy, and even ludicrous
appearance, for the fulness began just under the short
waistline. As the silhouette gradually lost all the grace of
the Empire style, it is not surprising that within a few
years a new mode, emphasizing the normal waistline and
calling for the corset, made its appearance.

During these same early years of the 1800's a very
unusual style, and one which has often threatened but never
materialized, stepped upon the fashion scene. This was the
wearing of pantalets. The cause of their adoption was due,
no doubt, to the lightness and transparency of women's
dress. Leading French and English fashions were now featuring dresses with pantalets and it seemed for a time that
pantalets had come to stay. It was not long, however,
before it was apparent that the various fashion reports did
not look with unqualified approval upon the new mode.
Rather than condemn the fashion outright, however, it was
simply pronounced a "distinct novelty." One of the French
magazines dared to prophesy, "The pantaloon will have a
short run, being truly ungraceful." Another, "A few of our

PHOTO L—PORTRAIT OF A LADY—*Beechy*

The fashionable dress of the early nineteenth century followed the mode set in Paris and came to be known as the *Empire* style. The long, easy-flowing skirt, with its high waistline and short sleeves, is in marked contrast to the hooped and boned figure of previous years.

haut ton have adopted the short frock and the trousers of the same texture edged with lace. This dress is much too singular to be graceful.''[5]

Certainly this was a clear forecast, for the pantalets have never been popular, and though they threaten they have never returned. At the same time that pantalets appeared, pantaloons for men's wear were ushered in.

Looking back we find the doublet and hose of Tudor times were replaced by knee-breeches and stockings. For nearly two hundred years these continued to be the favorite style of men's dress.

The nineteenth century marks the beginning of long trousers, the introduction of which was violently opposed. It is quite true that the ancient Britons, the Anglo-Saxons and Danes had worn a long garment similar to trousers, and that workingmen in both England and America wore a kind of trouser called "tongs" or "skilts." However, it was not until the nineteenth century that the long trouser proper was generally adopted.

In the early days while Fashion was evolving the new order in men's dress, the trousers passed through many stages of development. Sometimes they flared at the ankle, and again they were close. Sometimes they were made of elastic stockinet under which false calves were worn; others were of non-elastic corduroy and called "tights." The words of an old chronicler describes graphically the close fit of these tight pantaloons: "The pantaloons over which I wore boots, were of non-elastic corduroy. It would be unjust to the tailor to say they fitted like my skin, for they sat a great deal closer. When I took them off my legs were like fluted pillars grooved with the cords of the pantaloon." In 1810 trousers and gaiters were made all in one.

Large cloaks were worn by the very fashionable, and many of these were lined with bright colored silk. The high crowned silk beaver completed this very correct attire.

[5]Earle, *Two Centuries of Costume in America,* p. 774.

(*E*, Plate XXVII.) About 1824 the first signs of the frock coat became visible. The long coat-tails of previous years were shortened. Both coats and overcoats were long, fitted at the waist, and slightly full-skirted. Sleeves were long and snug at the wrist, the cuff extending over the hand. Collars were high and cravats of muslin and silk were worn. (*C*, Plate XXVI.)

The long cloak was also one of the favorite wraps of the women of the period and was worn as generally as the pelisse and the spenser. During the summer, shawls, short mantles, like dolmans, the long silk scarf, and the ever popular spensers, a necessary part of every wardrobe, were popular. All fashion plates from 1800 to 1833 refer to spensers. (F, Plate XXV.) One under the date of 1803 reads:

> Spensers are worn both for walking and carriage dress. Levantines, spotted silks, striped lutestrings[6] are the favorite materials. The trimming is always of satin. The Augusta spenser is one of the prettiest of dress spensers. The waist if finished in tabs is cut in the form of leaves. In velvet spensers, black, purple, and bottle green are favorite colors. The velvet is cut bias. Percale dresses are worn with these.[7]

The spensers, of course, varied in style. Some were shaped like a blouse, an eton, or zouave, and opened in front. (*B*, Plate XXVII.) They were all short, never going below the waistline. For summer the spensers were of silk and frequently trimmed with fur. The origin of the spenser is interesting. It is invariably recorded in every history of fashion. It had its beginning in a man's coat, a top-coat, invented by Lord Spenser. This gentleman, so the story runs, ventured to make a wager that he could set a fashion which would become popular inside of six months, and further, that it would be a form of dress wholly meaningless and unnecessary. He forthwith called for a pair of shears, cut off the tails of his coat close to the waist, donned his hat and went out for a stroll. He was a handsome man and one well known in fashionable

---

[6]Lutestring or lustring, a soft half lustred pure silk material which was generally worn.

[7]Earle, *Two Centuries of Costume in America,* p. 799.

AMERICAN COSTUMES, 1800–1850

A—Empire summer dress with contrasting ribbons and poke bonnet, 1810.

B—Girl's winter ensemble. The coat is made of blue wool with dark fur, 1814.

C—Woman's winter coat of maroon wool with black fur, grey muff, and tucked bands at lower edge, 1820.

D—Young man's attire in spring, 1829. Violet-blue coat, cutaway style, light vest, plaid trousers, high stock collar, tie, and tall hat.

E—Youth of 15 in 1837.

F—Woman at spinet, wearing an elaborate gown of 1835, with wide sleeves, silk bodice and skirt, lace ruffles, and ribbon bows.

G—Young girl's dancing dress with wide collar, fitted bodice, ruffled skirt, and pantalets, 1847.

192A

AMERICAN COSTUMES, 1850–1880

A—Man's attire in 1850—a tan wool overcoat, grey coat, checked vest, olive
    green trousers, black tie, and semi-soft hat.

B—Woman's dress, 1852, of blue taffeta with matching accessories—bonnet
    and parasol.

C—Girl's costume in 1861—a droop-brimmed hat, wide coat, and dress with
    pantalets.

D—Bonnets, hoop skirts, and cloaks of heavy silks were fashionable in 1854.

E—The lavish look outdid itself in 1873 because of the extended use of the
    sewing machine.

F—In 1874 a baby carriage was more elaborate than the baby's clothing. This
    "Grand Rapids" model was woven of rattan.

G—More unified and simpler lines than earlier marked this afternoon costume
    of 1879.

circles. In a few days several London dandies were seen wearing the spensers and in two weeks all London had donned the garment. All our boleros, zouaves and Spanish jackets have doubtless been evolved from the spenser.

In 1804 the poke-bonnets appeared. These were made of straw, willow and chip; they were also to be had in Leghorn and Tuscan. These straw bonnets were worn in winter as well as in summer and were frequently tied down with a red silk handkerchief or a folded silk or lace veil. Other shapes were also popular; the "Lavinia," worn from 1805 to 1815, resembled a gypsy hat with its broad brim and scant trimming; the "Troutbeck," a flat straw hat, was popular in 1803, and the Shaker-bonnets, which were small pokes of strawboard were also widely worn. Hats and bonnets were all large and really gave more shade to the face than the diminutive parasols that covered them.

The bonnets and hats so covered the head that little of the coiffure could be seen. In 1813 the hair was simply arranged in a low coil at the back, and short curls fringed the forehead. Flowers worn in the hair were very fashionable and were not removed when the bonnets were adjusted.

Foot-gear followed the same capricious fancy as in the eighteenth century. The shoes were generally low, though the ankle-boots laced at the back had been introduced. The year 1800, further witnessed the introduction of rights and lefts in shoes, and shoe polish and shoe blackening began to be employed. Previous to this a mixture of lampblack, suet, and tallow had been used.

Toward 1820 a change began to take place in the style of dress. The ladies began to tire of the clinging Empire, and dresses began to stand out from the figure. (*D, F,* Plate XXV.) The waist still remained high, scarcely a waist at all. This, with the bell-shaped skirt, heavily festooned, and the large poke-bonnet was the first step toward the 1830 costume. Later a change in the position of the waist took place. It was gradually shifted and soon reached the natural waistline, and now with the full skirt was much more charming. (*A, B, D,* Plate XXVI.) To keep the harmony of the *tout ensemble,* the hats and bonnets grew larger and were more heavily trimmed. So varied were the shapes of the popular bonnet that it remained in fashion well past the middle of the century. Sometimes it was high, extending out from the head, and the intervening space was filled with flowers and lace (Photo M); at other times it was low in the crown and close at the sides. A filmy veil was often attached to the crown and this could, at will, be easily drawn over the face. And now the coiffure had to have its changes! The hair was parted and the soft, front curls arranged at each side of the parting; the long hair was fastened up in loops interwoven with ribbon, erect upon the crown of the head. For very dressy occasions, feathers of maribou and the ostrich were often set amid these loops of hair and ribbon. The younger women wore flowers and large tortoise shell combs, and curls were everywhere arranged in all sorts of fanciful ways.

The leg-of-mutton sleeve appeared in France in 1820, but went out to reappear in 1830. The same sleeve appeared in America in 1827 but did not reach an exaggerated width until later. However, the sleeves continued to grow and the fulness reached to the elbow where it joined the deep, tight cuff. Padding was used in the top of silk sleeves, for they could not be starched sufficiently to meet the demands of fashion. For at all costs milady must be wide across the shoulders! The fashions of the thirties and forties continued to be exaggerations of the styles of the twenties. (Plate XXVI.) In 1830 skirts were short to the ankles, full and extended, and these with the huge sleeves made all other details of the costume fade into insignificance.

And now to add still more to the width of shoulders, bretelles and revers were introduced! (*B, E,* Plate XXVI.) These somewhat resembled a cape or perhaps a ruffle extending over the top of the sleeves. From a point at the waistline at the back they were carried over the shoulders at the sleeve seam and descended in V-shape to the center front. Between these broad shoulders and the breadth of skirt the poor little bodice was of slight consequence. It was

A	B	C	D	E

PLATE XXVI—AMERICAN COSTUME—1832-1884

A—1842—A fashionable belle of the period wearing the full triple skirt. Many petticoats were worn to give the bouffant appearance.

B—1832—A costume of the day emphasizing breadth of shoulder and the diminutive waist. Gloves and the flower-trimmed poke complete the fashionable dress of the time.

C—1850—The nineteenth century marked the advent of long trousers for men. Coats were short, with long skirts. High collars and cravats of silk or muslin were worn.

D—1834—A lady of fashion wearing the long full skirt, trimmed with bows of ribbon. The shawl at this time was very popular. Lace mitts alternated with gloves in popularity.

E—1834—A costume picturing the fashionable bretelle and the way in which it was adjusted at the back.

195

fitted as snugly as possible, not a sign of a plait or a pucker being allowed to creep in.   The materials were as beautiful as they were varied; embroidered cambrics were very popular, also cashmeres, muslins, and crepes.   A number of evening dresses of the period were made of tulle over satin, sarcenet or colored gauzes.

The period of 1830 is especially interesting in the development of American costume, for it was at this time that *Godey's Lady's Book* appeared.   This was the very first woman's magazine published in the United States.   It was founded by Louis Antoine Godey, who continued to be its publisher until its sale to a stock company in 1877. This publication was soon followed by the *The Union Magazine* and *Peterson's Magazine,* each taking its place among the leading fashion books of the country.   In 1867 *Harper's Bazaar* was offered to the public.   This fashion book was published by the noted firm of Harper Brothers of New York, which was established in 1833, and still continues in this the twentieth century to be managed by their descendents.

Toward 1837 skirts lengthened, ankles were no longer visible and only the toe of the shoe was seen beneath the undulating edge.   The skirts were beginning to be trimmed with flounces and bows of ribbon and many petticoats were worn in order to attain the desired effect.   (Plate XXVI.) Above all else, the waist must be exceedingly slender, and to secure such an effect without discomfort, advice like the following was given:

> Have your dresses made with very loose bands, cut on the crossway, and with a point in front, so as not to have the gathers under the point of your dress; let the petticoat be made of crinoline or wear what we call a *jupon à tournure,* which is a petticoat made of a thick and stiff cotton or thread material, not dimity, but a sort of honey comb pattern all over; this will make your dress appear sufficiently bouffant and form a proper contrast to the waist, thereby sparing the necessity and agony as well as injury of tight lacing.

In 1843 long trailing dresses were the vogue in Paris. A few years later they reached America.   It is almost im-

PHOTO M—MRS. JOHN CHURCH CRUGER—*Healy*

The fashionable costume of 1842 shows the flaring, open bonnet with dainty ruchings framing the face. The skirt is extended, the basque close-fitting with long sleeves, and the velvet mantle with long fronts is worn about the shoulders. Note the collar, cuffs, and handkerchief.

197

possible to believe that ladies once trailed through the city
streets. A Parisian paper of this date contains the following interesting account:

> The administration of la ville de Paris has it in contemplation to
> do away with the scavengers in our good city, as they say it is a
> useless expense to pay men for doing that which the ladies so kindly
> perform gratis in walking through the fashionable promenades.

In *Godey's Lady's Book* for 1852 we find the following
wholesome advice, which is decidedly interesting from an
American point of view:

> Apropos of the springtime but at the risk of incurring the dis-
> approbation of some of our lady friends, we venture a remonstrance
> against the still prevalent practice of wearing trains in the street.
> They may remember a picture of a "Punch" of last winter, where
> mounted cannon were represented as novel Parisian street-sweepers,
> but scarcely less formidable to us seem the skirts dragging their
> slow length along, cleaning the crossing at the expense of neatness,
> comfort and good taste. In the first place American ladies are
> noted for their lavish street toilets. Silks and even satins that
> no French or English woman would think of wearing unless in a
> carriage or drawing room, our ladies put into constant street service.
> The immoderate length of dress was never *intended* by its inventor
> to figure in this way before the public. The French woman whose
> immaculate white stockings have never a spot of dust would shud-
> der at the idea of walking with ankles—let us speak plainly—
> soiled and damp by the constant contact with the muddy drapery.
> We protest against it as a *Lady's Book,* in the name of neatness,
> common sense, and economy. Discoloration is inevitable; fringes
> are an ordinary sequence; and when such expensive silks are worn
> as we see at the present day, few purses can or ought to afford
> the outlay. Neither grace or expediency can be urged in its favor,
> and we trust the recent introduction of street sweepers into our
> large cities will preclude the necessity of our ladies' any further
> aid to the sanitary resolutions of the Common Council.

During the second quarter of the nineteenth century
mantles were of various materials, according to the season.
The long scarves of silk, crepe, and satin were trimmed
with fur in winter, and the pelerines took on various forms
and shapes; some just draped the shoulders, others covered the bodice and the long broad ends were allowed to
hang down in front. Long cloaks, the pelisse, the redingote
were also worn, and fur muffs and tippets continued in

vogue. Shawls were a general favorite at this period. For summer wear they were usually of crepe or printed berage of cashmere patterns. The center of these shawls was usually filled with a neat pattern on a white ground, and the borders were of dark rich Indian colors. Shawls, however were various; there were those with plain centers of white, green, or blue; there was the "gossamer berage" which was very delicate and beautiful; and shawls with and without fringe, all fine in texture.

Under "Fashion News" in the *London News* of 1845 is the following reference to shawls: "Nothing can be more graceful than the present promenade costume. The rich and soft cashmere shawl, so peculiarly fitted to the demi-saison, alone gives a peculiar character of elegance and distinction to the toilette."

Gloves were likewise in great variety. With short-sleeved dresses they reached to the elbow, while with the long-sleeved dresses they were short, usually with one or two buttons. Freqently the gloves were edged with frills of lace or ruching. Lace mittens were also worn through the thirties and forties.

Parasols almost usurped the place of the fan in milady's favor, and seldom did she emerge for a promenade or drive without her tiny fringed sunshade.

It was about the middle of the nineteenth century that the first step was taken toward one of the great inventions of the age. In 1846 Elias Howe, Jr., secured his first patents on the sewing machine. In 1851 Allen B. Wilson and Isaac M. Singer applied for patents. These early sewing machines have been so improved that there are now special attachments for making every conceivable article of clothing. In the United States the production of sewing machines has become a gigantic industry.

Approaching the second half of the century we come upon the great innovation of the period—crinoline.

There are flagrant follies in fashion which must be endured while they reign, and never appear ridiculous till they are put out of fashion.   —*Curiosities of Literature.*

To the critical of the twentieth century crinoline is forever dubbed as one of the "flagrant follies" of the past.
In fact crinoline ushered in a long line of "flagrant follies"
which stand forth silhouetted in the mind as the most un-
reasonable and ugly fashions that
ever   descended   upon   womankind.
Still, it is not left for us of today to
ridicule, anathematize, and excom-
municate; in its own day it met the
same response.   But of what avail?
Crinoline became the fashion.   Even
though the weight of starched and
flounced petticoats and yards of crinoline and horsehair would seem an intolerable burden to our American belles,
it was of no moment. *Fashion must*
be obeyed.   The subject of crinoline

Fig. 42.   The canezou

was a very serious one in Paris, and the style had its oppo-
nents as well as its supporters.   Though it was ridiculed
by everyone, and by husbands in particular, it became the
mode when the all-powerful Empress Eugénie set the
example and donned crinoline.   Then its reign became
universal.   (Plate XXVII.)

The previous years of full and flounced skirts, balloon
sleeves, and large hats had prepared the eye, if not the
mind, for the innovation; and when crinoline came it
seemed only the natural development.   Crinoline was a stiff
unpliable material, which was set around the lower edge
of the under side of the skirt to keep it sufficiently propped
out.   The width of the crinoline varied from six to fifteen
inches, and was frequently still wider.   With skirts four
or five yards in width there must have been no little weight
to support.   For those who followed the extreme in fashion,
entire petticoats of crinoline were to be had; while those
who did not take kindly to the new mode followed it at a
safe distance by wearing flounced and stiffened petticoats
of coarse muslin.   These petticoats were specially adapted
to summer and evening dresses of thin material.

The washable materials, such as fine muslins, cambrics, and other white stuffs, were exceedingly popular at this time, and silk also was a general favorite. In fact, the ladies of the period considered their wardrobes quite incomplete without the one silk dress. It was the day when women had their "best clothes." The silk dress was always in this class and was worn for church, for calls, and all important occasions.

Not only did the hoop and crinoline create a new mode in these days, but the style of the sleeve changed as well. They are now reversed and, instead of the fullness at the shoulder, it is found at the bottom of the sleeve. (Plate XXVII.) This brought in the fashionable undersleeve, which later developed into the bishop sleeve.

It was at this time that the parasol emerged as a definite accessory of dress. Previously sunshades had been large and unwieldly, and even as late as 1806 had weighed as much as ten pounds. By 1826 the weight had been reduced to two pounds, and then in 1850 followed the steel ribs with coverings of silk and other dainty materials. Handles, too, were of importance. Carved woods, vegetable ivory, and metals were generally used. Mid-century parasols were both large and small and often finished with fringe. During this period a small parasol with a hinged top that could be turned this way or that, was carried by the belles of the day.

In 1852 the canezou seemed to take the place of the dainty lace and embroidered capes. (Fig. 42.) This was a happy medium between the high and low corsages, and worn with skirts of different materials. Thus skirts whose bodices were partially worn could be utilized to advantage. For summer wear these were of the daintiest materials, and were edged with laces or bordered with the buttonhole stitch. With such a vogue for crinoline, the hoop seemed inevitable. Indeed our grandmothers looked quite askance at this second innovation of their time. The die was already cast. Soon crinoline was supplemented by the hoop. (Plate XXVII; Fig. 43.) A correct hoop

A   B   C   D

PLATE XXVII—AMERICAN COSTUME—1820-1865

A—1865—A belle of the hooped period. Diminutive hats and parasols were worn with this voluminous dress.

B—1865—A lady of fashion wearing the hooped skirt and the eton, a variation of the spenser. Gloves are always worn when milady walks abroad.

C—1850—A costume of the crinoline period showing the beginnings of the sleeve, full at the wrist.

D—1860—A fashionable dress with dolman-like sleeve set in low on the shoulder.

E—1820—An American gentleman of this period reflects in his dress much of the French influence. He wears the high neck-cloth, the broad-collared coat, the long tight trousers and the fashionable cape lined with bright colored silk.

consisted of "four narrow steels each covered with tape and run into the muslin or calico petticoat. The one nearest the waist usually measured one and three-quarter yards in length, while that at the lower edge of the skirt was two

Fig. 43. The hoop

and one-half yards in length. These steels with the exception of the top hoop were not allowed to meet in front, but a space of a quarter of a yard was allowed." Later, hoops were designed in various ways, many of them consisting of several covered hoops diminishing in size toward the waist, and held together by strings of broad tape reaching from the lower edge to the belt.

The year 1865 marked a change in shoes. They were now made entirely of kid or patent leather, and frequently the two were combined. The lacing was over the instep, the heels were high, and gradually became still higher.

In the early part of the sixties the hair was fastened up in a shapeless mass and held in a net. Silk nets were extremely chic, and many were spangled with jet. Frequently the front hair was parted in the center, combed down on each side making a loop over the ear, or arranged in masses of ringlets. Later the graceful side curl became the fashion and with it flowers were often arranged in the hair. (Fig. 44.)

Bonnets continued to be worn; in fact the entire nine-teenth century seems to be a period of bonnets. Hats, of course, were frequently worn, but the bonnet held first place. The size and shape of bonnets varied from time to time. Sometimes the fronts were fitted close to the head, and again they were very open. Frequently the open bonnets were trimmed with quilling of lace and ribbon just inside the brim, suggesting the colonial fashion of the little frilled caps under the hats. In summer, bonnets of tulle and fancy straws were worn. These were often large at the back, with curtains of lace covering the hair. In winter they were of velvet and beaver, and trimmed with fur, laces, and ribbon. Toward 1863 the bonnets became tall and pointed in front.

One of the novelties of the mid-century was the black silk sacque, which was worn by matrons and the more youthful as well. These were made both close-fitting and loose, with wide sleeves set in low on the shoulders, and were trimmed with fringes, lace, and ribbon.

There was a decided taste for jewelry at this period; ear-rings, brooches, necklaces, and bracelets were in vogue. In place of bracelets, black ribbons were frequently worn about the wrist.

The hoop-skirt and crinoline continued to be worn well on toward 1870. About this time skirts were cut in gores. This was ap-

Fig. 44.   Coiffure of the early '70's

proved as a point of economy. The sixteen or seventeen yards of material necessary for a correct gown were now reduced to ten or twelve. These were worn lined with horsehair or over horsehair petticoats, for the extension was still desired even after the steel hoop had lost somewhat in favor.

Then came the startling tournure, or petticoat bustle! At this time bustles were considered an absolutely indispensable part of all kinds of dresses, and often formed part of the skirt. Two shirrs, like those that had been used in the old-fashioned hoop-skirt, were run in the skirt linings, and served to hold the steel springs. When not a part of the skirt they were adjusted separately to the figure. Some of those of the period were made of a series of four or six spiral wires, resembling springs, about four inches in diameter and placed side by side vertically. These were encased in cloth, and attached to an adjustable belt. Bustles were worn high, and bustles were worn low. They were combined with the large hoop, and again with the small hoop. (*A,* Plate XXVIII; Photo N.)

In a fashion book of the time one reads: "The newest bustles are made of eight narrow frills of barred muslin or haircloth, very full, pleated on a V-shaped foundation of the same material that is curved into shape by strings tied across it—not by the objectionable bone or steel hoops. If anything more is needed, one or two steels are put in casings across the back breadth of the dress skirt."

Parasols continued important. We now hear of white silk parasols, braid-trimmed parasols, and fringed parasols. Braid, together with fringe and tassels, came into its own during the latter half of the century and, of course, the parasol did not escape. Large braided patterns filled the triangular space between the ribs, and silk fringe of various widths hung from the edge. Gowns were elaborate with braided patterns, and fringe was festooned over the skirt and hung in masses from the trussed-up overskirt. In fact, moderns look back to the 1870's as the period of braid, fringe, and the tassel.

A hat shape similar to the gentleman's round hat was worn, and on this was built up a pile of lace, flowers, and feathers to adorn the head. A sort of queue composed of

A   *B*   *C*   *D*   *E*   *F*

PLATE XXVIII—AMERICAN COSTUME—1873-1897

A—1873—The fashionable bustle dress which succeeded the hoop. The sleeves continue large at the cuff.

B—1883—A costume showing the popular vogue for combining materials. The draped overskirt and bustle are characteristic of the '80's.

C—1878—A costume picturing the fashion for combined materials in dress. The standing collar of linen and the bowtie were worn at this time.

D—1895—A lady wearing the princess dress, with skirt and bodice in one with no line to mark the waist.

E—1897—Toward the turn of the century, skirts of one color and material, and waists of another.

F—1895—The general costume of men, which changed very little during succeeding years.

flowing ends of lace and ribbon was fastened behind, over
which fell flowers and flexible stems. (Fig. 45.) With the
high hats that continued to be worn with the lofty chignon
and the excrescences of poufs and loops, milady was
expected to bend slightly forward in walking. Indeed she

Fig. 45. Hats of the '70's

must do so in order to maintain her equilibrium! Everybody affected the Grecian bend! The degree of grace with
which the tilt was managed was a passport to the realm
distingué.

The dress now became a construction of flounces,
fringes, loops, and puffings; and the great mass trailed a
yard or two after the wearer. And this was fashion!
(Fig. 46.)

By way of variety, came the bustle-skirt, combining a
bustle and petticoat in one. These had a hoop on the back
that stopped at the sides, and tapes attached to the sides
were tied underneath the hoop to give the desired effect.
This particular style was known as the "tilter." Later
tilters were made without the petticoat combination.

In those days of bustle and elaborately flounced and
looped skirts, shoulder straps were furnished to support
the great weight. These were frequently of elastic ribbon,
sewed permanently on the skirt back, and were passed over
the shoulder and hooked or buttoned to the belt in front.
These straps transferred the weight from the hips to the
shoulder.

PHOTO N—KATHERINE LORILLARD WOLFE—*Cabanel*

A handsome gown of the bustle period showing the fashionable combination of white satin and dark fur, highly favored at this time. Note the characteristic hairdress of this period. Painted in 1876.

The hair still continued to be plaited over pads in a
chignon worn high upon the crown of the head. False hair
was generally worn, and so great was the demand for these
tresses from foreign heads that great quantities were imported from France. This hair was chiefly procured in
Auvergne, Normandy, and
Brittany, and hair-cutters
made a special business of
collecting it in April and
May. The demand for false
hair naturally raised the
price, and those whose
purses were limited con-
tented themselves with tow
and other materials com-
monly used in lieu of hair.

From '70 to '75, while
the hoop was on the wane,
the silhouette changed. It
was difficult to give up the
full skirt; women had be-
come so accustomed to
yards and yards of mate-
rial that it was a real trial
to adjust themselves to less.

Fig. 46.   Hoop, tilter and trail
(Courtesy Marshall Field & Company)

Gradually all the fullness of the skirt was gathered at the
back. The skirts were drawn so tightly over the knees
that walking was difficult. That is the period known
as "tied-back" time. (Fig. 47.) With the large hoop losing
in popularity, and the tied-back effects gaining, the bustle
gradually assumed more important proportions. The
bustle, both with and without a small hoop, was worn well
into the next century. In fact, the distinguishing characteristic in the costume of the '80's is the bustle, the boned
basque, and the looped polonaise. (Fig. 48; *B,* Plate
XXVIII; Photos N, O.)

Fashion always swings from extreme to extreme, and
it is not surprising that, following the hoop, gowns which

moulded the figure became the last word in style. About 1882 the fashionable "jerseys" were introduced. In the early eighties these were of an elastic cashmere fabric similar to that known as stockinet, and closely fitted the figure. Their elegance of shape and finish was combined with a comfort and freedom of action in marked contrast with the preceding fashions. The jersey bodices were exceedingly popular, and as largely worn in America as in Europe, where they were adopted by the children as well as by their modish mothers.

Fig. 47. "Tied-back" time (After Kretschmer and Rohrbach)

So much for the bodice. The width of skirts was also reduced till they too were very much narrower. Soon costumes began to be designed in two colors, or in two different materials. (*B, C,* Plate XXVIII.) It was usual to have the skirt of one hue and the polonaise of another; or, a plain fabric for the basque, with flowered stuffs for the skirt. However, this was frequently reversed, the flowered or figured materials being used for the larger part of the dress and the plain for the skirt. Brocades, velvets, and silks were in high favor and these were elaborately trimmed with laces, fringes and passementerie. The thinner and more delicate materials were worn in the warmer season—printed India pongee, light-weight foulards, French cashmeres, and Chinese crepes.

Bonnets were still the last word from Paris. There were horsehair bonnets, proclaimed the "French novelty"; kid bonnets, in the natural leather color, the crown moulded into form and the brim covered with folds of velvet and felt; bonnets of velvet and silk in endless variety.

The dolman was a favorite out-of-door wrap. These varied in length and were made of the finest brocades, silks,

COURTESY, METROPOLITAN MUSEUM OF ART

PHOTO O—THE BOUQUET—*Diaz*

About 1878-9 the fitted and boned bodice extended well below the normal waistline and, with long, close sleeves and high neckline, was usually set off with white collar and cuffs. The pleated skirt was topped with an overdress sometimes looped at the back simulating the vanishing bustle.

and satins elaborately trimmed with puffing of silk, fringes, and passementerie. Outdoor jackets with short backs and long fronts were also worn.

Toward the end of the seventies several new movements in dress took place in London, Germany, and France which were destined to play no small role in the costume of succeeding generations.

The Æsthetic Movement had its home in London. The followers of this movement were interested not only in dress, but in art generally. The existing order of things in home furnishing, surroundings, civic conditions, as well as in dress were vigorously attacked. Wonderful w e r e the changes wrought. Color and color harmony began to have a new meaning. The more subtle hues which were hitherto known only to the few, began to appear. The most delicate hues as well as

Fig. 48.   The bustle (After *Harper's Bazaar,* 1883)

the richest tones in pleasing variety were now produced by the English dyers, who had adopted the ancient custom of using vegetable dyes.[8]

The Dress Reform Movement[8] began about the same time in Germany. It started with the idea that wool was the only proper covering for the human body. Everything must be wool, even the handkerchiefs. This period marks the beginning of the famous Jaeger Company. Previous to this the underclothing in both summer and winter had been of cotton, and naturally the soft warm wool was in great demand. Indeed it was impossible to keep up with

[8]Georgiana Hill, *A History of English Dress* (New York: 1893), p. 277.

the orders for woolen sheets, stockings, gowns, and materials generally. It was at this period that the ever-popular union-suit with its equal distribution of weight over the figure, was introduced. This movement merged into the agitation for a new system of dress. All the shortcomings of the modes of the day were taken up and vigorously attacked and great indeed was the feeling directed toward the corset. This new crusade was supported by doctors and sanitariums alike. The leaders were most radical, tabooing the corset as an instrument of torture. Further, they advocated the "divided skirt" as the only proper, sane, and sanitary garb for women. The new type was freely discussed and even demonstrated by a few of the more daring. The innovation succumbed, however, when she who ventured forth was stigmatized as "the new woman."

Though the aim of the movement was not entirely achieved, the discussion did much to awaken people to some of the existing incongruities of dress.

Just about this time the entrance of women into the athletic world did much to forward the movement toward a comfortable and easy dress. This was an English influence that had its effect in both France and America. English and French women rose early, donned short skirts, a comfortable blouse or jacket and stout shoes to walk, ride, or hunt. In America cycling, golf, and tennis, which necessitate an easy and comfortable dress, were the favorite sports of women. Time was when vigorous exercise of any sort was thought unfitted for women. A five mile tramp was unheard of, and cycling considered shocking beyond words; a young woman seldom engaged in any exercise more energetic than a prosaic game of croquet. Indeed, our grandmothers would stand aghast at the modern gymnastic costumes, the tennis frocks, boating flannels, and the "up-to-date" riding togs. Fig. 49 shows a riding habit of the seventies.

The entrance of women into the business and professional world has had an effect undreamed of in previous

centuries. Women began to adapt their clothes to their manner of living and their needs, demanding that they be useful as well as beautiful. Each of these influences in turn, has been most po-
tent in forcing the trend of fashion t o w a r d g r e a t e r simplicity. Moreover, it is the won-derful nineteenth cen-tury that gave birth to that great invention—the paper dress-pat-tern. It is this paper pattern, so universally employed today, that has contributed more directly than any other one influence to the de-velopment of feminine dress. *Pomeroy's Demo-crat* of 1871 said: "The sewing machine has

Fig. 49. Riding habit of the '70's
(Courtesy Marshall Field & Company)

done more than the piano to happyize our homes, and fol-lowing the sewing machine has come the Butterick pattern."

In July of the same year, the *Home Journal* comments: "They should be ranked with the benefactors of mankind, this firm that has worked out the problem of clothes."

It is due to these pioneers in the fashion world, Ebenezer Butterick and his wife Ellen Butterick, that this problem of the paper dress-pattern was planned and carried out.[9] Before this there had been only intricate diagrams which required the practiced hand of the skilled to trace and cut. Naturally this limited beautiful and well-made clothes to the more wealthy women of the period.

These interesting paper patterns began with an idea—an idea suggested by Ellen Butterick to her husband. One day she modestly proposed that a paper pattern for a

[9]*Delineator,* November, 1910.

child's dress might be a boon to mothers. The idea developed, resulting in a drafted and cut pattern for a child's Garibaldi suit, which was the first paper pattern offered to the world. Needless to say, all children were soon wearing Garibaldi costumes. Then came the desire for women's patterns. This soon became a demand, for the advantages of the child's paper pattern was being recognized the world over. In 1871 over six million paper patterns were sold.

Along with the paper pattern was the increased circulation of the popular fashion books, which not only pictured the present but anticipated the coming types, and discussed materials, trimmings, and modes in general. Thus the creating of fashions was becoming of greater interest to an ever widening circle. Moreover personal taste and decision were entering into the choices of line and color and the stern decrees of Dame Fashion were less blindly followed.

Another inspiration toward fashion-creating was awakened in France when the Historical Exhibition of the Costume of France was held in 1878. This was indeed a history of costume in concrete form. Curiosities which had hitherto been hidden away in private collections were dusted and presented. Many of the objects were of special interest in showing the earliest manufactures of France. There were garments of the Middle Ages and the early Renaissance, and of the sixteenth and seventeenth centuries. These were shown not only because they were objects of history, but as subjects for study. There were dress ornaments, bracelets, rings, pins, brooches, and ear-rings; women's hoods of various types, a fashionable doll dressed in the costume of the Medici period; women's hawking-gauntlets in chased steel, exquisite fans, patch-boxes, antique bags, and purse clasps, beautifully chased betrothal rings, diamonds in settings of old silver, curious Roman trinkets and quantities of rare Egyptian jewelry dating from the time of the Caliphs. Moreover, the Scandinavian Ethnological Museum of Stockholm forwarded a series of remarkable costumes dating about 1820. This was a wonderful collection and proved a great incentive to manufacturers, designers, milliners, and all concerned with the production of beautiful wearing apparel.

It was the growing taste for extreme simplicity that created the tailor-made gown, which even today holds first place for smartness and luxury as well. Though the tailored costume appeared simple, it was very expensive, for every detail must be perfect. Side by side with all this simplicity there was also much gay attire.

The decided taste for sports of all kinds did much to make the popular shirt-waist even more popular. These waists during the early days were very simple in line, full in front, with yoke backs and shirt sleeves. Frequently the standing linen collar was worn with the bow tie. This fashion for odd waists led to a taste for colored waists of red, blue and green plaid or stripes with black and white or dark-toned skirts. The wearing of skirts of one material with waists of another became quite the mode (*E,* Plate XXVIII), not only for everyday wear but for evening and reception toilettes as well. Many of these fancy-dress waists were of silk, grenadine, and other transparent fabrics, and lavishly decorated with lace and ribbon.

During the nineties, skirts attained a voluminous breadth, reaching in many instances seven to nine yards. Circular skirts divided honors with those cut gored, but whether circular or gored they must fall in great flute-like folds. (*D, E,* Plate XXVIII; Fig. 50.) To secure the correct fall of these great tubular folds, the skirts were lined with canvas, or with a heavy unpliable material called *fibre chamois.*

The sleeves again kept pace with the skirt, and reached the most extravagant dimensions. These too were partly lined with *fibre chamois* to make them sufficiently bouffant. Width of shoulder was the last decree of that ever youthful old lady, Dame Fashion, and to emphasize this width, berthas and fichus of various designs, laces, and ribbons were added to the shoulders. (Fig. 50, a, b, c.)

Fashion had set her seal upon all these little accessories of dress, and yokes, collars, fichus, and berthas were in

great variety. These were kept in readiness and were often
adjusted to an otherwise plain bodice, giving it that necessary touch to bring it within the realm of the fashionable.

Fig. 50.   Fashions of the '90's

To the very turn of the century, skirts continued to be
of great width.   Toward '97 the new distinctive note in the
dress was the sleeve.   In contrast with the sleeve of preceding years, it became close-fitting, with a large puff
or cap at the top.   (Fig. 50, d and f.)

Width of shoulder was still desired, consequently ruffles
of lace, ribbon, and other material edged the yoke and extended over the top of the sleeves, which were often
wrinkled *mousquetaire*.   With these sleeves all collars were
worn high, closely encircling the throat, and frequently
edged with a frill of deep lace or plaiting which stood high
at the back.

The new materials at the end of the century were various.   There were æolion, a mixture of silk and wool,
Pompadour sateens, jaconet, satin stripes, India prints,
Pompadour foulards, striped grenadines, and Italian silk,
Turkish, Japanese, Indian, and Persian stuffs, embroidered
in silk and glistening colors.   Vandyke red, lotus-blue, and
an undecided blue-green called Venetian heliotrope were
among the fashionable hues.   Well on toward the end of

the century costumes continued to be made of combined materials and colors.

Both hats and bonnets were worn, made in smooth straw and coming down close on the forehead. All head-gear was profusely trimmed with feathers and flowers. Golden poppies, tulips, magnolias, bachelor's buttons, and roses of every shade graced the covering of milady's bonnet.

A decided change in the arrangement of the hair marks these last years. The coiffure becomes more elaborate, and steadily grows to larger proportions until one almost wonders whether the extravagance of the eighteenth century threatens to overtake us. The Jubilee (1897) revived many of the early Victorian styles, and is said to be responsible for the new arrangement of the hair. It is now drawn up loosely over large cushions, that reach across the brow from ear to ear and secured at the back with pins and combs. To give a light and waving appearance the hair was often curled with hot irons or by means of a curling fluid. With this mass of waved hair raised over the huge cushions, milady came forth *à la Pompadour*. She who possessed a wealth of hair found herself highly favored, while she whose locks were scant took refuge in the "acquired."

The nineteenth century is a wonderful period in many ways. It is proudly marked as an age of science and progress. Many and rapid were the developments in every sphere, and so complete was the change in mental attitude and outlook upon life, that the nineteenth century seems a world apart from all preceding time. The growing conception of the appropriate in dress has completely changed modern costume. The new ideas regarding physical education, the opening of the business world, and professional life to women, the love of travel, and the complexity of modern living, have all played a part in revolutionizing the dress of both men and women. Woman has now taken her place in all the world's activities, and her dress is adapted to the life she leads. At the end of the century, the trend is marked by a simplicity of elegance and good taste, the gratifying outcome of the refining process through which ideas of dress have passed during this epoch-making nineteenth century.

REVIEW

1. What was the distinct type of dress worn in early 1800? When did the poke-bonnet appear?
2. What transformation took place in men's dress? When did the frock-coat appear? Describe the fashionable cloak. The beaver. The cravat and tie.
3. What change took place in woman's dress about 1830? What was the great innovation of 1850?
4. Discuss the use of shawls, gloves, and parasols during the century.
5. When did the bustle appear? The tilter? What period is known as "tied-back time"? Why?
6. Describe the hats of the 70's. The coiffure.
7. Describe the shoes of early 1800. Of late 1800.
8. How were sleeves and skirts made bouffant in the 90's?
9. Discuss new materials which appeared during the century.
10. How did woman's entrance into athletic life affect dress? How did woman's entrance into the business world affect dress?
11. What famous movement with reference to dress took place in 1880? Do you regard this movement of importance? Why?
12. When were the first fashion books published? Name them.
13. When were the first paper dress-patterns put on the market?
14. When did the sewing machine appear? Give a brief account of this and its great benefit to society.

CHAPTER TWELVE

American Costume (1900-1920)

I F "VARIETY is the spice of life" we must admit that
the world of today is well seasoned. Never has costume
been so varied and fashions so ephemeral as in the opening
years of the twentieth century. Though only a few years of
the century have passed, so numerous have been the modes
introducing wide variations in costume, and so immediate
their adoption, that only one conclusion may be drawn—
Dame Fashion still rules the world of dress. Indeed, so
potent is her word that even the most conservative must
submit in a measure to her decrees. Her sway is so universal that to be out of the fashion is to be out of the world!

> Oh, mighty fine it is to be the slave
> Of fashion! Mighty fine it is to brave
> Old Common Sense, that antiquated snob,
> Mix in gay crowds, and mingle with the mob,
> Whom love of show and love of pleasure, too,
> Lead where they can be rather viewed than view!
>
> Yes, to live thus, in some sea-beaten spot
> Is truly charming while the weather's hot,
> And while—kind friends, excuse this truthful song—
> Sport is the judgment and the purse is long.
> —PARKE BENJAMINE—A humorous satirical poem read before
> a fashionable audience in Newport in 1852.

It is true that her scepter's sway is not so haughtily
autocratic as in previous years. No, indeed, she is tact
itself, and now deftly subordinates her soaring instincts to
the feminine needs of her court. For woman has asserted
herself, and the intolerable, the uncomfortable, and the
grotesque are looked upon askance.

Fashions often overlap from century to century, the
opening years of the new era frequently clinging to the
preceding mode. So at the beginning of the century the

dominant types of the previous years still survived. The full skirt grew more clinging, fitting the figure snugly to the knees and then flaring out into great flute-like ripples, making the skirt at times as much as ten or twelve yards around. Often these rippling gores trailed behind in a kind of demi-train. Frequently the skirt was cut in two sections —the fitted upper section and the gored flounce. The latter was set on the upper section at about knee height. Such a skirt gradually became known as the "morning-glory" or "serpentine" skirt. Bodices were semifitted, and collars and stocks flourished. Jackets were snug in fit with long, close sleeves. (*A,* Plate XXIX.) Softer and more sheer materials were worn for afternoon and more formal occasions but the silhouette remained the same, resembling the ungraceful hour-glass type.

It was at this time that the "dip" became fashionable. The skirt, at the waistline, was cut with a decided dip at the center front and this downward tendency was shown in the girdle and in the fall of the skirt.

By 1904 skirts cut *en forme* may be said to have disappeared from the horizon of good style. At this period the skirts began to grow wider from the waist down, falling in an easy sweep over the hips, forming broad undulations about the feet. (*B, D,* Plate XXIX; Photo P.) The flowing line was the last word of fashion. Many of the skirts were as much as six or seven yards around the lower edge, and many of them touched the ground. With the long, flowing skirts, waists grew more easy in fit with long shoulder effects. All trimming aimed to give breadth and slope to the shoulders. Both horizontal designs and epaulettes were added to give this distinctive breadth. (*B,* Plate XXIX.)

The tailored suit continued to be a great favorite among all women who could afford it. The simplicity of line and the distinctive mark of the "tailor-made" put this popular costume in a class by itself. Though at first all skirts of the tailored suit were long, extending to the floor, they gradually began to shrink and soon reached the ankle, which in that day was considered quite correct.

A   B   C   D   E   F

PLATE XXIX—AMERICAN COSTUME—1902-1915

A—1902—The "serpentine," or "morning-glory," skirt. Jackets, blouses and sleeves were all very close in fit.

B—1907—The distinctive breadth of shoulder is attained by horizontal trimmings, epaulettes and bretelles. The lace yoke, or quimpe, was indispensable.

C—1915—The street and business suit. The coat is short, comfortably loose and double-breasted.

D—1908—A costume with overdress. Large hats and a generous arrangement of the hair accompanied this period of the flowing line.

E—1910—The tailored suit. The skirt was known as the "hobble-skirt." Cravats of lace and fine materials were worn.

F—1907—The tailored suit, showing the tight-waisted coat and full gored skirt. Waists were of linen and silk.

222

No matter how simple or how elaborate one's wardrobe, the *trotteur,* or walking-skirt was indispensable. The shirt-waist had proved itself of such value that its complement, the short skirt, was to be found in every woman's wardrobe. The walking-skirts were always finished in tailored effects and usually of serge, cheviot, or tweed.

The natural outcome of the shirt-waist and the short skirt was the shirt-waist suit. (Fig. 51.) No longer were the light waists and the dark skirts the mode; the fashionable women of the period had their shirt-waist costumes of silk, mohair, and other light-weight materials made *en suite,* and a most comfortable, charming fashion it was.

Ever since, women have owed much to the innovation which the shirt-waist made in the manner of dress. Its general comfort is still evident. Its loose lines have continued to be used in revising the mode from year to year, whatever the materials. However, in the early part of the century, the strictly tailored suit, coat and skirt continued to hold undisputed sway and it was not until 1914 that the almost rigid effects were somewhat softened by the vogue for the semi-tailored. During 1906 and 1907 the plaited skirt was the popular one for the tailored suit, and the jackets, all of close fit, were either short or three-quarter as milady preferred. (F, Plate XXIX.)

Fig. 51. Shirt-waist suit

In 1907 the French influence was especially seen in the tone and beauty of the colorings offered. Taupes, lovely smoky tones, purples, yellows, browns, and peacock were the hues particularly sought and with these were combined trimmings of hand embroidery, beaded design, and fringe.

This was the day of high and close-fitting collars and guimpes. (Plate XXIX.) The linen collar was invariably worn with the shirt-waist, but with the more elaborate attire

PHOTO P—TEA LEAVES—*W. M. Paxton*

The moderately full skirt, blouse with high or low neckline, and short sleeves, together with the large hat set over the lingering pompadour, is typical of the fashions of 1908–10, and preceded by a few years a radical change to the "hobble" skirt and the smaller hat.

AMERICAN COSTUMES, 1880–1900

A—Man's wool suit with narrow shoulders, matching trousers, and Derby hat, 1884.

B—Woman's surah silk dress with fitted bodice, over-draped and pleated skirt, and feathered bonnet, 1888.

C—Girl's bolero style coat and its balloon sleeves, over a plaid dress, with plumed hat and lace collar, 1896.

D—Woman's lavish winter coat of velvet, trimmed with fur and gold embroidery, 1891.

E—Girl's pink and brown summer dress, worn with long ribbed stockings and high boots, 1898.

F—Man's attire, 1890. A lightweight summer coat, high collar, four-in-hand tie, and straw sailor hat were in fashion.

G—Boy's "sailor suit" with knee length trousers, long ribbed stockings, and button shoes, 1894.

224A

AMERICAN COSTUMES, 1900–1920

A—A high school graduate, 1902, wearing a white organdy dress, ribbon sash, and long gloves.

B—Small boy with sailor suit and "puffed" trousers, 1906.

C—Girl's lavender cotton voile dress, trimmed with white braid, 1908.

D—The man is in spring attire with lightweight wool suit, vest, and straw hat, 1912.

E—The woman's dress is of pink bordered, dotted voile, with deep rose sash and wide fichu, 1912.

F—Woman's motoring costume, 1910. The straight-lined coat was long. The Merry Widow hat was tied with an auto veil.

G—A secretary in 1919. Employment for women increased in offices, stores, and teaching, 1919.

H—Young man's two-piece wool bathing suit, 1916.

guimpes of finest laces gave the daintiest touch to the costume.

The hats of these early days of the century were set well up on the head and were often raised by means of a bandeau. Plumes had a triumphal career, and the barbaric use of birds and wings was given second place. This use of birds and paradise feathers was temporarily discarded because of the satire directed against it; and it was the fond hope of many that this style would never again be approved by fashion's decree. However, a few years later it peeped above the horizon of fashion for a brief period in the guise of "chanticleer." (Fig. 52.)

Again it is an instance of the stage setting the mode, for it was the popular and unique drama *Chantecler* that set the barnyard fowl upon the heads of dainty woman. Women audaciously wore chanticleer perched upon their pretty heads, the tail feathers drooping at the back, and the head erect ready to announce his presence.

Fig. 52.   Chanticleer

We are amused today over *la Belle Poule* and the *pouf au sentiment* of Marie Antoinette, but can these be more ridiculous than the poultry head-gear of our enlightened women of the twentieth century?

No longer can it be said that one type of hat is the fashion, for hats are as various as the occcasions for wearing them. The curves and graceful lines of the Gainsborough effects were especially adapted to the long clinging diaphanous gowns. The Gainsborough is a large picturesque type of hat that sat tilted upon the head. It has become associated with the name of the artist Gainsborough, because he painted the portraits of famous women of his day, wearing this very becoming large hat.

Just the airiest, fairiest, slip of a thing,
With a Gainsborough hat, like a butterfly's wing
Tilted up at one side with the jauntiest air,
And a knot of red roses sown under there
Where the shadows are lost in her hair.

Then a cameo face, carven in on a ground
Of that shadowy hair where the roses are wound.
—JAMES WHITCOMB RILEY, *Love Lyrics.*

The small toque simply trimmed was indispensable with the tailored costume or shirt-waist suit. Further, sports and outdoor life had created head-gear appropriate to its own world. The broad brimmed sailor was a general favorite for the warmer part of the year, and later it was replaced by soft white and light colored felts in various styles.

The following year (1908) the emphasis fell most decidedly upon the tunic or drapery, a Greek idea which was sought in both evening gowns and day toilettes. (*D,* Plate XXIX.) The most pronounced features of these draperies were the overskirts, which offered many possibilities for trimmings, for they were invariably bordered in one way or another. With these flowing robes, a taste for large hats and a most generous arrangement of the hair was indulged in. Crowns were high and trimmings were high. This tendency toward height gave the final touch to the costume inclining toward the Empire or Directory. The long curve from the tip of the hat to the lowermost edge of the flowing skirt produced that pleasing and picturesque effect which made perfect the *tout ensemble.*

Toward 1910 we find another revolution imminent in the matter of dress. The change began to be visible in Paris toward the latter half of 1908 when the question, "to be or not to be," was fiercely debated by the *couturières* and the public. The birth of a new fashion often wavers long between oblivion and the vogue, and it was not until the matter had been definitely settled that the new mode reached America.

The most pronounced innovation was the skirt which had shrunken to almost unbelievably small proportions. It became flat and narrow, ignoring the hips and keeping the lines of the figure as straight as possible. The silhouette had completely changed, skirts were not only narrower and high-waisted, but shoulders were narrower, and sleeves were narrower, in fact the styles of the Directory, the Consulate and the Empire were again becoming established. (*E,* Plate XXIX.) Not only were the skirts narrow, but they reached such exaggerated scantiness that many of them measured only from thirty-two inches to a yard and a half at the lower edge. In fact they were as narrow as they possibly could be and the wearer be able to walk. The hobbling, toddling gait of the geisha was fashionable because it could not be otherwise. This gives some color to the theory that the narrow skirt descended upon us from the Japanese.

Never since the time of the Louis' had fashion been so assailed as was this close-fitting skirt. It was ridiculed as the "hobble-skirt," the "halter-skirt" and the "sheath."

> Hobble, hobble, little skirt,
> How I wonder what thou wert.
> Perchance, maybe a papa's pant
> Now for him a trifle scant.
> —From a set of parodies issued by the Carol Press, Boston.

Pulpit and press alike heaped ridicule and abuse upon the mode. And yet, Fashion will do as Fashion always has done, the more she is assailed, the more she asserts herself. Consequently the hobble-skirt continued, became even more scant, until it was impossible even to hobble; then my fair lady shocked the pulpit and press still further by slashing the binding of the lower edge. Sometimes the slash was at the sides, sometimes every seam was left open to knee depth and sometimes only the front and back were slashed. These openings were often filled with a narrow plaited panel of silk, cloth, or chiffon. However, this was not always the choice of the feminine world, for many adopted the bright-colored silk petticoat and the more daring ventured the satin trousers of the Turkish harem.

No wonder the world stood aghast! No wonder bills were introduced into the State legislatures aiming to correct and regulate women's dress!

But not so ruthlessly is Dame Fashion's world invaded. In the fate of one such bill introduced into the Virginia legislature we may read the fate of all—"It is a shame," said delegate W. M. M. of Richmond, commenting on the defeat of his bill in the Virginia legislature regulating woman's dress. "I introduced the measure in all seriousness and I insist that it was worthy of better consideration than it received at the hands of the house, which killed it with an overwhelming vote."

With the narrow skirt came the collarless blouse with the open, flowing sleeve. This sleeve resembled those worn by the peasants of Roumania and Bulgaria. These simple blouses were made of soft, clinging materials which emphasized the fine lines of the shoulder and the arm.

With this scant and narrow silhouette there was only one possibility for hats—they were high and set well down on the head. (*E*, Plate XXIX.) Tall plumes added height to the silhouette but very soon the vertical tendency was reversed and trimmings of flowers and ribbon kept the crown low. The hat, nevertheless, continued to be set well down on the head. About 1912 the "willow" plume, the uncurled ostrich feather, was very popular. The coiffure continued elaborate.

With the elaborate hairdress, hats grew large in the crown and wide of brim. These were fabric hats made of silks, straw braids, velours, and panne velvets. During this period of large fabric hats, the automobile was in the heyday of its popularity and, to save the hat from dust and wind, milady adopted the enveloping veil two and one-half yards in length. This entirely covered the big hat, was tied under the chin, and the free ends left to the breeze.

The narrow skirt continued to be played upon in varying ways, as if Fashion were toying with the old in the effort to

A   B   C   D   E   F

PLATE XXX—AMERICAN COSTUME—1913-1916

A—1916—The short, full skirt succeeded the long, close-fitting skirt of the earlier period. With the short skirt much care and attention was given to footwear.

B—1913—This lady of fashion wears the new basque dress. The over-dress is now added to the "hobble skirt."

C—1914—Fullness is now at the top rather than at the lower edge of the skirt. The extreme lower edge is left open.

D—1914—The peg-top silhouette in evening gown. The evening head-dress is typical of the time.

E—1915—The dress suit of a gentleman of the period. The short waist-line and well-opened fronts still continue.

F—1916—A costume showing the short bouffant skirt.

evolve the new. Shortly tunics were added to the narrow skirt, (*B*, Plate XXX.) They were usually of chiffon, crepe, or net and inclined toward much fullness. Frequently they were banded at the lower edge thus preventing the tendency

to fall away from the figure, and again, they were allowed to fall and fly unconfined. (Fig. 53.) Beads and bead trimming were used in profusion upon both skirts and blouses. The bands which confined the tunic were often of beaded design, beautiful in color harmony. The simple blouses were also artistically ornamented with beaded patterns.

Toward 1914 the narrow skirt still lingered, though the silhouette gradually changed. Instead of the straight figure, the "drooping boneless pose" took its place before the footlights of fashion.

Gradually more fullness was creeping into the skirt, but at the top rather than at the lower edge, thus giving every hint of the atrocious bustle of the eighties. (Fig. 54.) The new figure, narrow at the foot and full at the hips, was termed the "peg-top silhouette." (Fig. 55.) Often the fullness of these skirts was laid in plaits around the hips or arranged in gathers. The extreme lower edge was left open at the front that it might slip up over the instep in walking. (*C, D*, Plate XXX.) This simple plaiting about the hips of these skirts merged gradually into huge puffings, ruffles, and draperies, giving the panier effect. In fact, caution in the use of drapery was thrown to the winds and the queen of fashion was simply wrapped up in material.

With the evasive waistline and the flow of drapery the fitting of a costume was not a matter of accuracy as in former years, but became a matter of artistry in the subtle

Fig. 53.   Dress of 1912, showing basque and tunic.

harmonies of line and color. Materials were usually supple and clinging, revealing the graceful lines of the figure and suggesting the Orient. Charmeuse, messaline, chiffons,

Fig. 54. Revival of the styles of '83

silk mulls, silk poplins, moire, gaberdine, embroidered and printed crepes, crepe meteor, and other charming stuffs in sufficient variety to please the most fastidious were offered. In evening dresses trains were worn narrowed to a point, a veritable *queue de serpent*. (*D,* Plate XXX.)

After a period of drooping blouses with the vague indeterminate waistline the fashion world awoke to find itself in the most unexpected attire—the new basque dress. It was indeed the old basque of the thirties but so tempered with the modern feeling for comfort and ease, and so charming in line that it immediately became the vogue. Slenderness was still the distinctive note, for the favorite skirt to be worn with the basque was narrow, decidedly narrow, with the full tunic overdress. The new basque did away with the blouse effect at the waist and dropped the waistline to the hip. It subtly suggested the curves of the figure without accentuating them and kept the long line from the shoulder to the hip unbroken. (Fig. 53.)

At this time, a reminder of the war in the Balkans was seen in the Balkan blouse with its belt girding the hips. (Fig. 56.)   The bright colors of Bulgarian peasant art were also seen in the vivid hues of the period's trimming.

Though women's fashions were as inconstant as the will-o-the-wisp, there continued to be little change in men's dress. Still the Prince Albert, or frock, and the cutaway, which have passed through varying phases of popularity for almost two hundred years, continued to be first choice. Dark browns as usual were favored; also, black, blue, gray, and the black and white mixtures.   During 1915 odd waistcoats again appeared.   These, however, had only a short season and were seen chiefly in dark silk or in white washable stuffs made double-breasted with a roll collar.   The efforts to change the style of evening tailcoat proved unsuccessful, and the short waistline and well-opened fronts still continued.   (*E*, Plate XXX.)

Fig. 55. The peg-top silhouette

There is an old adage to the effect that the longest road has its turn.   So it is with the way of fashion.   Three years is said to be the lifetime of any particular mode, but the narrow skirt in either tailored or draped effects had survived for twice that period, and toward 1915 a welcome change appeared in the skirts flaring a little at the lower edge.   By the end of 1915 the new mode was at its height—the full skirt and the well-defined waistline with the faintest suggestion of crinoline. (*A, F,* Plate XXX.)

The modes of 1916 plainly point to the fact that there is nothing absolutely new in a style.   The conventions of dress have developed year by year, all the possibilities of costume have found expression and now nothing remains but to adapt the old to the conditions of today and thus relate it to the life and society of the present.

The fashions of 1916 take us decidedly back to the basque and crinoline of 1870, the period of the French Louis', with little suggestions of the Directory period, especially as seen in the hats. Skirts were full, and their width emphasized by horizontal trimmings and panier drapery. They had also become short. (Fig. 57.) Crinoline was imminent and already the new frocks had two hoops of whalebone between the hip and knee to make them sufficiently bouffant.

With the very short skirts a new emphasis was placed upon the footwear. Boots were of various colors, gray, tan, pearl, blue, and bronze; indeed the all-black shoe seemed relegated to the past. Boot tops were made quite high, just meeting the edge of the short skirt.

Hats also go back to the time of the French Louis' when ribbons were much in evidence. Not only were there wide brimmed hats, trimmed with ribbon, lace and flowers, which point to the Louis Seize period, but the Watteau of the time of Louis Quatorze and the Directory

Fig. 56. The Balkan blouse

came in for its share of popularity. Much in evidence was the cockade of the French Revolutionary period. This was seen in ribbon and feathers and was evidently indicative of the times. (Fig. 58.)

Four years of the Great War made their inevitable demands upon the fashion world. Women must adapt themselves to a wartime schedule. Clothes must be economical. The great problem in the feminine world lay in selecting the clothes which might reflect in their dignity and simplicity the seriousness of the time. With the strict conservation of wool; silks, satins, crepes, and chiffons became the mode. Lines were simple, colors subdued and unobtrusive. The quiet and subdued tones were not a matter of choice but of necessity. The dye situation in the dye markets of the world had become acute and a shortage of dyestuffs with which to color materials threatened. These quiet colorings were called "sympathetic hues," suggesting the mental tone of the world under the stress of war.

Fig. 57.   Styles of 1916

The first season of the Textile Color Card of America resembles in tone if not in name the French color cards. A blue with a violet cast is called "heron"; gray, with a suggestion of taupe is "dusk"; a beautiful leaf-green, "tyme"; and a shade between fawn and brown is "gazelle." "Spring green" is the tone of the first new leaves; "mist," a tint of gray; and "blossom," pink with a violet tinge.

It was during the war period that the strictly one-piece dress became the favorite. For morning war work a one-piece frock (*C*, Plate XXXI) of satin, cloth, or wool jersey was selected. The attractiveness of these war-time dresses grew out of their simplicity of line and the lack of trimming. The coat-suit and the one-piece frock, slightly trimmed, were the "all-occasion" costumes of war time. (*A*, *B*, Plate XXXI.)

The many avenues of service open to women during the war gave rise to an entirely new departure in clothes. The woman skilled in driving her own car offered her service to the Motor Corps or the Ambulance Service. She of business experience found her place in the ranks of the Naval Yeoman Reserves. Many women skilled in domestic science entered the canteen kitchens, while others took their places in the Red Cross Service. In all these departments of service, regulation uniforms were authorized by the United States government. (Plate XXXII.) The material of outdoor uniforms was strong durable stuff—serge and whipcord, often leather trimmed. Leather coats with removable fleece linings were often worn over the uniform. The Red Cross nurse, in her service at home, wore a uniform of fine white cloth; overseas, a gray chambre took

Fig. 58.   Hats of 1916

its place. Coifs of red or blue according to her duty added the note of color to the costume. (Fig. 59.)

With the signing of the armistice in November 1918, the world looked for a return to normalcy in dress as well as in affairs. But with an upheaval so gigantic, adjustment lay only in the hand of time. A sudden transformation in fashion is unknown to history. The transition from the style of Louis XVI to that of the Directory is the most rapid recorded and that was born through a Reign of Terror.

As the aftermath of the French Revolution brought forth the *incroyables* and *merveilleuses,* so now new and strange fancies appeared. It is said that the incredibly short and scant skirt of 1920-1921 was the direct expression of the unsettled condition of the world. All women, irrespective of age, height or width donned the scant skirt reaching just below the knee. (*E,* Plate XXXI.) The women of sixty, fifty, and twenty were wearing, with an effort at equal grace, the abbreviated costume, formerly restricted to the growing girl of ten or twelve years. Notwithstanding the warning of skillful designers—"a woman should gauge the length of her skirt by her physique, not by Parisian styles''—the short skirt continued. Along with the short skirt came the unbridled use of cosmetics. The "vanity-case" with its powder, rouge, and lip-stick enjoyed a reign rivaling that of the French queen, Marie Antoinette. Added to those of the past were new beautifiers which were rapidly coming into the market. These luxuries of the toilette, which in former times had been only the privilege of the few, were now becoming available to the many. The great economic changes in the position of women in the professional and business world had much to do with the modern beauty shop which began to be established about 1918. It was necessary for women in the business world to be not only well-dressed but well-groomed, and these demands were met by the numerous beauty shops which sprang up all over the land.

Along with the increase in the use of cosmetics was the conspicuous change made in the manner of dressing the hair. Milady's locks were now clipped and the fashion for "bobbed" hair rapidly became general. Of course, styles in cut were different, for the hair-dresser of that day strove for "personality" bobs suited to the lines and contour of the head and profile. This treatment and dressing of the hair introduced an unlimited variety of tonics, shampoos, and rinses which added to the ever-widening business of the beauty shop. About this time the "flapper" made her bow before the footlights of fashion. "Flapper" was the popular term applied to her who followed the dictates of fashion to the limit. Then again history, true to type, repeated itself. Our makers of laws arose in their official dignity and denounced these follies of fashion. Again laws threatened regulating the dress of women. But, as in the past, the mode continued until woman herself decreed the new.

The war, the automobile, and the world of sport have all contributed to the costume of postwar days. All periods of dress have furnished ideas for the postwar fashions. Directory, Louis Seize, Moyen Age, and Oriental influences elbow one another. The Directory was suggested in the short, scant skirt, and in the knee-length, perfectly straight, close

A   B   C   D   E   F

PLATE XXXI—AMERICAN COSTUME—1917-1921

A—1917—The tailored suit which has proven itself an all-occasion dress for women. The attractiveness of this costume lies in its simplicity of line and lack of ornamentation.

B—1918—A simple afternoon dress of the war-time period. This was usually of silk or satin crepe.

C—1918—The one-piece frock which rose to popularity during the World War.

D—1919—An afternoon dress carrying out the one-piece idea in the tunic. At this period all dresses were short.

E—1921—A woman wearing the short and scant skirt of the period.

F—1921—A costume showing the influence of the military idea upon dress in the large full cape and the Napoleonic hat.

237

coat. Louis Seize styles were reflected in the bouffant skirts
of 1916. The Moyen Age ideas were seen in the long panels,
front and back, and side fulness at the hip line. (*B*, Plate
XXXI.) Oriental influence was reflected in the long, scant
skirt with slashed sides. With these various influences of
the past was the distinctly modern note contributed by the
American sport world.

The sport clothes of postwar days were far removed
from those of a generation previous. Clothes had been
"adapted" to tennis, golf, riding, swimming, and other
numerous activities. No longer was the tennis enthusiast
hampered by corset and petticoats! No longer was the
water enthusiast weighed down with bloomers, skirt, blouse,
and stockings! Sports had indeed contributed much to the
style and cut of clothes; much also in distinct sport accessories—knitted woolens, sweaters, hose, gloves and scarves.

The element of athletics in the life of the American
woman had greatly influenced her education and taste in
all matters of dress. Comfortable clothes were an outward
expression of woman's ideals and indicated much of the
trend of the times. The contrast between feminine apparel
in 1848 and that of 1920 is well portrayed in the following
excerpt from *Equal Rights:*

> The hoop-skirt, the small waist and the general impracticability
> of the clothes worn at the first Seneca convention interpret far more
> graphically than words can phrase the position of women seventy-
> five years ago. The artificial helplessness, the wretched discomfort,
> the denial of nature, all are emblazoned in sartorial terms. The
> absolute dependence of woman upon man was blazoned forth in
> her clothes. . . . The frailty and incompetence inherent in an
> eighteen-inch waist and a hoop-skirt stimulated the male ego to an
> unconscionable extent. It was not difficult to feel superior to that.
> Probably there is no more wholesome encouraging symptom of the
> times than is to be found in woman's clothes. They indicate that
> women are no longer doomed to live on sex, that men are no longer
> such impossible egotists as they were, and they predict the girls of
> the future will enter life booted and spurred for the fray as they
> never have been before. (Fig. 61.)

The contrast in clothes of the modern world is a precise
counterpart of the contrast in feminine thinking in the year
1848 and in that of 1920.

A   B   C   D   E   F

PLATE XXXII—AMERICAN COSTUME—1917-1918

A—The regulation overcoat worn by American women in foreign service during the war was made of durable stuffs, serge and whipcord, and leather trimmed.

B—A leather coat with removable fleece lining was a popular coat worn in both foreign and domestic service.

C—The uniform worn by the Naval Yeoman Reserves. This was the practical business suit for American women in yeoman service.

D—Foreign service uniform, American Red Cross. The black leather belt was worn only by commissioned officers.

E, F—The regulation overcoat and uniform worn in the American Red Cross (Motor Corps) in domestic service.

239

By the close of 1920 women's dress had become as varied as the world itself. No longer does she wait for the coming of the Parisian doll to announce the new mode from Paris, or borrow a much-prized fashion-sheet from her neighbor

to glean the coming styles. Not she of the twentieth century! Months ahead the buyers and designers of the big shops of North and South America, England and the continental countries have invaded Paris and brought back the word. This is broadcasted through innumerable magazines, fashion books, style shows, and the "movie." These buyers and designers, advance agents of style, come into Paris during the weeks of early spring and late summer. Their interest centers around the salons of the unrivaled French creators, Poiret, Callot, Paquin, Cheruit, Lanvin,

Fig. 59. Red Cross uniforms Worth, Redfern and others.

Though a few of the names long cherished as French are not French at all, these creators have risen to fame under the stimulating influence of the French capital. Paris is the inspiration! But why Paris? The answer is unmistakable. It is found in the French national character. Here is a people who have behind them traditions of color, traditions of design, traditions of artistic feeling. A people with a refined sense of form and color, who from time immemorial have given attention and thought to the adornment of the person. In Paris culture and society life developed earlier than in any other city, and fashion is essentially a product of social life. Under the French kings, the women of the court enjoyed a position and power which made them patronesses of fashion, and an inspiration to creative endeavor. With this heritage of background who will say that this is not the stimulus which every artist finds in this historic beauty-loving city?

Long has been the hope for American fashions, and strong has been the agitation for a world's fashion center in America—a fashion center where ideas of dress especially adapted to American women may be fostered and developed. Since the war the idea of a greater Americanism has taken a profound hold upon the mind of the people. Not only does a greater Americanism

Fig. 60.   Sport suit

Fig. 61.   Riding clothes of 1924 (Redrawn, courtesy Marshall Field & Company)

center around the legislative problems of the country, but it also enters into the commercial life. In industry the new note is "American Art for American Industry." This has led as never before to a greater emphasis upon the term "Industrial Art." The efforts now being made by designers and manufacturers to use American designs and American materials make apparent the common interest of these two powerful agencies in producing strictly American types. Our de-

signers have always gone to France, not only for the fashion
but for the design of fabrics as well. In 1916 the first American design contest for women's wear was held at the Art
Alliance of America in New York City and promoted by the
paper called *Women's Wear*. During the same year the first
instance of a manufacturer calling upon American artists
for designs was that of the Albert Blum Contest.* This was
a contest for hand-decorated fabrics. This manufacturer
put his emphasis upon *designs created in America*. Many
of the designs submitted were inspired by the study of
primitive American design including Mexico and Central
and South America. The museums and galleries of America
have entered heartily into this movement for the development of American design. Through these institutions a
co-operation of artist and manufacturer is being fostered.
The artist tells the expert in industry the effective use of
form, line, and color, while the textile expert tells the artist
whether the designs can be carried out by the machine, and
whether the colors can be obtained. Others are lecturing
upon costume design and the effects of the various lines,
colors, and proportions upon the figure. Experiments in
dyeing have been conducted and specimens of dye stuffs and
textiles, native and foreign, have been shown. In 1917, the
Metropolitan Museum of New York City, recognizing textile design as a part of our national art, opened a new
textile gallery. In this gallery embroideries, hand-decorated
fabrics, and eighteenth-century garments were displayed.

The co-operation of art and industry is recognized in the
organization known as the Fashion Art League, representing the dress-makers of America. The Dress and Skirt
Designers' Association is another commercial group emphasizing American designs. At a recent exhibit forty-nine
model skirts were shown. The cloth, the designs, and the
skirts themselves had all been made in America, and though
this organization had always featured Parisian models,
their advertisement now reads: "American designed,
American manufactured, American made."

---

*Journal of Home Economics, May, 1918.

A B C D E

PLATE XXXIII—AMERICAN COSTUME—1900-1920

A—The popular bathing suit of the day. These are carried out in
    various and gay colors. The caps are rubber, harmonizing in color
    with the costume. The large cape adds the finishing touch to the mode.
B—A sport frock showing the comfortable shoes, walking skirt, sleeveless
    vest of gay color and sailor hat of rough straw.
C, E—Types of sport costume.
D—Riding togs of the twentieth century.
B, C, E—Redrawn, courtesy Marshall Field & Company.

243

The educational institutions of the country have taken hold of this matter of clothes. Not only is the making of clothes an accredited course in the schools, but the line, the color, and the beautiful in the dress of the past is rapidly becoming a vital part of the educational curriculum.

With all this impulse toward the beautiful in dress, it would not be surprising should American women, in time to come, create as well as wear beautiful clothes, though the art is not easily wrested from the hand of Paris. The French designer has supplied the world from an age-old heritage of artistic feeling, and he will doubtless maintain his supremacy until some other people, some other time, from a garnered heritage of the same age-old aesthetic instincts, can, with the intuitive facility of Paris, divine the beautiful in the realm of dress.

REVIEW

1. What demand does modern woman make in reference to clothes? Contrast the modern attitude with that of 1830-1870.
2. How did the tailor-made suit probably originate? What is your reaction to this type of costume?
3. Discuss the popularity of the walking-skirt. The shirt-waist suit. Describe the neckwear worn at this period.
4. Date and describe the "morning-glory" skirt. "Hobble" skirt. "Peg-top."
5. Discuss the after effects of the Great War upon dress.
6. Name fashionable materials of the twentieth century.
7. What influence in American life has forwarded the knitting industry?
8. What fashions of the century suggest the French Directory? The Middle Ages? French 1700? Bustle and tilter time?
9. Discuss French *couturières* and their methods of introducing new fashions.
10. Give several reasons why Paris maintained her place as the world's fashion center.

CHAPTER THIRTEEN

American Costume (1920-1940)

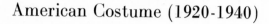

IN A backward glance through the years immediately following the World War (1914-1918) it is clear that no distinctly new styles appeared. Every style seemed, as it came upon the fashion scene, to be a revival of some bygone age. About 1920-21, after a period of very short skirts, a distinctly new silhouette appeared. This was a one-piece frock with the waistline set low about the hips, and the skirt knee length or shorter. The costume was perfectly straight with no suggestion whatever of the natural waistline. (Plate XXXIV.) Street frocks and formal gowns alike appeared in the same short and straight silhouette which remained practically unchanged until about 1925-26. By-and-by sashes and panels began to appear. These dropped below the hemline, breaking this severe edge and giving more softness to the formal dress. (*A, B,* Plate XXXIV.)

With the fashion of the straight silhouette women continued to wear the hair cut close, in the style of a mannish bob. This demanded a small hat. The small, close-fitting hat of the early twenties was set low on the head, covering the ears and shading the eyes. (*E, F, G,* Plate XXXIV.) Oxfords and pumps with comfortable heel were usual for street wear, while various styles in strapped sandals with high heel were the choice for more formal occasions.

The plainness of this very fashionable mode was somewhat saved to femininity by the use of ornament. The great novelty was the new costume jewelry. Fashion had at last conceded that all that glitters does not necessarily have to be gold to qualify as smart jewelry. Synthetic stones and vegetable ivory, simulating lapis lazuli, and other opaque stones were now set in brooches, bracelets, pendants, clips, and rings of new and attractive design. The cost of costume jewelry was so little when compared with the value of its contribution to the ensemble that milady felt no qualms of conscience in purchasing a generous supply for her many costumes.

Women began to give considerable attention to the ensemble—the complete picture. Fashion demanded that all accessories, hats, gloves, bag, and scarf match or at least harmonize with the gown. This demand for the harmonious ensemble went still further and milady decided that her "make-up" which, in her grandmother's day had only aimed to correct shortcomings of nature, should enhance the personality. With the assistance of the specialists of the beauty shop, she was not long in achieving all the mysteries of make-up and especially those which particularly aimed to build up her personal charm.

The modern beauty shop began to develop toward its present state of importance about 1918, and succeeding years have witnessed a truly phenomenal growth. At no time in the history of the world have the luxuries of the toilet been so easily available to all women, no matter what her economic status may be. The modern beauty shop with its vast array of powders, creams, tissue builders, rouge, lipsticks, astringents, masks, tonics, brilliantines, rinses, and waving fluids must outstrip the wildest dreams of a Pompadour or Antoinette!

About 1928 the silhouette showed signs of a flutter in the hemline. This could mean only one thing—the monotony of the straight silhouette was beginning to tell. Some fullness was creeping into the hemline. Pleats, gores—anything to give a little fullness! This tendency increased more and more until the skirt grew quite full around the lower edge. The waistline, however, still remained low, with little indication of the natural waistline. Then what did milady do but lengthen the back of the skirt to within a few inches of the floor and keep the front knee length. (*D, E,* Plate XXXV.) This was, indeed, an unusual mode and had its greatest popularity in afternoon and evening

A   B   C   D   E   F   G

PLATE XXXIV—AMERICAN COSTUME—1920-1926

A—1925—Evening gown of velvet, lace, and crepe in the prevailing straight silhouette, showing the long back panel introduced to break the severe lower edge of skirt.

B—1925—A crepe evening dress with sash knotted at hipline; ends extending below skirt succeeds in giving a softer effect to an otherwise severe silhouette.

C—1926—A formal gown with surplus closing, showing a single tassel at front and back as the only trimming.

D—1926—Fringe makes the skirt of this dress, with a fringed scarf forming a bertha effect in front, and falling from the shoulders at the back.

E, F, G—1926—Smart one- and two-piece dresses of simple design worn with the high, close-fitting hat set well down over the ears.

247

frocks. This tendency toward fullness and the bouffant silhouette overthrew the straight, mannish fashions of the twenties and they soon withdrew from the fashion scene. Now, with the more feminine lines in costume, the boyish bob of the previous years began to soften and was quickly replaced with a style of hairdressing harmonizing with the changed modes in dress. Hats ceased to cover the ears and shade the eyes. Indeed, hats revealed the forehead! By 1931 the "Princess Eugènie" was extremely popular. This was a little hat with a round, low crown and brief brim similar to the small hat of the sixties. The name "Princess Eugènie" was given this particular hat because during the sixties the Empress Eugènie, the most popular fashion leader in Europe, had worn with great distinction the little hat of that day.

The introduction of fullness in the hemline continued for many seasons, during which the waistline reached its natural level. It was only a matter of months after the back hemline had dropped that the front followed. Then the long skirt was upon us!

It is said that confusion began with the new mode. The flapper of short-skirt days scarcely knew how to conduct herself with so much material swishing about her ankles. Indeed, much was said for and against the long skirt! By-and-by it was decreed that the long gown belonged to the evening or formal field, and that the shorter frock should remain for daytime wear. The "shorter" skirt was, however, by no means a knee-length skirt but by the early thirties had dropped several inches below the knee. The proper length then decreed was ten inches from the floor. From the early to the middle thirties, lines were lean and long. Formals, particularly, aided the slim effect with a clinging instep hem. (*B,* Plate XXXV.)

Waistlines continued at normal level, and the particular modes of the day emphasized high necklines, full sleeves, wide shoulders, collars, scarves, and bows—anything to keep the interest above the waistline. (*A, C,* Plate XXXVI.) These fashions reflect in a modern way the

A   B   C   D   E

PLATE XXXV—AMERICAN COSTUME—1929-1937

A—1937—Crepe evening dress showing fulness at lower edge.

B—1937—A slender evening gown and tailored jacket of acetate crepe. The smart costume to wear from 5 o'clock to midnight.

C—1935—A draped evening gown. Side panels are twisted into a knot which spreads out, making the train. Note sleek hipline.

D, E—1929—Evening gowns, the fashionable knee-length front and long back which brought in the long skirt.

249

Medici costume of the time of Henry III, late sixteenth century,* when wide sleeves, small waists, and high neck-lines with ruffs dominating the fashion held sway. In other words, the modern silhouette followed the lines of the inverted triangle, resting on the apex—all interest above the center. During 1935 the silhouette began to change. The triangle was gradually reversing itself and was beginning to rest on its base. The silhouette widened at the bottom and interest diminished above the waistline. Skirts were now on their way to a fuller hemline and grow-ing shorter.

With the long skirt taking first place for formal wear, drapery appeared and other lines of beauty came into the costume. Many evening gowns showed a classic treatment, reminding one of Greek drapery effects. These long lines and drapery, which frequently terminated in a slight train, made the figure appear slim and rounded. (*C*, Plate XXXV.) Satins, transparent velvets, soft crepes, taffetas, and lamés, rich in gold and silver thread, were the choice materials for strictly formal wear.

During the early thirties many new materials were coming into the market—acetates, rayons, and all syn-thetic fabrics which for the first time were being manufac-tured. Printed crepes, printed silks, and printed linens seemed to take the place of embroidered fabrics. The new note in printed materials was the color on color combina-tion instead of the usual color on white or white on color. These printed materials were usually gay and "splashy" in both color and design. If, however, milady preferred, a quiet design in subdued color could be chosen. The Chi-nese legendary prints, a demand for which arose about 1937 when war brought sympathetic attention to China, are an excellent example of the inspiration for design and color which may grow out of a country's own national life. In-spired from the realm of Chinese legend, these prints rep-resented twenty-five separate designs, with each a legend of its own. Such patterns carried suggestive names, as

*See pages 113, 115.

"Lotus Maiden," "Temples in Moonlight," "China Forever." Some designs represented familiar Chinese subjects —jade teapot, fish patterns, Confucius, or others equally Chinese. Typical oriental colors predominated—Peiping green, lotus pink, pagoda red, and bamboo. These printed fabrics were used for both daytime and evening gowns, for house coats, beach wear, parasols, bags, turbans, and other apparel. A part of the proceeds was planned to go to Madame Chiang Kai-shek for Chinese relief. So popular were all printed materials in this day that one could not escape a print! Each following year new designs and color combinations were presented the fashion-minded public and, what is more, purchased with the same admiration as when first introduced.

During 1935-36 the tailored and semi-tailored suit, useful for so many occasions, still led the parade. These were sometimes seen in three-quarter coats with a smart inside jacket of harmonizing color or a gay plaid, depending upon the type of suit. The tailored suit, vary as it may, is one that continues to hold high favor in the hearts of woman-kind. So it is with the popular shirt-waist suit which first

Fig. 62. The shirt-waist suit, 1937

came upon the scene about 1905-06.* In its day it was considered the indispensable feature of every wardrobe. It, too, returned and, in 1937, much modernized, appeared as one of the leading types in the smart and comfortable dress of that period. (Fig. 62.)

By 1935 the boyish bob of the early twenties had just about disappeared and the hair, though still considered short, was arranged in soft ringlets. Gradually some leaders were allowing the hair to fall to the shoulders. Hats remained small. Vary as they might, however, in crown

*See page 216, Fig. 51.

or brim, they remained distinctly the small hat, and continued so until about 1935-36. Then the broad-brimmed hat became a reality. In the new hat the crown was very low and small in circumference and the brim of exaggerated width. Many were not willing to give up the small hat, and the middle thirties found both the large and small hat the vogue.

Fig. 63. The strapped low shoe, the toeless sandal, and the pump, 1930-40
(After *Delineator*)

With the continued popularity of the short skirt, milady's shoes and hose assumed first importance. Though both styles and materials covered a wide field, the fashion world still clung to the low shoe. The high shoe, so fashionable during 1916-18, had passed definitely out of the picture and, moreover, seemed destined to remain out. More and more, shoes, hat, and frock are related to the occasion for which they are worn. Consequently, one finds specially designed shoes for walking, for sport, and for formal dress. The new feature in all shoes which came in about 1937-38 was the open toe. In fact, so completely did the open toe usurp the field, that it was well-nigh impossible to purchase shoes with the closed toe. The oxford, the pump, and the sandal in a variety of styles, made up in suede, leather, or gabardine, with leather trim, were most popular for daytime wear. Sandals in fabric, often in beautiful colors, and a multiplicity of straps, and always the open toe, were chosen for formal dress. (Fig. 63.) In sport shoes, the toeless sandal in a variety of styles and colors held first place.

And what shall we say of hosiery! Since the low shoe has become a permanent fashion, the hose is of utmost importance. The most highly favored hose of the postwar period was the gossamer silk chiffon. The great demand for this popular silk hosiery led to much experimentation in the effort to produce a substitute for silk. Vegetable silk made from wood fiber was one result of this experimentation. This hose, however, did not succeed in taking the place of the all-silk stocking. Then toward 1940 another miracle thread, spun from the chemical elements found in coal, air, and water, produced a new era in the hosiery industry. The new textile discovery has been termed *nylon* and nylon hosiery has assumed a leading place in the fashion world.

During the period between 1937-40 women seemed to tire of bobbed hair and, for a time, it appeared that long hair was destined to return. Soon the "up" hairdress became a leading fashion and many women let the hair lengthen to achieve this latest line. This they did by carrying the hair up to the crown of the head, where the ends were rolled under or arranged in curls and held in place by small combs or pins. Some women unwilling to surrender their short hair, even to fashion, permitted the side locks only to lengthen and, carrying these in an upward line, achieved practically the same effect.

About this time the new designs in hats held the spotlight in millinery. Seldom before had such unusual and "queer" shapes been given to hats. It so happened that many of the hat shapes resembled familiar objects seen in everyday life. Some suggested the lowly flower pot filled with colorful posies and banded by a silk ribbon and bow; others ran up to a high point; while some appeared as a diminutive crown set at a pert angle over the left eye and secured by a strap about the head. It is said that back in 1860 a similar style was created when a lovely young crea ture set off to a picnic wearing a wide-brimmed leghorn. During the evening a pet dog dined on the tasty leghorn but left the tiny, rose-covered crown. The young lady, undaunted, retrieved what was left—she set the crown at a pert angle and became a leader in the fashion for small hats!

Hats in 1940 were set far back on the head—big hats, little hats, and the demure bonnet. (*E*, Plate XXXVI.)

Fashion forecasts indicate that hats of the future forties are all destined to be worn back on the head, and that this will return the popular hatpins of the nineties. During the late thirties and continuing through 1940 veils attained great popularity. Every hat, it seemed, was draped with a wiry veil, softening an often otherwise severeness.

Fig. 64. Fashionable tennis shorts, 1937 (After *Delineator*)

During the thirties the active participation of women in all phases of sport activities led to many innovations. Changes are seen in every type of sport clothes. Clothes for comfort, clothes properly adapted to special activities, no matter what they might be, seem to have been the aim of the designers of sport clothes. Today the unmistakable sign of the trained designer's hand is seen in the fine lines and tailored output of clothes for the sport world. Slacks, one-piece play suits, shorts, the *culotte,* or divided skirt, have each its particular niche. (Fig. 64.) Sweaters, beach capes of terry cloth, sun hats, toeless sandals with flat or medium heel, and other sport accessories also belong to this highly favored department of clothes. No longer is milady hampered by clothes as she takes off for a swim, a tennis match, or a round of golf! This is, indeed, a long, long stride from the period when the usual street dress was worn for tennis, and the inevitable skirt, bloomers, blouse, and stockings appeared as the proper outfit for the swimming enthusiast! (Fig. 65.)

Toward the close of the thirties, milady's silhouette showed signs of a striking change. Skirts became definitely shorter, ranging from 15 to 17 inches from the floor, and of equal importance was the fitted bodice which was designed to reveal the fine lines of the shoulder, bust, and waist.

A   B   C   D   E   F

PLATE XXXVI—AMERICAN COSTUME—1935-1940

A—1935—A dress for daytime occasions. The draped collar is of style
  importance. Sleeves have their fulness caught up below the elbow.

B—1937—Printed crepe afternoon dress with jacket. Blouse is shirred to
  give bodice fulness. Large straw hat with small, low crown.

C—1936—Rough woolen three-quarter coat, the jacket big-checked plaid.
  Note the muffler and felt hat.

D—1940—Fitted jacket with pockets of fur. Fulled skirt is 18 inches
  from floor. Small hat with wiry veil.

E—1940—Gentleman's street suit. Coat semifitted, felt hat.

F—1940—Fitted crepe dress. Skirt 18 inches from floor. Note bonnet,
  gloves, and large envelope purse.

Daytime frocks showed high necklines and short sleeves. In 1940 fitted clothes reached their peak in the torso jacket, a snug jacket with a long, slim line over the hip. In fact, the torso interest was uppermost, and yokes, pockets, fur— anything to accentuate the torso idea — were seen in the modes of 1940. (*C, D,* Plate XXXVI.)

During the passing of the years little change was seen in gentlemen's clothes. The silhouette scarcely varied from year to year either for business, for sport, or for formal dress. In the late thirties, however, a leaning toward gayer hues was seen, and bluish greens, greenish blues, sand tones, and other hitherto unusual hues were much in evidence. During the early forties a pleasing variety in men's clothes was seen in the choice of one color for trousers, a harmonizing tone of another color for coat, and a hat blending with these. Many of these combinations were a distinctly charming note in the clothes of the modern world. Lighter-weight straw and braid hats with gay silk or crepe bands added another happy note to masculine attire.

In the history-making business of fashion-creating, America is rapidly attaining an ever-widening sphere of

Fig. 65. Fashionable clothes for the beach, 1936 (After *Good Housekeeping*)

AMERICAN COSTUMES, 1920–1945

A—A spring dress of lightweight dark blue wool. Hats were veiled and worn
at eyebrow level, 1920.

B and C—Couple dancing in 1927, the time of ''Flaming Youth.'' The girl's
dress was the shortest to date, low waisted, and sashed. The man's evening
clothes were styled in the English manner.

D—Woman's double-wrapped wool coat with fur collar, and closely fitted hat,
1932.

E—School girl of 1940 in woolen coat, berét, short socks, and boots.

F—Woman wearing a winter suit with vest, scarf, and Alpine style hat, 1939.

G—School boy in hand knitted woolen sweater, knickerbockers, and long hose,
1933.

H—Young lady's two-piece swim suit, to date (1943) the most abbreviated.

AMERICAN COSTUMES, 1950–1965

A—Man's business suit, 1964. Shoulders, sleeves, and trousers were narrowed. Fabrics were chemically treated to prevent wrinkling.

B—Boy's winter ensemble, 1953. Long trousers with knitted cuffs contrasted with the plaid coat.

C—Young woman's autumn wool suit with grey fur stole and felt hat, 1951.

D—Young lady's soft red wool coat with black velvet trimmings, 1958.

E—Woman's "shortie" wool jacket, worn with a plaid skirt, 1952.

F and *G*—Flower girls in pink and blue organza dresses, holding the bride's train.

H—A 1965 bride, wearing an ivory satin gown with antique lace bodice and appliqués. The veil was nylon organza, and the train was detachable.

256B

influence. American creators of fashion have long since demonstrated their skill in distinctive fashion creating and are constantly scaling new heights in designing achievement. Today these outstanding American designers are well known to the fashion field and to the buying public as well. Looking toward the future, established schools of fashion are launching young designers on their chosen careers in fashion creating. The unlimited opportunities afforded by American libraries and American museums for research is supplying these designers of no distant day with a superb background. Thus the oncoming style creators will continue to furnish the fashion world with distinctive American designs, and steadily reinforce the American claim to fashion leadership in the world of clothes!

REVIEW

1. Describe the silhouette of 1925-26.
   What details later introduced gave more femininity to the fashion?
2. What is *costume jewelry?*
   Why has it been accepted?
   Give some interesting details about it.
3. When did the beauty shop become of business importance?
   What led to this development?
   Compare today's use of beauty aids with that of past centuries.
4. About what year did the long skirt return?
   What place was assigned to it? Why?
   What unusual fashion bridged the gap between the short and long skirt?
5. What period witnessed the coming of rayons, acetates, and other synthetic materials?
   When did printed materials make their appearance? Describe these with reference to color and design.
6. When did the boyish bob of the twenties begin to disappear? Give a general review of styles which followed.
7. Give an interesting review of skirt lengths through the thirties to 1940, inclusive.
   What effect did this have upon the importance of shoes and hosiery?
   What is the modern development in hosiery?
8. What great change has taken place in sport clothes?
   Name various types new to the century.
9. What interesting change in color appeared in men's clothes during the late thirties?
   What can be said about men's clothes in general?
10. Give a brief account of the striking change in the silhouette of 1940.

RNK

CHAPTER FOURTEEN

American Costume (1940-1966)

AT the outset of the 1940's, the late styles of the 1930's changed in details and were influenced by the beginnings of the war in Europe. The lines of women's clothing began with accentuated slim torsos and wide shoulders. Padding was used in coats, suits, daytime and evening gowns, and even in blouses, to extend shoulder widths. The newest rayon fabrics in crêpe weaves gave a clinging hipline, ending at the hem with wide circular folds. The evening jacket, made from sparkling lamé, came into fashion. Buttoned down the front, it was worn over evening gowns or became part of an evening suit in velvet or crêpe.

Designers in our larger fashion centers were in full agreement on the elegance of lines for coats, gowns, jackets, and furs, when World War II struck the United States in 1941. Hemlines were shortened, skirts were narrowed, and sleeves were tightened. Influences from faraway places on our country's fashions were replaced with "plain American." But the shoulders remained broad and were even extended in both women's and men's wear. The influence of uniformed women's attire accounted for an almost masculine appearance of women's clothing. Shorter skirts were influenced by the fact that suit and dress materials in wools, silks, and rayons became in tight supply. Cottons, too, were scarce. The Federal Government limited the required yardage in manufactured women's wear, and narrowed the widths of skirt hems to 2 inches.

Styles of women's hats and hair fashions, however, reached ludicrous exaggerations. The hair began to drop from the modest waved coiffures of the 1930's down the back of the neck and shoulders, while extending itself upward from the forehead into a roll-back pompadour. The hats were very small, nestling over one eye, or they were over-large, odd-shaped, and angled. Designers used available materials not required for the war effort, in unrelated shapes. Furs, wings, feathers, beads, sequins, veils, felt, and velvet, were included in the materials for winter; laces and straws were used for spring and summer. "Hats" appeared in the forms of snoods and scarfs, tied into knots at the front of the head while draping over long bobbed hair at the back.

The activities of women increased outside of the home. Many were employed in factories and business pursuits to replace men at war. Women's clothing began to borrow masculine features. To save on material, however, short skirts, ending at the knee, contrasted with wide shoulder lines. Topped by strange hats at acute angles, the costumes of this period between 1940 and 1945 were somewhat violent, in effect, as if to echo the stridencies of war.

Rainwear was designed to harmonize with the lines of

Bags, gloves and shoes of the 1940's and 1950's to 1961.

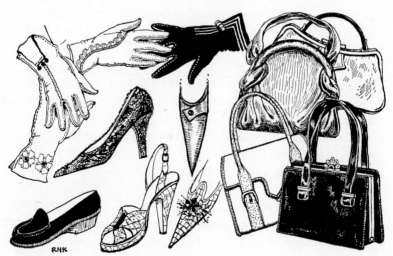

dress in use, although of necessity for protection, it was longer. Materials such as rubberized cotton, rayon, satin, and parachute cloth (nylon) gave added protection. Later, in the 1950's, nylon, plastics, polyesters, and acrylics were added to cottons and woolens, singly, or in combinations.

Shoes were practical, with medium heels and rounded toes. For summer, open toes were worn universally and straps exposed the foot. Silk stockings were laid aside for the newer nylons in the early 1940's. But the war had produced such a scarcity of nylon that rayon and cotton lisles were substituted. Dyed an intense copper tint, most hosiery at this time was inharmonious with the rest of the costume.

At the same time, men's suits, which had been manufactured previously with two pairs of trousers and a matching vest, were limited to one pair of trousers and no vest. Matching or contrasting vests were sold separately.

Although 1945 saw the ending of World War II, scarcity of materials continued. It was not until 1947 that the designers could make full use of their talents. Among the more creative and daring designers, starts were made in a luxurious direction, and the public began to talk about the ''New Look'' in 1947. In that year skirt lengths were called ''the dropped hemline,'' falling halfway between the knee and the ankle. Acknowledgment of the feminine figure was back, accenting the rounded bosoms, slim waistlines, and molded hips. Sweeping grace succeeded the angled pre-1945 fashions. The backs of garments were especially featured, including draped folds, almost to the floor. Materials were used lavishly in wide, circular folds for coats, suits, dresses, and skirts.

Fashion people talked of ''pyramid effects'' in women's garments, of draped necklines, and glistening sequins. A bustle effect returned, imitating the styles of the 1880's in corded taffeta, with fitted torsos in one- and two-piece styles. Earrings were featured in small, round forms, and in pendant drops of metal and stones. Costume jewelry began to increase in importance, to enhance the glamour of the attire.

A   B   C   D   E F   G

A—1940—Fitted suit with wide shoulder jacket and skirt length just below the knees. Small, draped hat with inserted quills.

B—1943—Wide-brimmed hat in felt with pheasant feather. Broad-shouldered, wool plaid coat. Skirt length the same as in 1940.

C—1945—Box coat of blond soft wool with wide shoulders. Small, draped turban with single curled feather. Skirt length still short.

D—1946—Flat, veiled felt turban with quills, worn with hair coiled softly at the back. Fitted coat with one-button side opening.

E—1947—Man's double-breasted, drape suit, popular in 1945 and holding sway for almost a decade. The pocket handkerchief was arranged in four points.

F—1947—The "New Look," which changed women's styles from meager to lavish in the cut and use of materials. This was an evening gown of nylon chiffon, with a flowing, lined cape of velvet.

G—1949—Neo-bustle based on the dress of the 1880's. Deeptone taffeta with velvet trim and close-fitting, veiled bonnet hat. Skirt length was just above the ankle.

Men's suits at this time became more generous in cut.
The shoulders, which began to widen in 1945, went to wider
extremes. The "drape" was more important than the fit.
Coats were double breasted and not only wide, but long, with
broad lapels. Trousers, too, were wide. These suit syles
continued well into the 1950's. Men's shirt sleeves were designed with double or "French cuffs." Cuff links returned
to fashion and, along with tie clasps, offered further interest
for the designer.

By 1949, the flow of new details in all of women's garments was steady. That year, the small hat in various designs was much in evidence. It hugged the top and sides of
the head and, with covered wire side loops, remained in
style for years. Achieving the practicality of the close cap,
it was manufactured for both daytime and evening wear in
a variety of materials. The page-boy cut and other long
bobbed hair styles were gradually replaced by shorter,
closer cuts, waved or curled. With close-fitting dark velvet
hats, berets, or tams, these styles were easy to adapt, and
were generally becoming.

School and college fashions drew much attention because
of the increasing number of young people in higher education. The same styles were adopted by women in occupations and in the home. With more women driving cars, the
practical and youthful appeal of such college fashions combined to end the elaborate "New Look" lines of 1947-1949.
Suburban living at the fringe of large metropolitan areas
gave the newer clothing designs ready acceptance. Wool
plaids, tweeds, cotton corduroys, gabardines in wool and
rayon, and "wrinkle-shed" cottons were great favorites in
ready-mades and home-mades. The ever-present sweater,
in all its forms and colors, continued to be a strong favorite.
"Separates" grew in popularity. Blouses, skirts, jackets,
and slacks or shorts could be mixed or matched for ensemble
harmonies. This styling increased wardrobe usefulness,
and simplified laundering and dry cleaning. It continued
well into the 1960's.

Such practical styles in clothing could not be universally appealing without a great forward push in chemistry, creating new man-made fibers and fabric treatments. The simple list of cottons, linens, silk, and wool fibers supplied by nature and used by man since records began has been supplemented in so many forms and variations that it is truly difficult to keep them all in mind. In use, some of the man-made fibers surpass the older natural ones for clothing, industrial applications, and interior decoration. The big point to remember is that their quality and performance can be controlled by science.

Today, the consumer is protected in his fabric and clothing choices by labeling, which describes the content and methods of care. With much extensive fiber varieties under various trade names, directions for laundering, dry cleaning, and pressing are a real necessity.

Some Examples of Trade-Marked and Basic Fibers

Acele: Man-made textile fibers composed of cellulose acetate, and the yarn, thread, or textile fiber. E. I. du Pont de Nemours and Co.

Acetate: Man-made textile fibers composed of cellulose acetate; the yarn, thread, or textile fabric made of such fibers.

Acrilan: Trade-mark for acrylic textile fiber made by the Chemstrand Corporation Division of the Monsanto Chemical Co.

Acrylic: A manufactured fiber in which the fiber-forming substance is any long-chain synthetic polymer composed of at least 85% by weight of acrylonitrile units.

Antron: A registered du Pont trade-mark for its trilobal nylon.

Arnel: Trade-mark of the Celanese Fibers Co. for a cellulose triacetate textile fiber.

Avicron: A triacetate rayon yarn with latent crimp, activated by normal bleaching and dyeing. FMC Corp., American Viscose Division.

Avisco: Trade-mark of FMC Corp., American Viscose Division, identifying fiber content of its rayon, acetate, or vinyon. (Vinyon is any of the various synthetic textile fibers in filament or staple form that are long-chain polymers composed of at least 85% by weight of vinyl chloride units.)

Avron: FMC Corp., American Viscose Division, high strength rayon.

Caprolan: Trade-mark of the Allied Chemical Corp. for a polyamide fiber (nylon).

Celaperm: Trade-mark of the Celanese Fibers Co. for an acetate; color pigmented in solution before the fiber is spun.

Cellulose: A carbohydrate of complex molecular structure which forms the chief framework of plant cells and walls. Used as a basic raw material for making rayon.

Chromespun: Trade-mark of Eastman Chemical Products, Inc. for a color-locked acetate fiber.

Creslan: Trade-mark of the American Cyanamid Co. for an acrylic fiber used in yarns and fabrics.

Dacron: Trade-mark of the Du Pont Co. for a polyester fiber and yarn.

Dynel: Trade-mark of the Union Carbide Chemicals Corp. for a textile fiber made of vinyl chloride and acrylonitrile (for pile fabrics), classed as a modacrylic.

Estron: Trade-mark of the Eastman Chemical Products, Inc. for white acetate fiber.

Fortisan: Trade-mark of the Celanese Fibers Co. for a modified rayon textile yarn of super-strong filament.

Fortrel: Trade-mark of the Celanese Fibers Co. for a modified polyester fiber or yarn.

Kodel: Trade-mark of the Eastman Chemical Products, Inc., for a polyester fiber.

Mylar: Trade-mark of the Du Pont Co. for a polyester film used to coat metallic fibers and textile trimmings.

Nylon: Generic name for a long-chain polyamide capable of being formed into filaments. (A polyamide is a compound composed of more than one amide, a crystaline compound derived from ammonia.)

Olefin: A manufactured fiber in which the fiber-forming substance is a long-chain synthetic polymer composed of at least 85%, by weight, of ethylene, propylene, or other olefin units. Used for upholstery, Venetian blind tapes, industrial products, and, recently, women's hosiery (Vectra).

Orlon: Trade-mark of the Du Pont Co. for an acrylic textile fiber produced in both spun and continuous filament form.

Rayon: Man-made textile fibers composed of regenerated cellulose, and the yarn, thread, or textile fabric made with such fibers.

Spandex: A manufactured fiber in which the fiber-forming substance is a long-chain synthetic polymer comprised of at least 85% of a segmented polyurethane. (Polyurethane is a substance used in making rigid forms (foam type) and resins for coatings and adhesives.) Spandex makes a strong, flexible, elastic textile in which the spandex core is wrapped or spun with the same textile fibers from which the garment is woven, thus appearing as part of it. Spandex is used for foundation garments, bathing suits, hose, and webbings.

Triacetate: Thermoplastic material capable of being spun into textile fiber. Contains three acetate compounds.

Verel: An Eastman trade-marked name for a modacrylic long-chain polymer fiber, used alone or for piled fabrics.

Vycron: Registered trade-mark for Beauknit's polyester fiber.

Zantrel: American Enka Corp. trade-mark for a new high-modulus rayon. (Modulus is the ratio of the elongation strain and stress within the elasticity of the material.)

Ze Pel: Trade-mark of Du Pont for a fabric fluoridizer to repel fluid stains.

By 1953, the amount of material used in women's costumes began to lessen. The trimmer look in shoulders and waistlines, with longer, straighter skirts returned. Evening gowns, although not changed much in line, were shortened to 4 inches above the ankles. Materials of the luxury quality were more in evidence. The popularity of costume jewelry created an industry in itself, extending to male accessories in such items as cuff links, tie clasps, and belt buckles.

Throughout the 1950's, skirt styles were divided into two classes, plus the full, permanently pleated skirt. These were the sheath and the regular full skirt, gored or gathered. The sheath skirt used a deep pleat or double pleat in the

A   B   C   D E   F   G

A—1950—Spring suit of soft navy wool with detachable "capette." The veiled bonnet hat is of cream straw with black velvet trim.

B—1954—Black and white tweed suit with box jacket, worn with a black felt sailor hat and black accessories.

C—1954—After-six gown with tightly fitted bodice and ankle-length, ballerina skirt of warp-printed acetate taffeta.

D—1958—Linen chemise dress with peach-basket hat, flowered gloves, and a straw tote bag.

E—1956—Evening stole of soft fur, worn over a long, fitted gown of metallic satin.

F—1957-1958—Man's "Ivy League" suit, single breasted with narrower lapels, longer slim coat, narrow trousers, and straight or informal handkerchief folds in breast pocket.

G—1957—Afternoon or street dress of silk Shantung, featuring a side open collar line and diagonally crossed belt. Closely fitted, with waist darts and narrow, calf-length skirt.

back to give stepping or walking width. For evening wear, the draped skirt was featured in luxury materials such as rayon, taffeta, or velvet. Some wide skirts were extreme, and flaring, with bias or circular cuts, and were called "ballerina" styles. The two contrasting styles of skirts, the straight and the wide, persisted into the early 1960's.

In 1955, styles for street and occupational wear had been simplified. Materials were elegant and varied. The design and cut of garments truly could be classified as inspired. Foundation garments were improved. Nylon was used more with cotton, rayon, and elastic, adding strength to give support to the bust, abdomen, and thighs. Variations in sizes available for these garments gave better fitting qualities. Early in the 1960's spandex fibers developed. They were manufactured under trade names such as Lycra, Spandelle, Blue "C", Vyrene, Darlspun, and many more. (See fiber list.) A core of this strong, flexible thread, synthetically made through chemistry, was wrapped or spun with the same fiber from which the entire garment was made, thus making the spandex and the textile one material in appearance. The most delicate lace for a foundation garment could become the strongest "stretch" fabric, by the combination of spandex and the textile threads.

Nylon tricot was used to add strength and fit to undergarments. It resisted stretching out of shape, and retained its original daintiness of detail. Sizing for short, medium, and tall figures in undergarments, petticoats, and slips widened the choices and variety of selections.

At this point, let us consider the marked acceptance of women's slacks, pants, shorts, and the in-betweens. For practical uses, they became so popular often appropriateness of "where" and "when" was forgotten. It is interesting to note that as time progressed from the late 1950's into the first half of the 1960's, the wearing of every type of women's trousers and shorts was seen in public. The longer pants and trousers were designed in a variety of materials, and also with a content of spandex fibers. This gave the gar-

A   B   C   D   E   F

A—1958 to 1960—Man's continental model suit, showing distinct European influence—closer shoulders, shorter flared coat, and tighter trousers than its predecessor, the Ivy League model.

B—1960—Lightweight, wool-and-man-made-fiber coat with matching, deep-dome hat. The coat is cut with circular folds and loose fit.

C—1960—High hair style with long earrings. The upper part of the evening gown featured a scoop neckline with a ruffled bertha in black nylon chiffon.

D—Late 1950's and 1960—Separates in pleated-wool, plaid skirt and harmonizing wool or orlon sweater.

E—1960—Taffeta stole worn with a matching evening gown of the same material, and featuring an upturned ruffle effect at the back waist line.

F—Late 1950's and 1960—Separates in short-sleeved blouse and tight, striped cotton pants, popular with high school and college girls for leisure wear.

ments closer fit, and added flexibility and comfort. Ballet lessons for all ages added leotards and tights to the list.

A great deal of attention in garment manufacturing was given to sport and play clothes—sweaters and slacks for cold weather sports, bathing suits, jerseys, and shorts for warm weather, for men, women, and children. Two-piece play and street dresses with removable jackets were popular for the summers of 1950 and into the 1960's. Sleeveless dresses with removable jackets helped to solve temperature problems. Designers of fabrics for sports wear used all sorts of color combinations and designs, some of which were "borrowed," in 1964 and 1965 from "Pop" and "Op" art.

In 1958, fashion news, which had been smoothly progressing in relatively good taste, suddenly became revolutionary. The chemise was revived as a dress, a style popular in the late 1920's. It had no waistline, and was loose, straight, and, if belted, the hipline carried the belt. Like the sheath skirt, the dress was constructed with an extra pleat or pleats at the back, below the knees. The box jacket, worn with it on occasion, added a hipline division. Hemlines were raised to 16 inches from the floor, giving prominence to the long vamp shoes with high heels and pointed toes. These spring fashion effects caught on with young fad followers, but women who had devoted thought and effort to keeping their waistlines slim rebelled. Almost as suddenly as it came, the chemise went out! By autumn of 1958, dealers were left with quantities of new dresses in stock, and there were few interested customers. Women just would not accept a style which hid their waistlines. But—what happened in the early 1960's? The chemise returned in various forms and names. It was still a chemise in cut even though called a sheath, a shift or, later, a skimmer. In the fall of 1963 it took the form of a jumper dress (without sleeves) to be worn with a blouse underneath.

Evening wear still appeared in many forms, among them the long overdress, using a contrasting blouse with long sleeves. The A-line skirt (slightly flaring) returned to popularity to add width to the vertical skirts. The A-line skirt in 1966 was extremely acceptable, because of the shorter styles.

Although the draped look of the late 1940's still persisted in men's clothing, coats in the early 1960's became narrower in the shoulders, with much less padding. They were shortened and made to fit the waist more closely. The styling was single breasted. Trousers became narrower, and separate vests were designed either to match, harmonize, or contrast in material and color. Chemical treatment of fibers, and actual new man-made fibers, helped to make the press in clothes last longer. In fact, by the beginning of the 1960's, permanent creases in trousers, accomplished through a "baking" process, and permanent presses in coats and vests were appearing. Some of the newer man-made fibers added to pure wool helped to make them wrinkle-proof. Built-in creasing also helped the pleating in women's skirts to remain permanent.

Men's neckties narrowed in the early 1960's, and most bias cuts, which produced bias stripes, were replaced by ties of straight cuts of fabrics, and therefore horizontal stripes. The wide, garish, handpainted ties of the late 1940's and early 1950's disappeared. In their places were ties of small figured challis in soft wool, silks, rayons, or newer synthetic fibers, figured, striped, or banded. Color schemes were carefully planned and harmonious on backgrounds of predominant colors. Paisley and other decorative all-over designs in harmonious colors returned, giving an opportunity to choose wider ranges of color schemes in neckwear. In 1965 and 1966, wider stripes and diagonal cuts returned.

The double-breasted coat again began to make its appearance, both as a separate coat and as part of a suit.

Men's shirts for business wear continued in white with wrinkle proof materials. "Easy-care" fibers were added to cottons, and fabrics were processed to be wrinkle-free. In the 1950's and early 1960's colored shirts in light tints were used sparingly for business and some occupations in the larger cities. It was interesting to learn that in a large city like New York, various districts had their own styling. The financial district kept to white shirts. The light colors were found "on Broadway" and neighboring streets. Shirts with larger, bolder schemes and patterns were in vogue for casual or sports wear. Plaid shirts in deeper color schemes were universal favorites. Also, in the latter part of the 1950's and in the early 1960's, a man could wear his suit in summer with more comfort. The newer fibers and treatments made the launderable suit possible. Short sleeved, low-thread-count shirts were used with summer suits for business and occupations. Light, airy hats of straw or synthetic straws added to the comfort of the summer months. Men's leisure and sports clothing permitted a new sense of physical comfort without loss of appearance, because of permanence of press. Sweaters, knit shirts, shorts, slacks, and bathing wear were made from cottons, wool, and synthetic mixtures, "stretch fabrics" being used for action and appearance. Casual footwear for men was designed as open, slip-on, or sandal styles for leisure use. For occupational or business wear, men's oxfords were designed in the usual laced classic styles, with moccasin style slip-ons, and plain-toe styling, in black and brown.

The review of costume for both men and women would not be complete without a look at cosmetics and toiletries. Face powders, lotions, creams, rouge, and lip coloring, as well as eye make-up, have been used for centuries. In the United States, in our own history, such uses seemed connected, somehow, with morality. Then, in recent years, cosmetics became accepted quite universally, enhancing both appearance and outlook.

The colorings of women's cosmetics changed rapidly at the end of the 1950's. In earlier uses, bright lipstick was purchased in rose, deep reds, and bright to deep pinks. Rouge, which had not been used for years, returned in delicate "brush-on" form. Lipstick, in some cases, became almost colorless. Pale lips and sophisticated eye make-up

A—Draped beret of 1949.
B—French roll hair style of 1956.
C—Draped fur fabric hat of 1960.
D—"Bee hive" hair style of 1959-1960.
E—Velour pillbox hat of 1960.

F—Long hair bob of 1942.
G—Modified "pony tail" of 1952.
H—Velvet cap of 1950.
I—Stitched silk hat of 1961 (spring).
J—The "tossed cut" of 1959.

took the place of lipstick and became the vogue in the middle of the 1960's.

Polished nails were not new, although methods for achieving results in 1910 contrasted with those of 20 years later considerably. In 1910, an arduous buffing with light pink powder was used to give a clear high polish. In the 1930's when colored nail enamels were introduced, liquid nail polish was simply brushed on and allowed to dry for any tints or shades from pale pink to rose-red. With this system, at first, nail tips were left white, but later the style was to cover the entire nail.

Early, in France and England, cosmetics helped to give social status. For the same reason, our own women in the United States began to use them. At first they were all imported. Later, drug firms here began to manufacture creams, lotions, powders, shaving creams, and other cosmetic preparations for both men and women. From 1940 through 1966, the arts of packaging and promoting sales added much to the enhancement of the use of cosmetics. Lipsticks were designed ingeniously so they could be controlled by a simple twist of the "cartridge." Containers were designed to simulate jewelry. The lipstick colors varied almost infinitely with the exception of the darker shades, which were not so popular. Compacts for carrying dry powder in cake form were elaborately and tastefully designed both in metals and plastics. Each year cosmetic manufacturers promoted new lists of colors and names, and redesigned their containers. In 1966, as said, tints were more popular than the deeper colors. In fact, in 1966 tints were promoted for lips and complexions which ranged in color from the lighter golden tints—orange, "blonde," tans, beige—to deeper tan tones. In 1965 and 1966 most lipsticks created a moister look. Creams and lotions appeared in ever-increasing varieties. These included cold creams, oil emulsions, moisture creams, powder bases, toning lotions, dry-skin creams, astringent creams, throat creams, bleaching and all-purpose creams, as well as "youth" creams, purported (but not guaranteed) to disguise or retard aging effects.

Men's shaving creams and lotions became popular, and at holiday time, particularly, were promoted with great vigor, as were deodorants for both men and women. Shampoo liquids and soaps became highly competitive, aimed at normal, dry, and oily hair. These went along with all kinds of hair care and styling between 1940 and 1966. Men, who had heretofore brushed back their parted hair vigorously, began to give consideration to the many new longer styles as they sprang into fashion. For women and girls, lotions and devices for waving and setting hair grew in number and variety, as they began dressing their own hair. Then waving styles were simplified as the straighter, smoother effects took over, and both shorter and longer hair, once again, came into style. The younger men, seeking ways to be "different" especially in the "rock-and-roll" world purposely allowed their hair lengths to be *the* feature.

By 1965, hair styles began to change from the high teased style to a more natural, lustrous look. Some of the more acceptable styles for young women in school or in occupations had their hair arranged in a variety of gently curved rhythms. Extremes will always put in their appearances, and the very long bobbed style was one of these. Hair tinting and dyeing were becoming so popular that one of the largest manufacturers of hair coloring products used three successive pages in a prominent magazine, directed to women, in advertising his products, part of which was a fold-back of the cover. In the late 1950's, hair tinting and dyeing had been on the increase. In the 1960's, one could meet a friend with chestnut brown hair one week, and the next week scarcely recognize her with her new blonde decor!

Hair styles and hair cuts underwent many changes from the 1940's to 1966. To review the early 1960's, "teased" hair acted as a cage under the surface, allowing high-built styles. From the very close curls of the 1950's to the gradually enlarging and extending coiffures of 1958 to 1963 styles passed through many phases. There were close and wide styles, Italian-boy bobs, pony-tails, moppet cuts, beehives, tossed cuts, short bobs, curved bangs, upsweeps with top-knots, tipped bob cuts with curved ends, teased hair for high styling (as said before), French knots, braided topknots, and others. In 1964, the rhythmic lines of smooth curved tresses returned and continued into 1966. Hair pieces were added to natural hair in curls, short and long braids, in chignons, bangs, and topknots, braided and twisted. Earrings in both close and pendant styles were widely used. In some parts of the country hats were almost done away with because of the prominence and elaboration of hair arrangements.

From the end of the 1950's through 1965, fashionable eyes took precedence over the lips, especially for dress occasions. They were like the eyes which the French artist, Renoir, painted. Eyebrows were gently curved, tapered, and accented with eyebrow pencil. Both upper and lower lids were tinted with colored eye shadow in violet, brown, blue, green, or silver. Some extreme stylists tried actual designs and patterns on the upper lids. Lashes were touched with mascara, or false eyelashes were added. Plucked, penciled eyebrows and contact lenses contributed to the general effect, allowing the centering of the make-up on the eyes.

In the 19th century when perfume and cologne were ascending, odors were chiefly floral, such as rose, lilac, violet, and jasmine. In the years that followed, perfume chemists experimented with synthetic odors, which emerged in the 20th century. Perfume names such as "Black Starlight," "Formula 10," "Chanel Number 5," or "My Sin," were considered as having intoxicant qualities and moods. During the twenty-five year period from 1940 through 1965, it is interesting to note the growth of synthetic perfumes in full strength, as colognes, in soaps, sachets, face and dusting powders. Colognes and lotions for men gained in popularity and were used regularly.

In 1959, fashions for women became extremely diverse. There were so many fibers, fabrics, color modes, and garment styles that even the manufacturers themselves curtailed the number of new modes per season. Some firms divided the year into four rather than two seasons. Added travel and resort living for both winter and summer had necessitated this. Considerable designing thought was given to seasonal styles without extremes in line and cut. Full, long, or wide cut clothing did not pack well for travel. Variety was obtained with different materials, colors, textures, and accessories, without added bulk.

Millinery, of necessity, followed current hair styles, particularly from 1958 on. Hat crowns were generous and varied, fitting well down on the head. Turbans of knitted and woven materials as well as of furs made their appearance. A certain free-lance designer was heard to remark, "Hats are not designed this season, they explode!" Pleated and buckled, wool jersey was draped and wound, brown mink was used as trimming, and black Persian lamb was fashioned into tall fezzes.

Women's hand and shopping bags must be considered part of the costume ensemble. They vary widely in material and shape. In the early 1940's, because leather was scarce, bags were designed from other materials. The shoulder bags of women in uniform were imitated for street wear in plastic and cloth. They proved very popular. Around 1945, the pouch bag returned in varying designs. Drawstrings, run through pleated leather, served as both handles and closing devices. Suede and velvet bags accompanied dressier daytime occasions. There was always the small evening bag or clutch purse in various colors and materials, beaded or bespangled with sequins. For shopping, there were tote bags, wide and deep, in cloth, straw, or reed, sometimes trimmed with leather or plastic. Plastic bags came into wide use during the late 1940's, and remained popular thereafter, chiefly because of the high cost of pure leather. Plastic was made to look like leather of all grains and colors, and, like patent leather, wore well. In the early part of 1966, shoulder bags for women returned; it coincided with war times (Vietnam).

From 1950 on, the bag, woman's necessity, was a target for many new designs. The deep bag with clasps and straps; the long horizontal bag, shallow but modish, the satchel; and even muff bags added variety to the list. Most bags were rectangular in shape, made of genuine leather or plastics. Each was provided with linings, inner pockets and fasteners, a change purse, and a small mirror. Later, some of these added accessories were omitted, and were purchased as separate items. Summer bags in 1959 and 1960 were trimmed with artificial flowers and covered with transparent plastic films.

From 1959 to 1962 shoes became only an excuse for higher and higher heels! For evening wear and some street styles, women's heels were the highest and the narrowest in the history of contemporary footwear. Hotel managers com-

A—1966—Corduroy sport coat, with open neck shirt.

B—1964—Jac-shirt of lightweight Merino wool.

C—1964—Discothéque singer with high hair style, sleeveless short evening gown.

D—1966—Girl's quilted cotton granny robe puffed with fiber-fill.

E—1962—Evening gown of printed surah silk with self stole; blonde wig and long earrings.

F—1962—Woman's spring coat of soft ivory wool; black straw hat, black leather gloves and shoes, and straw bag.

G—1962-1966—Men's ties—diagonal stripe and paisley, 1966; horizontal striped, narrow, 1962-1966.

H—1966—Girl's fall costume with double-breasted coat, visored cap of wool, mini skirt, stretch nylon hose, and high, simulated leather boots.

I—1965—Man's over-the-calf, long, spun nylon hose.

J—1961-1966—Man's tapered felt hat, with slight modifications.

K—1963—Woman's built-up coiffure with added coils and curls.

L—1966—Young lady's long-type, exaggerated coiffure with added ''fall'' and single, exaggerated style pendant earring.

plained about the holes dug into their lobby carpets by the metal lifts of these highest heels. Although high heels became common in offices in the 1960's, the styling gradually changed to lower stacked and covered heels in 1964, and the extremely high heel was reserved for evening and party wear.

"Corfam," trade-mark of the Du Pont Co., a manufactured substitute for leather came into use by 1964. It passed all tests for the utility of leather, and can be cleaned with a damp cloth, still retaining its original finish. Being square cut rather than a carcass hide, it saves waste in the cutting. It promises, now that manufactured shoes are made from it, a dependable material for manufacturing both men's and women's shoes.

Because in the 1940's leathers became scarce, woven gloves in knitted stitch were in demand. The man-made fibers such as rayon had already replaced silk gloves many years before. Now, heavier sueded cottons were used along with wool and woolen mixtures. Toward the end of the 1940's, sueded nylon was used for winter gloves for women in all varieties of colors. They wore and laundered well, and one could match or contrast them with any ensemble with the wide color choices. Also, at this time, gloves of varying lengths were in stock for all seasons and color choices, including wrist, gauntlet, and below-and-above elbow lengths. For special occasions, women might go hatless, but never gloveless!

For many years, from the end of the 19th century on, women's gloves never varied much in design. Three stitched stripes appeared at the back. Variety was obtained in material, length, weight, and colors. Later, in the years following World War II, designers who were challenged by the sameness of glove designs, began to create new features. In the early 1950's, gloves were cuffed with buckles, partial straps, and buttons; stitched stripes ran from between the third and fourth fingers to the wrist; light, short gloves of white or pastel tints of nylons were beaded or spangled;

others were embroidered with floral patterns for spring and summer wear. For autumn and winter, tweeds, plaids, checks, and fur touches were used on heavier fabrics for gloves. Gauntlet and elbow lengths took on decorative touches in the colors for the season; edges were pinked, scalloped, or stitched; embroidery, buttons, buckles, tucks, sequins, simulated gems, and beads were added. Men's gloves were heavier; more of the practical variety in machine knit fabrics and leather were worn, some with non-slip palms for driving use.

Leather in polished and sueded finishes will be used for gloves perennially unless in the increasing demand through population growth it becomes a scarcer and more costly item. The new strides which have been made in simulated and man-made chemical ''fabrics'' and ''leathers'' will give us other satisfying materials for gloves and footwear.

For men's and children's uppers for shoes, a new material called ''Morimer'' made of vinyl foam—a vinyl sheet, covered on one side, and with a woven fabric on the other—was announced in the mid 1960's. It can be cleaned with a damp cloth.

Other vinyl coated fabrics were being substituted for leathers in use for children's and women's shoes and boots, such as ''Patenlite,'' and ''Pattina.'' Leather in soles was sometimes being substituted by the various man-made materials, such as ''Avonite,'' ''Hypalon,'' and ''Neolite,'' trade names for man-made materials.

The amount of all types of hosiery manufactured in the United States in 1964 (the latest available information) is 189,215,000 *dozen* pairs. Women's and misses' full and knee length production was 83,899,700 *dozen* pairs. This same year, 92% of production of women's stockings were seamless as compared with only 8% full-fashioned hose. This was certainly a ready acceptance of a seamless style. A new type of women's hosiery, named ''Vectra'' (trade-mark of the National Plastics Products Co.), was made from a strong fiber called olefin. (See the fiber chart.) It was marketed in 1964. It appeared to be the best manufactured fiber since nylon for women's hosiery. Men's hosiery production climbed to 50,652,000 *dozen* pairs in the same year of 1964. Boys', infant's, children's, and younger misses' production reached 54,663,000 *dozen* pairs in the same year.

In the winters from 1959 to 1966, new costume trends were created by talented designers, each with his own ideas of projected styles. These were not always accepted by the mass of the population, when they represented ideas too extreme for the general public. Sometimes these extreme fashions would be worn successfully by eccentrics with a daring flair for the new and different! Their photographs would scream their way across pages of our most important newspapers and magazines. College and university youth had their own fashion extremes, not alone for creative effects, but rather for their novelty appeal. But changes came so rapidly, it did not prove feasible to accept extreme new ideas, from where the manufacturer viewed the picture. Ready-to-wear, one must remember, has to be manufactured in various sizes, lengths, widths, etc., to fit varying figures. This in itself is an expensive risk, and if clothing designs are not accepted much can be lost.

Some of the newer designers, however, were responsible for up-and-down changes in fashion lines, and they were employed by manufacturers for new ideas, new uses of materials, colors, and textures. Foreign styles, especially from the initial showings, were usually modified before being manufactured in quantities.

All in all, discounting extremes, such as skirts 4" above the knees in 1966, and higher, the women of America, after purchasing and wearing a few extreme fads, have come back to those styles which are practical as well as becoming.

Men's clothing remains more conservative than women's. The very nature of the fabrics used, the universal demands of vocations, occupations, and travel, social usages and customs still dictate less changes and less individual choices at this writing. One must remember, too, that in selection of their color schemes and accessories women are allowed more personal choices. Nearly 100% of all men's clothing and accessories are factory manufactured, with perhaps some hand-knitted sweaters as the exception!

When new clothing styles are designed, the past offers much in the way of selections. Coupled with our newly created materials and passing through modern methods of manufacture, these styles appeal as "brand new." The fall of 1966 offered much in regenerated styles of men's clothing. Going back to the 1930's, designers re-created double-breasted suits, blazers, overcoats, outercoats, sport coats, jackets, slacks, and rainwear. However, men's and youth's clothing, though reminiscent of past times, never repeats styles in quite the same forms or details. The reasons are obvious. Each age or period of time has its own ideals and activities.

For cooler weather, 1966, worsteds and woolens were worn in dark muted colors, club checks, and plaids. Woolens were often combined with polyesters such as Dacron, and were permanently pressed. Contrasting or harmonizing coats and trousers gave a man a wider choice of daily clothing. Overcoats were adaptable to more colorful styles with softer textures in the fall of 1966. Some were pure wool or worsted, others were of pile fabrics which combined wood and man-made fibers. The outercoat was popular for informal wear, styled generally with wool plaids and lined with pile fabrics. The bush jacket was being offered in cotton poplin, wool flannel lined with acrylic pile, or in double knit wool. This was belted and had four flap pockets. The return of corduroy, in both wide and narrow wale, was popular in suits and coats. Once made of cotton fiber only, it was now a combination of 50% cotton and 50% polyester.

We cannot leave the scene of changing styles without mentioning the "tent" dresses and coats of 1966. They were cut close to the shoulder, in dress styles, and swung away from the figure in circular folds, with lengths just above the knees. In coats the cut was narrow at the shoulder and swung away into fullness at the hemline, just at the knee. With these styles were worn small fur toques, or helmet-shaped velour hats, close fitting and contrasting.

The tent styles seemed to have been influenced by world happenings, which is often the case. Since they were shown with high boots, high waistlines, and double-breasted effects, one could conclude that the military had a great influence.

As each new season comes along, why not visualize what you would like to wear if you were designing your very own clothes! One cannot wholly shut out what is admired for the immediate past and the present, but it is a real test of one's creative ability to project one's imagination and judgment.

INDEX

Acele, 263
Acetates, 250, 263
Acrilan, 263
Acrylic, 263
Aesthetic Movement in London, 212
Aigrette, 38, 116, 176
Albert Blum Contest, 242
A-line skirt, 269, 270
America as fashion center, 241
American costumes, Colonial, 176A; 1700-
    1804, 176B; 1800-1850, 192A; 1850-
    1880, 192B; 1880-1900, 224A; 1900-
    1920, 224B; 1920-1945, 256A; 1950-
    1965, 256B
Amonieres sarrasinoises, 77, 84
Amusse, 82
Ancient costumes, 32A, 32B, 64A
Antron, 263
Apotygma, 41, 42
Ankle-boots, 193
Ankle-rings, 17, 27
Appliqué, 81, 99, 180
Apron, 165, 167, 173; Egyptian, 15, 17
Armlets, 17, 27
Armor, 83, 84
Arnel, 263
Art and industry, co-operation of, 244
Artisans, 78, 85
Arts and crafts movement of Middle Ages,
    113, 134
Asp, the royal, 16, 17, 23
Avicron, 263
Avisco, 263
Avron, 264

Bagnolette, 139, 145
Bags, 82, 146, 259, 276, 277 (Also see
    Purse)
Basque, 233; boned, 209, 210
Basque-dress, 229, 230, 231
Basquine, 105
Beads, 14, 28, 230
Beard: Asiatic, 34; Egyptian, 22, 23;
    Greek, 50; "Imperial," 121, 122;
    Middle Ages, 75; Persian, 37, 38
Beauty shop, 246
Belt, 14, 37, 82, 85
Biblical costumes, 32A
Bills, regulating dress, 228
Bliaud, 83, 84
Blouse, 213, 221, 228, 230; Balkan, 232,
    233
Blue "C," 267
Bodice, 112, 130, 152, 177, 185; boned,
    105, 117, 123, 124, 141, 178;
    pointed, 102, 173, 182
Body, ornamentation, 11; painting, 9
Bolero, 193
Bonnets, 139, 170, 179, 193, 202, 204,
    210, 218
Books, fashion, 215, 240; Godey's Lady's
    Book, 196, 197; Harper's Bazaar,
    196; Peterson's Magazine, 196; Un-
    ion Magazine, 196

Boots, 24, 33, 56, 102, 104, 120, 233;
    great-topped, 120, 122, 136; half,
    Asiatic, 33, 34, Greek, 56; high, 119,
    159
Boston, a center of fashion, 176
Bracelets, 27, 38, 57, 76, 78, 156
Breeches, 109, 119, 120, 124, 137, 164,
    186
Bretelles, 194, 195, 206, 222
Brooch, 41, 49, 73
Buckles, 139, 146, 168, 186
Buckram, 177
Bustle, 104, 205, 206, 208, 211, 230; re-
    turn in 1940's, 260, 261
Bustle-skirt, 207
Butterick, Ebenezer and Ellen, 214
Buttons, 95, 96, 112, 114, 125, 137, 163,
    165

Calash, 179
Cambrics, 201
Camlet, 76, 134, 175
Canezou, 200, 201
Capes, 124, 133, 187, 202, 237
Capillamentum, 69
Caprolan, 264
Caps, 106, 108, 146, 175, 181; Charlotte
    Corday, 155, 157; cylindrical, 38;
    Mary Stuart, 109, 111, 112; Phry-
    gian, 32, 34, 36, 73
Caul, 50, 69
Cavalier, 168
Celaperm, 264
Cellulose, 264
Chain stitch, 99; stitching, 114
Chemise, 95, 115, 266, 269
Chignon, 185, 207, 209
Chinband, 77, 88
Chinese prints, 250, 251
Chiton, 39, 42, 45, 47, 51; Doric, 39, 42,
    44; double-girded, 42, 44; Ionic, 44-
    46; knitted, 45
Chlamys, 49
Chopines, 125, 126
Chromespun, 264
Clasps, 31, 36, 43, 47, 48, 73
Clays, use of colored, 10
Cloak, 121, 157, 163, 165, 198
Coat, 124, 133, 163, 168, 186; cutaway,
    186, 188, 232; double-breasted, 270,
    277; full-skirted, 137, 139, 177, 178,
    195; Prince Albert, 232
Cockade, 137, 155, 185, 233
Coiffure:
    American, Colonial, 166, 177, 179; 1813,
    193; 1830, 194; '60's, 203; '70's,
    204, 207; '90's, 218; 1921, 236
    Carlovingian, 82
    French, middle 17th century, 131, 132;
    late 18th century, 146-149; following
    Revolution, 156, 158
    Gallo-Roman, 73
    Grecian, 44, 48, 50

283